JOHNO and the Blind Chick

Sue-Ellen Lovett

Published by Sue-Ellen Lovett in 2021

Text copyright © Sue-Ellen Lovett 2021

Cover design by Belinda Crawford (www.DesignedByBoots.com)
Cover photography by Prue Crichton, 2CPhotography
(www.2Cphotography.com.au)
Matt and Johno illustration © Amy Naef (www.inkypony.com)

ISBN: 978-0-6488298-2-9 (ebook)
ISBN: 978-0-6488298-3-6 (paperback)

A catalogue record for this book is available from the National Library of Australia

*I would like to dedicate this book to Libby Sander,
who came into my life when I was six months old.*

We spent two years together and then I went from your heart.

*I would like to share with you the past two years of my life that
I shared with The Blind Chick.*

This is the story of our journey together.

*Loads of Love
Johno*

Preface

Would you like to see more? Really see?

Would you like to listen more? Be a better listener? Really hear ALL the layers to life that are there to hear?

Well read on!

If you had told me that the person who'd be able to teach me to see, to listen, to enrich my day-to-day life with a joy, a laughter, and an ability to celebrate life, even the suckiest moments, was a Blind Chick, I'd never have believed you.

But it's true!

What you experience here isn't just words on a page.

It's not because the Blind Chick's eyes don't work that she sees the world in such color, it's because at her core, her vision is way more than seeing. It's who she is.

Allow yourself to immerse, savour, reflect... these pages contain the stuff of fairy tales and magic. Let them help you declutter and be available to some of the day-to-day mysteries of life. Goodness that escapes most of us because the pace of life gets way to busy and cluttered.

Be prepared to be shocked, joyously surprised.

Like me you'll be blinded by the light that Sue-Ellen, the Blind Chick, Cancer Survivor and Adventurer illuminates. Her vision is heartfelt, skin tinglingly hair raising. I lost count of the light bulb moments this glorious woman shone into my heart and mind for me to discover.

If you think this book is about training a horse, think again.

This journey is about how to take off your mask, take off your blinkers, get free flowing and generous with your praise. It's about getting your vision absolutely rocking.

Welcome to your brave step into how to live life – all the highs, lows, farting, belching, ugly and beautiful bits. Come grab life with both hands and get connected to your best self. A part of you you may not have even known has been quietly waiting, waiting for you to see it.

A truth.

This book made me a better version of myself.

It will do the same for you... if you let it.

Thank you for being here.

Now mount up, it's time for the ride of your life.

Jacqueline Thompson

Scene Setting

Matt, the Blind Chick and I © 2CPhotography

Let me share with you what it's like to walk in my Blind Chick's shoes, for just one day.

I'll describe what a typical day is like. I'll probably add in a few other little things as we go along, but I will try to keep it to what her life is like on a day-to-day basis.

Most mornings start at 6am when the Blind Chickie babe gets up and gets her husband Matthew his breakfast; puts the jug on and makes a cuppa tea. Just this start is an awakener for her, for anyone! Why? For the Blind Chick to pour a cuppa she must put a finger in the top of the cup so when the boiling water meets that finger, she knows to stop pouring, Ouch! Now she's very much awake.

Then she comes down to feed me. That involves walking out the back door, putting her boots on and picking up her trusty white cane. Never ever did she think she'd rely on a white cane. She had a

Guide Dog for 38 years, she never liked using the cane. I remember her telling the story of before she got a Guide Dog, she'd had to do white cane training. She'd called her cane Fred. He's buried it in the backyard somewhere in Victoria. Why? Because as soon on as she got the Guide Dog, no more white cane. But these days it's white cane all the way around the farm.

I will digress in a little while and tell you a couple of white cane stories, but let's continue for now with the morning routine. She heads out to the tack shed, tap, tap, tap, tap with the white cane, I hear her coming. She measures out my supplements, mixes the feed then off to my paddock to feed me. Watching the Blind Chick finding the paddock gate is sometimes really funny for me, not for her. If she isn't holding the cane's rubber handle, she's holding the long metal part, Zappo! My fence has a hot wire running around it. Some mornings I hear her get zapped. Her second ouch for the morning.

Probably not the best way to totally wake up with a zap from the electric fence, but it happens reasonably often. I admit to having a wee chuckle to myself, I know the Blind Chick laughs about it too, later. Right at that time, it's not that funny for her.

I'm always conscious of anytime the Blind Chick goes outside, she's very dependent on the sun shining for her orientation. The morning sun comes up from the east, she can feel the warmth of the sun's rays on her face. This warmth helps her knows where she is. As she walks through the garden to my paddock the white cane finds the trees, but the sun on her face orientates her so she can make her way down to my paddock quite easily. Except for one electric fence shock or two.

After she gives me my hard feed she walks down to the stable block and into the spare stable. There she breaks off a couple of biscuits of hay which she puts outside the gate. Once I finish my hard feed, she gives me these.

⌒

Oopsy, I missed sharing a funny thing. Luckily, it only happened once.

The Blind Chick has a favourite pair of lovely blue linen shorts. They're really comfy so she often pops them on first thing in the morning with a clean shirt and down she comes to feed me. Well, one particular morning she came down, how she looked was hilarious. She'd put her shirt and shorts on inside out! She looked like an elephant! The two pockets of the shorts are quite large, so she had elephant ears. Naughty Matthew didn't bother to tell her that the shorts were inside out, but I sure noticed. I had a quiet chuckle to myself. Thankfully when she cut the string of the hay and went to put the string in her pocket, voila! Right there in the hay shed she quickly fixed her wardrobe malfunction before anyone else saw her.

These little things that you take for granted, like dressing yourself without looking like a weirdo, can have serious hiccups for my Blind Chick. Clothes being inside out, socks not matching. She's clever with what she buys though, like her socks. She's got about six pairs of the same colour and same brand, so she doesn't have to worry about wearing odd socks. Not that that matters most of the time, but it can look pretty funny when you have visitors. She's been known to do it.

Back to finishing up my day-to-day feeding routine. She goes back up and washes out the buckets then heads inside to clean up the kitchen and do her domestic goddess duties.

Once inside she has a quick breakfast and a coffee, of course. Then she gets her phone to read her a bit of Facebook and catch up with all the comments that people are putting on my page. After that she's off to the bathroom to clean her teeth.

Be warned, teeth cleaning can get a bit precarious!

The first totally hilarious time things went pear shaped was when she was getting ready to go and do a radio interview with a local radio announcer Leo De Kroo at 2DU, the Dubbo Radio Station. After the Blind Chick had a shower she went to brush her teeth. She put the paste on her toothbrush and put that in her mouth. Oh, my heavens what's on the brush? As well as the toothpaste a daddy long legs spider had stuck to her toothbrush! Yuck. Yes, there was a lot of spluttering and gagging that followed. So now, when the Blind

Chickie babe cleans her teeth, she puts a bit of toothpaste in her mouth first, then the brush. Voila!

It pays to smell things before you put them in your mouth or on your face! With her new routine of putting some toothpaste in her mouth first, one day she felt in her beauty case, found the toothpaste, didn't think to smell it first then gee whiz! She'd squirted some hair conditioner in her mouth. Again, lots of spluttering and gagging. This not seeing gig can sometimes suck, literally.

My Blind Chick is big on applying sunscreen. Our Aussie sun can be deadly. One day instead of grabbing the sunscreen, she applied her husband's Pinetarsol gel. Man, oh man, definitely not effective sunscreen and holy cow does it stink. Aaagh! Sometimes it's not easy to do simple things when bottles feel the same.

With being totally blind, she also doesn't have the best radar system. So often as she goes down the hall it's a little bit like a pinball hitting one side, then bounces off and hits the other. Generally, it's a crash with the left shoulder then a shuffle to the right. So quite a few bruises can result from a simple walk down the hall.

As a finale to that hall catwalk, she typically walks through the dining room to the kitchen, which often results in a corked thigh! Yes, she walks straight into the corner of the dining table. Ouch!

After finishing cleaning up the kitchen, it's about time for the girls to arrive to come and work me. If the sun is out the Blind Chickie babe will try to have me up at the tack shed, brushed and with fly spray on before they arrive, so they don't have as much to do. Sometimes when the Blind Chick comes to find me, if I wanted to be naughty, I could hold my breath or stop my feet from moving. She won't know where I was! But being the nice lad that I am, I don't do that. Plus, I know she has a carrot! So, I typically meet her halfway, or she comes to my usual haunt, which is down in the bottom paddock looking out at the river.

Once she finds me, she gives me a carrot. Imagine what it was like the first few times she walked towards me though. A new person in my life waving a white cane, coming at me! Naturally at first, I was very wary of that white cane. Yes, she got me around the legs with it a few times, but now once she hears me, she puts her hand up with the carrot. I then walk to her. We worked out that this is a much less dangerous way for me of getting together, I don't get walloped with that cane.

Then I guide her back up to the gate and up to the tack shed. Sometimes I can get a little distracted, which can be a bit difficult for the Blind Chick. While she's not able to see what I'm looking at or what I'm thinking about shying at, she can feel it through my body that I'm anxious. This can be a little bit hard to orientate, depending on whether it is a sunny day or an overcast day. Sometimes on the overcast days the Blind Chick will wait till the girls get here, they catch me. When it is overcast it's exceedingly difficult for the Blind Chick, as she has no orientation to work by.

The other thing I've noticed about our day-to-day routine is the Blind Chick never works me of an afternoon, it's always mornings. Again, this is to do with the sun. When she goes into the arena to ride me of a morning, she starts on the right rein with the sun is on her left cheek when she rides down the long side. I think it's incredible how she can rely on the sun for her orientation, it rocks. Finding a way to do something you love, when you can't see, helps heighten your other senses, like your feel.

In the tack shed everything has its place and everything goes back in its place. If not, the Blind Chick can't find it. I know she's quite anal about her gear being clean, particularly my beautiful saddle cloths. Everything is clean and washed regularly, including my boots and rugs. I'm especially lucky in summer when I have a clean rug on every day! Ok, I understand that might be unusual, but there's only one of me. I know the Blind Chick spoils me a little, she loves me, a lot.

Now taking my rug off is no big deal for my Blind Chick. Undo the three straps on the neck rug, undo the chest strap, undo the back legs, do the buckles back up and pull the rug off. Voila! But it is a big deal, hilarious in fact, for the Blind Chick to work out which part of the rug she is holding at the time. Once she finds the fury little bit of padding which sits on my wither, she's fine. It's the finding that and positioning it that's fun to watch. Yes, my rugs are massive, I'm 18.3 hands high. It's like putting a tent up. So sometimes she has her leg in the strap, sometimes a foot on the rug, but eventually she gets it on me. I typically stand ever so patiently, except when I pinch the odd leaf off the Paulownia tree. I've got to, to stop the boredom! Because these things do take time. That's one of the things I learnt early on. Nothing with the Blind Chick happens quickly.

Matthew has spent a lot of time trying to get her to slow down, she was running into things because she was moving so quickly. When she goes to fast, the white cane hasn't time to pick things up, so BAM! Another bruise.

Now we're tacked up we go to the dressage arena, the Blind Chick orientating herself with the sun. Jenelle gives her a riding lesson and Jacqueline stands at the letter C. From C Jacq helps orientate the Blind Chick on where the Quarter Lines and Centre Line is. Anytime they do work on the Centre Line Jacq sits and calls out the letter C, C, C, C, C. So instead of the Blind Chick seeing the letter C, she rides towards the sound. Jacq will call out "Drifting to the right" or "Drifting to the left" and the Blind Chick will fix up her Centre Line.

I think out of all the things we do in the dressage arena, the Centre Line is the hardest for the Blind Chick, as she has absolutely nothing to go on. When we're on a long side it's easy and when we do, say a leg yield, Jacq will call out Quarter Line, Centre Line, then Quarter Line and the Blind Chick will turn down the second quarter line and do a quick yield to the left. Easy peasy. But when you're in no mans' land heading for the letter C, it's hard. There's no point to focus on. That voice calling the letter is it. That voice is especially important.

How's this for surprising. The Blind Chick can ride really good circles! Her wonderful coach from years ago, Judy Cubitt, gave her a few tricks to riding a circle and she applies that knowledge well. Her circles are quite symmetrical. This is intriguing considering she can't see. But as long as she has someone calling on either side of the arena, she orientates herself brilliantly.

Guess how we work out where X is when we're coming down the Centre Line, where we need to halt? The Blind Chick counts the strides. It's the technical details of how to do what most people take for granted that we are practising and play with, often. While we may not get to do a dressage test, I'm hopeful that such miracles do happen.

There's a lot more counting when we're doing lateral work. Let me explain. Say we're doing a shoulder-in from F to B, then we do an eight-meter circle, then half pass to the left; this equates to 12 strides shoulder-in, listening for the B to be called, then at B we do our rock star circle. Ok, I admit it, sometimes my circles are a little big, but we're getting better at the eight-meter circles.

Once the living marker calls B we're back on the track, then the H starts calling and we do a half pass to the left. Then it's 12 strides till we get to G. As soon as the Blind Chick leaves B the person standing at H is calling H, H, H, H so the Blind Chick knows the angle to go on to get our half pass exactly right. Then Jacq will start calling the C, C, C, C about two strides before she gets there and then keep calling C, C, C, C to get the Blind Chick on the Centre Line and travelling straight so we can track left and do our extension. Phew! Yes, there's a lot going on in my Blind Chicks brain all at once.

She must listen, count, guide me, be mindful of her own posture and not just correctly riding the movement we're doing, but getting ready to set me up for the movement that comes next. All at the same time! I know my brain would explode with all that going on. Would you cope juggling all that? And if it all gets a bit overwhelming the Blind Chick can't just open her eyes. They're already open. They don't make a difference.

So, as you can see for the Blind Chick to ride, it's incredibly involved. You may wonder why we train so hard to perfect our dressage movements if we can't compete right now? But that's the thing. The Blind Chick's ultimate goal is to get back to competing in Open top-level dressage again. I'm sure we will one day. How can I be sure? Because I see her day-in-day out. She can be incredibly determined and so resilient when she sets her mind on something.

Yes, we will struggle with doing a dressage test if it has backing in it because of my Equine Shivers. Shivers makes me back up like I'm doing a weird goose step. But like I say, miracles do happen. One day there might be a cure.

When the sun goes away and it's overcast, everything changes for the Blind Chick. On such days she isn't nearly as adventurous or as bold. Typically, she doesn't ride at all. Why? Because of the confidence thing. I know that C word it a sensitive topic, but I wanted to share it with you, it's an important thing to talk about.

The last time the Blind Chick competed was in February 2019 at Dressage by the Sea at the beautiful Willinga Park, she rode her previous horse, Desiderata, Desi for short. They competed in the Prix St George, Inter 1, plus they did a Grand Prix demonstration. Pretty impressive, pretty hectic.

Yes, it's been a long time since the Blind Chick has competed. Add to that her losing her confidence from her unceremonious dismount off me and you start to understand why this rebuilding her confidence gig has been a biggie.

I think she feels embarrassed. The fact that she was riding at quite a high level, in the top 10% of able-bodied riders in Australia, and now she's frightened to ride on an overcast day or if it's really windy!

Sometimes she calls herself a fair-weather rider. I can tell she's extremely hard on herself. She's actually quite relentless on punishing herself, but as one of her lovely coaches said to her years ago, "You have nothing to prove." But I think deep inside all she wants to do is keep proving to herself that she can do it. But her determination, guts, bloody mindedness, and inner strength can sometimes fail her. It's gut wrenching that she can't do something that she loves so much. I know she's determined to get her confidence back, beat the niggling "Itty-Bitty Shitty Committee" in her head that makes her doubt herself. We'll see how things go.

If I could talk, I'd ask her to "Cut yourself some slack", "Give yourself more time", "What's meant to be will be." I know my Equine Shivers hasn't helped the situation. It's made me quite anxious and overreactive and sometimes quite naughty. That hasn't helped either of our confidences, but we're on this journey together, one day at a time. We'll see how things play out.

Ooops, I digressed. Back to our day-to-day routine.

Generally, Jenelle brings Johno in from being worked and Jacqueline guides the Blind Chickie babe back to the tack up area. There, it's like being a Formula 1 car coming into the pits, a veritable pit crew converges on me. Boots off, saddle off, bridal off, I'm washed, rugged and in amongst all this activity the Blind Chickie babe wanders off in the wrong direction, and has to be called back. But that's part of the fun I suppose. Yes, maybe not such fun for the Blind Chick, maybe frustrating, but it is what it is. Like with the diary entries we share with you, this is the reality of life for us; the good, the bad and the ugly.

Then comes the bit I like very much. The girls, Janelle and Jacq, put me in my paddock and I get to relax for the rest of the day. They go and sit together on the veranda; have a drink, discuss the days ride, and work out the program for the next ride two days later. It's such fun listening to them giggling and rehashing what has happened and working out a better way to do things, so it is easier for the Blind Chick. How cool are they! What they're doing is so important for us.

Oh, I've got to tell you a Blind Chick funny. She admits it's funny now, but at the time I'm sure it wasn't so. The dressage arena had been blown down, so the Blind Chick went out with her trusty white cane to find all the arena pieces and run a string from end to end to help ensure the arena sides were straight. Then she got busy finding all the blown away bits strewn across the paddock and reassemble them all. When Matthew and the Blind Chick do this job together, it's 30 minutes tops. When the Blind Chick does it by herself, it's easily 2.5 hours. She and her cane: find everything, find the string, get caught up in the string, trip over the string and trip over the dressage arena pieces. It's hilarious to watch. But onwards she persists, determined. Yes, often the dressage arena edges aren't straight, but the arena is standing, just maybe not quite a rectangle.

But I have to give her 10 out of 10 for having a go.
Another time wasn't quite so funny, it was actually really quite sad. It was getting late; the sun was in the west which didn't help the Blind Chick with any orientation. She was in their garden, 2 acres of lots of big trees. Nothing felt familiar, she felt like she was in no man's land. The Blind Chick had gotten lost, she was in tears. So, what could she do? She had to ring her husband Matthew who was out on the tractor to come and get her.

This really shook her up because she takes great pride in thinking she knows where she is. It was a confronting reality check getting lost in your own garden! Then there has been the odd occasion she has been lost in my paddock. Thank heavens for mobile phones. She rang her father-in-law John; Matthew's parents live in the neighbouring property. He came and saved the day.

These days of getting lost typically happen on overcast days, not sunny days. If she's going to get lost it will be of an afternoon when she has no sun to work by. It's those days that the electric fence tends to get her as well, double ouch.

Did you know the Blind Chick is a bit of a snake charmer? In the 20 years she's been married to her wonderful husband Matthew, she's been bitten by them and fallen on them!

Yes, bitten by three brown snakes! Thank heavens their fangs didn't penetrate her boots or her riding breeches. She fell on one whilst leading a horse called Mr Bojangles. Matthew was out the back but heard her screaming over the noise of two loud irrigator machines that were watering the lucerne paddocks. He came and annihilated the Gazania garden looking for the snake. He never found it.

One of the other snake encounters happened when she'd walked next door to talk to Matthew, he was at his mum and dad 's place. After she spoke to him, she started down the pathway back home. I tend to think they thought she was a little girl calling wolf, looking for attention, but next thing there was screaming and yelling and more screaming and the Blind Chick impaled across a rosebush in the garden! Matthew came running, "What's wrong" and learnt she'd stepped on a slithering something that hissed loudly. It struck her on the outside of her breeches three times!

Everybody came out of the house to help look for the snake. The Blind Chick was a bit in shock. At first, I think everyone was dubious whether there was a snake or not, until …… all of a sudden Matthew's mum Lee spotted it. John and Matthew carefully dispatched it off the property. What was it? A six-foot brown snake, potentially deadly. The Blind Chick was so lucky the fangs didn't penetrate her breeches.

Then there was the time Desiderata had dirtied his stable, so she picked it out with the poo rake, and let the stable dry out, shutting the stable door so he didn't go back in during the day. That evening she went down to make his bed; went in with the bedding fork, opened the door and straight away stepped on … another brown snake! She didn't realise she was standing on its tail. Mighty annoyed he was swishing and swishing in the bedding making seriously scary sounds. It was only when he flicked back and struck her on the inside of her boot, she realised what she was standing on. Once again lots of screaming and yelling. Again, Matthew came and saved the day, but because there was so much grass around, he couldn't find this one. Again, a rather shaken Blind Chick.

The other time was years ago when the Blind Chick had her beautiful stallion Hecco. She'd finished riding him and was going around the other side of the house to turn a sprinkler off, so she could have more pressure for Hecco's wash. When she was walking back, she heard a noise down at the river, so she stopped. She didn't think twice about the thing under her foot, she assumed it was the hose. No! It was another snake. This one was a three-foot brown snake. Luckily, Matthew was close by to save the day yet again. I think living on the river doesn't help the snake situation.

One particular day was especially funny, all in hindsight of course. It was the day the Blind Chick fell on the snake and Matthew annihilated the garden searching for it. After her heart calmed down enough, she rang her dad. All she could get out was "I fell on a snake", that's all she kept repeating. "I fell on a snake". All her dad wanted to know was did it bite her. But all she could get out was, "I fell on a snake". That night when her dad rang to check on her, he asked Matthew if he could speak to the...

Snake Charmer. Thank heavens people have a sense of humour.

You can appreciate why I'm quickly coming to the conclusion this blind gig isn't much chop. When you're blind living on a farm comes with serious risks. So many things can go wrong.

But my Blind Chick wouldn't change any of it.

What had the biggest impact on me when I first met the Blind Chick, before they bought me, was how she lives for her horses. It's her reason for breathing and living.

Now I've lived with her a while I understand more this incredible passion she has for horses. We give her freedom; we give her independence. She loves being able to do the things an able-bodied person can do. Okay she might need some help but that's okay, if there's a will there's a way. I know sometimes there are days of great frustration for her. She can't just get in the car and drive into town and pick up some horse feed when it's needed. She's at the mercy of other people, all the time.

When I hear her crying, I'd love to be able to give her my eyes. Maybe not both, but she could have one! I don't blame her for shedding tears. Imagine how frustrating it must be to be sent beautiful photos? Weddings, birthdays, the celebration of new life reflected in amazing baby photos. She can't enjoy them.

I know when she received my baby photos she just sat in the chair and cried. She so wanted to see how I looked. More tears when she was sent a video of my rather magnificent father, Gymnastic Star. She sat and listened to the beautiful man's German accent as he spoke of my dad being the last horse from hundreds he inspected, with a view to purchasing a Hanoverian stallion worthy of importing to Australia. The background music, the sound of my dad's hooves as he danced in the arena and his owner, Holger Schmorl's impassioned words narrating dad's movement, unleashed a flood of happy and sad tears from my Blind Chick. My heart breaks when things like this happen.

It happens so often. People saying beautiful comments about me, saying how lovely I am, how perfect I am. Recently the Blind Chick was saying to a friend how she was so sad she can't really enjoy any of that. Her friend made the comment which I thought was so right – "You lay your hand on that beautiful horse and you feel his beauty."

Yes, the Blind Chick knows this. But sometimes I think she needs to be reminded that she feels so many other things, things most people don't get to feel. See feels them in a very deep and meaningful place deep in her heart. I know when she rides me her smile never leaves her face.

Where does my Blind Chick feel most at home? In the saddle. That's where she belongs. Her smile comes from so deep down inside. Isn't it amazing something like riding a horse can be so special, so precious, and be the thing that makes everything else in one's life, work?

What other things does the Blind Chick love? My list in answer to this is growing with each day we're together. She loves people describing a sunset, a starry night, the swans on the river. All the things that cost you nothing, that you take for granted. It's the little things that count. It's the little things that mean the most, like a smile. As you can tell the Blind Chick is a lover and a hugger. She will always give someone a hug. Until then, she sends her love.

Feel is so important. On so many levels they talk about feel when you're riding. The Blind Chick gets that, but she also gets a feel from people in a handshake, a hug. They tell you so much about a person that we will never know.

But the Blind Chick feels it all.

Does this sometimes get the Blind Chick down and distress her? Yes.

Are there days there are tears? Yes.

Are there days of frustration? Yes.

But very rarely do you see it publicly or is it shared, because I know the Blind Chick wants you to see strength and ability, not a disability.

So, I take my hat off to my Blind Chick. She soldiers on through thick and thin. She makes the best of everything she can. Her philosophy of 'Just one step at a time' totally rocks! Why? Because if you keep doing that, soon enough you may actually find yourself standing at the top of that beautiful mountain having achieved all of the things you wanted to.

I know she's a big dreamer. She believes in dreams. She believes in magic.

I know the Blind Chick and I being on this journey together is total magic and full of dreams. Thank you for coming along with us and sharing in our amazing journey.

And remember – vision is much more than seeing.

2
First Anniversary

Handsome me & the Blind Chick © 2CPhotography

Well, what a year! It has totally flown.

Can you believe I have been with the Blind Chick for one year! It has been the most amazing experience getting to know my lovely Blind Chick.

Learning to lead her around, having her rely on me and my two beautiful brown eyes to guide her safely from my horse paddock to the tack shed, and then out to the arena, and then to look after her as we are riding around the arena, wow! I'm still totally blown away. Who would've thought that an 18.3hh warmblood would be the Blind Chicks choice?

I am so awfully glad she chose me. It was meant to be.

In our past year we've tried three different coaches, looking for something special. Looking for that someone to match the something the Blind Chick has in her head and the way she wants to train.

I know in the past, the Blind Chick has trained Dressage the German way. I would say not knowing very much about this, I can't have an opinion really, but I know the Blind Chick has been looking for something different. She wants to do more work with me on the ground and to train a different way in the saddle. Hence, she's gone down the road of classical dressage. Which I think is Spanish but her amazing coach who she has now, José Mendez, is a master on the ground and in the saddle. We are progressing well and loving it.

In this past year, the Blind Chick has had an eye operation. After this she had a bit of time doubting that she could keep riding. The "Itty-Bitty Shitty Committee" got in her head and undermined her confidence. But she rose above it, onwards and upwards. I tend to think this confidence thing is going to be an ongoing issue, especially if she keeps training by herself. I think this is not the ideal situation for a Blind Chick to be in. Training solo!

I am really hoping she will put the feelers out for someone who is Dressage orientated to help her with her day-to-day riding. In my heart I know this will make a difference to her confidence, having someone give her positive support.

It is an interesting concept to think of what it would be like riding totally blind.

How about you give it a whirl! Just something simple like walking around the house, putting the washing on, hanging the clothes on the line, and then coming in and packing the dishwasher with your eyes closed? I hear her husband Matthew often has to repack the washer after the Blind Chick has done it, but that's beside the point. She still packs it.

Having the courage to go out into the paddock with your white cane and find the feed bin with the white cane; get the hay and feed your horse, put the rugs back on, check each leg – are there any injuries, and take the fly veil off. Think of how much trust and schooling must be in doing this when you are totally blind. I bet sometimes it's pretty scary.

Keep in mind also how much the Blind Chick relies on the sun. Feeding the horse on an overcast day there is no sunlight to tell her which way she's heading. The sun helps orientate her. The sun is on her right cheek when she walks down to feed me of a morning and then when she feeds me in the afternoon the sun is on her left cheek. Finding the opening to go into the yard where my stable is, is also a challenge. My Blind Chick does this stuff day in day out because she loves it. It's food for thought for those of us who can see.

We have accomplished a lot of really cool things this last year. The Blind Chick riding me bareback with a riding pad! That was cool fun. She even tried a couple of canter pirouettes. They were great. I went nice and slowly, so she didn't slip off the side. You could get a little disorientated very quickly, doing too many spins.

I know she's been doing lots of work on my flying changes. I was getting a little anxious with them, especially the sequence changes. But after a sequence of three, three times changes, we'd come back to a walk and relax. She just lets me breathe. This has made a huge difference to my stress level. I'm coping with this much better, now there's no issue with my flying changes or sequence changes. But who's to say when we up the ante and do two times changes that things won't change? She might have to take my training a little slower then.

Our exercises with our canter pirouettes are coming along well. I have good strength in my hindquarters and find the canter pirouette no issue. But sometimes a little tension can sneak in so again the Blind Chick does the movement and then a reward and backs off. This has really been a wonderful way of training me. I am responding well to it and really appreciate it.

Our lunging is also coming along well. Sometimes if I have had a couple of days off, I may play a little bit on the lunge; buck, kick up and try to go amazingly fast when the Blind Chick is lunging me. I think it might un-nerve her and give her a fright sometimes, but she copes and eventually I slow down and put my head down, bum up and work properly. I do some beautiful work on the lunge. So she tells me!

I know the Blind Chick puts a lot of time into my lunging. She thinks it's a wonderful training aid, I agree. It's a time when I can use my back and be engaged with nobody on top interfering with what I'm doing. I have very expressive movement in the trot and the canter. In the walk I'm still a little bit lazy! But I can't be perfect at everything, can I?

It has also been interesting observing the Blind Chick going from summer into autumn. In summer she doesn't go outside alone much. She is absolutely petrified of ...... snakes!

In the 20 years her and Matthew have been married she has managed to walk on three snakes and fall on a snake! So, knowing she's not a cat with nine lives to risk, she's super careful and conscious of having people around her when she is outside in summer. Personally, I don't blame her. I think they're horrible slippery things.

But since the weather has got cooler it has been transformative. She is in the garden most days. I must say the plants look extremely nervous! Especially when she has those secateurs and loppers.

Matthew has given her some lovely lucerne hay to mulch into the garden, so she's spent a couple of days mulching and weeding. I think her next aim might be my paddock, doing a bit of weeding. I hope she doesn't bring the loppers with her!

It has been lovely getting so much rain. Finally, the drought has broken and wow, what a difference! Not dust everywhere, instead it's lovely green grass. Absolutely spectacular. My first year with the Blind Chick was mainly in drought. Over the last two months the drought broke and everything changed. It's now a different feeding program and having days so hot, up around 44°C day after day, meant such stinkers were no pleasant for man or beast. Definitely not nice weather for riding and doing dressage!

During the drought, the Blind Chick kept the sprinklers going in my paddock for me and to keep the grass growing. It was heaven having somewhere I could stand under the sprinkler and keep cool. Sometimes I was lucky a lovely breeze would come along and cool me even more. It was just shocking heat, take your breath away heat. Certainly, much hotter than where I came from.

And then came the rain! Yippee, it was amazing. The first lot of rain was four inches deep, my paddock was soaked, the grass started jumping out of the ground and the birds were so happy. It was such a beautiful time. Everything seemed to be smiling. Everything was so clean and smelt so fresh.

Mind you, this did put a bit of a dint in our dressage training! The dressage arena was totally flooded for about 10 days. This was when the Blind Chick's lack of confidence really set in.

Consistency would be one of the main things the Blind Chick needs with her riding. With it raining and the dressage arena being flooded we weren't getting the consistency working together. With this came the "Itty-Bitty Shitty Committee" who got in the Blind Chicks head and started undermining her. I hadn't done anything to upset her. It was just her lacking in confidence and not having anybody with her when she was training, this makes a big difference.

During this time, we've had this deadly thing called the Corona Virus start affecting you humans. It hasn't affected me. It's mainly affected the Blind Chick by not being able to get anyone to come and help her. People are in lock down. This has also contributed to her lack of confidence.

But I'm sure she's going to look for someone to assist her that has dressage training. This will make a big difference. Someone who knows what they're looking for and can help her on the ground, be her eyes on the ground. But she hasn't done anything about this yet.

But what she has done, is book me in to go and do training with the amazing trainer José Mendez! He is a Master Horseman on the ground and in the saddle. We have had lessons with him before the Corona Virus hit, but we had to stop because of the virus. Things are loosening up a little bit so the Blind Chick and her friend Jenelle are taking me down to the Southern Highlands. I'll have some training for a couple of weeks, then the Blind Chick will come down and join me.

I'll be sending daily updates to the Blind Chick. José's wonderful wife Fay will take photos of me working with José. So, I'll keep sharing with my wonderful Facebook friends and keep you in the loop with what we are doing with my training. It was such an exciting time last time when I was down there. In three days, 10 minutes each day, just with the lunging cavesson on, the amazing José had me doing very handy piaffe and a lovely elevated passage. The Blind Chick was so excited. So, things are on the move again. All we need to do is get the Blind Chick's confidence back and we'll be on a roll.

3
Riding or Training?

© 2CPhotography

I suppose you'd think it's a simple enough thing, to get on a horse and go for a ride, for your coach to arrive, put the earphones on you and voila, you have a lesson! But none of this works for the Blind Chick! For her to have a lesson isn't that simple.

There needs to be quite a bit of preparation for the Blind Chick to have a lesson. Especially if she is riding by herself, even more things need to play out the right way. One biggie is, the weather!

Let's take the sunshine and what time you would normally ride. For most of us the sunshine is lovely just because it makes it a lovely day, instead of a windy, cold, overcast day. The sun plays a big part in making the day pleasant for man and beast.

This is far from being the case for the Blind Chick.

The sun is a major part of her being able to get her orientation in the dressage arena. We generally walk across to the dressage arena, me guiding the Blind Chick, with her right hand on my neck and the left hand holding the reins. I guide her quietly to the mounting block where she mounts. She typically starts off on the right rein. By doing this the sun is on her left cheek and she rides inside leg into the outside rein, keeping me straight and travelling along the edge of the arena.

The Blind Chick did a lot of work when she first got me, lunging me, and making sure I wouldn't leave the arena as it's lucky to be 12 inches high, maybe 15 inches. It's white plastic and looks like a normal dressage arena edging that you'd find at a competition. But that height is nothing for me to step over. Then voila! I'd be free to roam in the paddock the arena is built in. But I don't. It's especially important for me to stay in the arena and look after my Blind Chick.

So, remembering we started on the right rein and the sun is on our left cheek, we get to the first corner up near H and I turn right. It is my responsibility to turn in the corners. The Blind Chick has put a lot of time into establishing this. Then the sun goes from being on her left cheek to onto her back. This is along the short side. Then we turn and then the sun is on the Blind Chick's right cheek.

So, you can see the importance of the sun when you are totally blind. It helps with the orientation and knowing where you are in the arena. It's not as precise as knowing exactly where you are or what letter you are near, that comes from counting strides, but it gives you an approximation of where you are. Because I turn in the corners this makes a huge difference to the Blind Chicks riding. It's one less responsibility for her.

Keep in mind this is all done with the Blind Chick riding me by herself at the moment. She is looking for someone with dressage training to help her each day as that will make it much easier. Especially easier when she's practising movements like a shoulder-in. Having someone on the ground telling her if she's correctly on three tracks and the same thing if we are practising our flying changes. Someone telling us if I'm late behind will make a big difference to the Blind Chick's training.

The other thing to consider is how hard it would be to do a centreline when you are totally blind! This is exceedingly difficult without someone there to help you. Having someone stand at the centreline where the C marker is and consistently calling out the letter C, C, C, C, allows the Blind Chick to use her hearing to keep her straight on the centreline. This is often quite difficult because sometimes you drift a little to the right or a little to the left. So, it's really important you're set up on the centreline. As you turn at C down the centreline you must be perfectly straight. Those first three strides are critical.

Also having someone on the centreline with a lovely big clear voice is so important. I think when the Blind Chick is training, a consistently straight centreline is our hardest thing to do. Then you bring in halting at X! How does the Blind Chick do a cracker of a halt right at X you ask? She counts the strides from when we turn up the Centre Line to our halt at X. Generally, it's about 14 strides, but this can differ. She must adjust the count if I'm not relaxed, if I've got a little or a lot of tension. Tension makes my strides a little shorter or a little longer. All of these things make a big difference on the count.

So, training by yourself brings in a whole lot of other difficulties not unsurmountable for the Blind Chick. She's been doing Dressage for 30 odd years but I'm a new horse and we're working out new movements. She's constantly trying to adjust for and feel if we need more sideways, more forwards, is the sideways with the correct angle, or not? Having those eyes on the ground make the world a difference to this and it helps the Blind Chick get the feel for the actual movement, and the correct set up of the movement.

Straightness is also especially important. Not having too much bend to the inside, having the horse lovely and straight through the neck is the aim. To achieve correct straightness the Blind Chick uses another sense, a lot. That sense is... feel. Because the Blind Chick can't see whether my neck is straight, feel is really important. I think this must be one of the hardest things for her. Like most horses I am straighter on my left rein then on my right. When I'm on the right rein I probably tend to have a little too much bend and hence I'm not working straight. So, we do quite a lot of work on this to correct it.

Then we add in, maybe doing a diagonal across the arena. Now, unless we have someone at the spot we're aiming for, calling that letter as a living marker, we end up hitting the other side of the arena! Which is not a drama, it's just white plastic, it'll survive. We then proceed on into the corner. It's been remarkably interesting with the Blind Chick riding into the corners in a canter.

Because I'm so large this has been quite the challenge for the Blind Chick to collect me up, so we don't stride out over the edge of the arena. It makes for a really deep corner, which I can understand totally.

All our work together is improving with time. It's amazing the difference working together each day makes. With this a level of understanding between horse and rider it's really quite a cool journey.

So, wow! So many extra senses are being used by the Blind Chick so she can ride. We all have and probably don't utilise them to the maximum all our senses. This makes for great food for thought, I think.

Then we bring in having a lesson with a coach. Now it gets really interesting. It's rather surprising how many coaches don't realise by putting earpieces in a blind rider's ears so the rider can listen to the coach's voice, means that rider now has no way of orientating themselves. That coach now has the possibility of being run over by the blind rider!

I have found that the Blind Chick responds very well to an analytical coach; someone that is big on accuracy, counting of strides and preparation for a movement. Because when you know exactly where you are in the arena, you have the time to prepare for a movement. This is especially important at the level the Blind Chick and I are riding at the moment, which is Medium-Advanced. The movements come up quite quickly, so your preparation for of movement is so important. Being accurate and knowing where you are is also extremely important. Especially when you are setting up and doing these more difficult movements like positioning your canter pirouette and having your sequence changes evenly spaced on the diagonal. Doing these things well, all get you extra marks in a test.

Let me give you an example of a lesson with our wonderful coach José. He calls to the Blind Chick about two strides before she is getting to the corner. This way she has time to do inside leg into outside rein, riding me into the corner. Then we go across the top of the arena towards the next corner, 2 to 3 strides, set up inside leg into outside rein, then straight.

This is so extremely helpful and after time this becomes automatic. The Blind Chick fills in the queues from me as I am getting closer to the corner my body starts to bend a little, I'm giving her feedback from what is coming up. I'm sharing this with you because I want you to understand I'm conscious of what you call teamwork. The Blind Chick and I are a team, we're working together. It's important that she is totally focused on what I'm letting her know, and that she is listening.

José is also very analytical in his teaching of the shoulder-in, renvers and travers. He teaches using the analogy of a face of a clock as a circle. This is very cool; the Blind Chick got the concept extremely quickly.

We don't have consistent coaching at the moment, which is something I know the Blind Chick would love to be having. Generally, we get to see José every four to six weeks for three days. Which is just so cool. But it would make the world of difference if we were able to have more consistent coaching sessions. Why? Because it doesn't take you long to get into bad habits and be doing too much angle in your shoulder-in or having the quarters trailing in your half pass. With a knowledgeable coach being eyes on the ground, those habits do not happen, and you move forward more fluently and consistently.

Also considering we are in Corona Virus lockdown now, we're way behind with our lessons. This hasn't been a good thing for the Blind Chick as it has made a very big gap in our training, plus we've had lots of rain and the dressage arena is in flood! Hence the Blind Chick hasn't had the days in the saddle. This makes a big difference to her confidence level. Currently her confidence is waning, but with the help of José this will all be fixed very quickly. It's not a new thing, it rears its head every time she's not in the saddle at least five days a week.

Confidence is one of those things that are just so very brittle and fragile, and which we often take for granted. But I suppose as you get older that "Itty Bitty Shitty Committee" can get in your head and start undermining you, which creates issues. But the Blind Chick is on the job and getting it fixed by firstly by sending me for training with the wonderful José. She's come down and started building on our relationship with Jose's guidance there. On the ground we have no problem. It's just a little bit of lack of confidence in the saddle, which is understandable when you appreciate my Blind Chick is totally blind.

I'm confident this dint in confidence is just a small glitch which will be overcome very quickly. We'll then be moving right along with our training.

4
Just Nervous !!!

© Amy Naef

Wow isn't autumn just the most beautiful time of the year!

We've had some spectacular rain. Thick lush grass is everywhere instead of dust from the horrific three-year drought.

The days are slowly getting shorter and cooler. It's been a little bit of a wicked summer; the heat has been horrific up around 45°C for quite a few days on end. So, we're really enjoying this awesome cooler weather.

It's like everything has been refreshed after the rain. Everything is so clear and clean. The birds sound so happy, the grass is growing and trees that we thought had died from the drought are coming back to life. It's like magic.

The other thing that's happening is my coat is growing! I'm getting ready for winter.

I was enjoying my beautiful Monday morning; I'd had my hard feed and carrots and was standing enjoying my lucerne hay when the Blind Chick comes down to my paddock carrying a bucket. Oops, no! She's forgotten something. She goes out of my paddock, another five minutes or so goes by, then she's back again. This time she grabs my halter.

I wonder what she has in the bucket, maybe treats for me, some carrots? She puts the bucket down with her goodies in it and I follow her down to the edge of the yard. She proceeds to un-rug me. Perfect, it's a rather lovely, beautiful day and the sun is beaming down, a great day to get some vitamin D don't you think?

Then the Blind Chick starts delving into her bucket. Oh darn, no carrots! It's a brush. She proceeds to give me a lovely brush, I just stand enjoying the sunshine and getting pampered.

Then she dips into the bucket again, maybe a carrot this time? No! She has the clippers; she must be going to do my mane again.

The Blind Chick turns the clippers on and slowly starts to do my mane. Now there wasn't much hair there to start with, but I suppose a tidy up is a good thing. When she finishes my mane, she starts on my body! Wow does she realise what she's getting herself into? I'm going to look moth-eaten. I'm sure the Blind Chick and clippers are not a good combination.

She diligently starts on my neck with her clippers, the blades are lovely and sharp, so my winter woollies are dropping off very easily. She goes back and forth over my neck many times because she can't see, trying not to miss anything. Then she starts on my shoulder, my back and part of my legs. Things seem to be going okay but I still think I will look moth-eaten. I'm sure she is missing bits and pieces.

At this stage I should point out I'm just standing there. She hasn't put the halter on me. I admit this clipping thing isn't such a bad a gig. I quite like the vibration of the clippers on my skin and they're not noisy which is a bonus.

My Blind Chick is such a clever cookie. To makes sure the hair that's coming off isn't blowing in her face there she's positioned me, so the breeze blows the hair away from us, not into us.

She finishes one side, or let me say partially finishes one side. My neck on the near side is done, my shoulder and belly the Blind Chick has done a little bit under my tummy, now it's time for me to turn again so the wind will blow that hair away. She can start on the off-side again, starting with my neck.

Gosh my body feels so lovely where she's taken the hair off. I'd started getting quite itchy with the extra hair especially during these beautiful autumn days and lots of lovely sun. I'd get a bit sweaty. Things are looking up, but I still think I will look moth-eaten!

After 2.5 hours of diligent clipping the Blind Chick gives me a lovely brush and then I lead her up to the tack shed. She gets the wash gear out and gives me a lovely bath. Oh, I feel so fresh, and the breeze is drying me off super quick.

Okay kiddo, I think the job is only half done, what happens now? The Blind Chick appears in the tack shed door with a clean rug which she proceeds to put on me and then my fly veil. Then I lead her quietly back to my paddock. Yay, this time I get a carrot, I've been such a good boy. But, I still have hair on me, the job is not finished. What's going on?

The next day the same thing plays out. The Blind Chick comes down with the halter and her little bucket with no carrots. Ripped off again! She takes my two rugs off; gives me a lovely big brush and it is just beautiful feeling the spectacular sunny day on my skin. Then, out come the clippers!

Well, I must say she did struggle getting to the hair on the top of my back and rump being 18. 3hh, 187.5cm. Definitely she needs the mounting block to finish the job properly. She slowly did around my flank area and then my rump and it was feeling so good getting that itchy hair off. Again another 2.5 hour session with the Blind Chick going over and over where she'd been making sure she'd left no hairy lines anywhere. So now I'm left with four hairy legs and a hairy head!

I felt a little bit like those poodles that have those specialty clips. But I'm quite grateful that the Blind Chick didn't take the power tool to my face or legs, that was left up to her wonderful friend Jenelle.

We're visiting her on Monday to get my clipping job finished, plus I've got a date with the dentist.

So, after a weekend looking quite moth-eaten, the Blind Chicks lovely friend Jacq and her sister Sally picked us up to go to Janelle's place. It was a little bit of a brisk morning, but it was turning into a spectacular day. Janelle finished clipping me and then I had a lovely big brush and waited for the dentist.

It was remarkably busy at Jenelle's. She's a professional showjumper and has quite a few horses in training as well as giving lessons, so it was an interesting morning for me watching the horses coming and going and those training over the jumps. A lovely time.

Ashley arrived about 10.30am. Ashley is the Equine Dentist, a lovely young man from out near Mendooran.

5
Check out my smile

© 2CPhotography

You may ask, what is an Equine Dentist? What do they do? Why do we get them to see our horses?

I'll endeavour to give you the short answer, and then I'll share with you my experience with the wonderful Ashley.

Equine Dentists help maintain the health of a horse's continually growing teeth. They also correct problems such as uneven chewing surfaces, which can lead to inadequate nutrition and poor performance. Equine Dentists spend most of their time performing preventive dentistry on horses.

The most frequently performed procedure is called floating. It's a procedure that smooths the sharp points from a horse's tooth, the points that cause mouth pain and cuts to the inside of their mouth. These sharp points often cause difficulty riding and controlling the animal. The modern horse's diet typically lacks traditional grazing, consequently normal even tooth wear from a traditional diet doesn't occur.

When Ashley first came to meet me, he chatted with me, patted me, and gently placed his hand along my cheeks. Next, he put a leather thing similar to a halter over my head. It had a metal gadget as part of it, that he put in my mouth. This specific Equine Dentistry halter is called a gag.

The gag is really well designed. The metal bit in my mouth can be clicked open a little or a lot, to make sure my mouth stays open. This allows Ashley to gently put his hand in my mouth and feel my teeth, to see what they were like, without fear that I could bit him.

Thankfully, Ashley seemed rather pleased with what he felt. He said that I didn't need a lot of work, I just had a little rough spot at the back of my offside bottom row of teeth, and that could be easily fixed with a bit of rasping. He floated the rest of my teeth, which made sure there were no rough edges, and that nothing could grab when I chew.

I admit my first impression of Ashley was a good one, but that didn't last long. I wasn't a fan of the gag holding my mouth open. It felt really strange when he then put his hand in and felt everywhere. If that wasn't weird enough, he put a flat metal thing in my mouth and used it to start rasping my teeth. Well holy cow Batman! So unimpressed was I, I proceeded to walk backwards every moment I could. In his quiet voice Ashley reassured me that it was okay, slowly but surely, I settled, and Ashley got to work levelling my teeth. Thankfully this didn't take long.

I admit I did make it more difficult for Ashley. Every now and then I'd lift my head up. I couldn't help it. Remember I'm over 18hh, 187.5 cm, I'm quite tall. What I did must have made it like trying to treat a giraffe!

But like I said, after a while I settled down and Ashley was able to rasp my teeth more easily. Then he put his hand back inside and felt my upper and lower teeth to make sure everything was just right, and nothing was going to catch when I ate. He was very pleased with the job he and the gag did. I was really happy about how my mouth felt. He finished by giving me a big pat and ….. a carrot, of course.

I had a couple of other horsey friends that were done at the same time. There was a lovely horse called Zeke. He and I become quite good mates, just standing in the yard waiting for Ashley. Zeke is a racehorse and he had only been off the track about six weeks when Ashley put his hand in Zeke's mouth. What he found wasn't pretty. It was all cut up and scarred from his teeth being so sharp for so long.

Soon Ashley had the gag on Tommy and began rasping his teeth. Voila! In no time at all the rough edges were gone and now Tommy won't be losing any feed when he eats, and he won't be getting cut inside of his mouth. Eating or being ridden must've been very, very painful.

It was interesting watching Ashley do Tommy's teeth. Tommy was much better behaved than I was, he just stood there and let Ashley get on with his job.

Well, all is good. Our teeth are done and dusted for another year. I'll try and be better behaved when Ashley visits again next year to do our teeth.

6
Yippee a Road Trip

Smiles all round © 2CPhotography

Well gee whiz, it's an exciting time right now.

I can't wait. I'm going down to spend some time with the amazing José Mendez, our coach. After a little while the Blind Chickie babe will come down and do some training with us.

But there are lots of things that have to happen before I can be put on the horse float and taken down to the Southern Highlands to train.

Firstly, the Blind Chickie babe has to organise a driver to take us down in the Ranger. She has to make sure it's okay with Matthew that we take the Ranger, because doing so means he becomes carless for a few days. Typically, he borrows his mum or dad's car for the time we're away. These types of things are the first bits of organising that needs to be done.

Then its coordinating with the amazing José and his wife Fay, the dates that suit them best for us to arrive.

Yippee! The big things have been organised. Dates confirmed, driver for the car arranged and float organised.

Our amazing friend Jenelle Waters, a professional showjumper who typically wouldn't be available to come with us, is able to spend this time with us because of Covid. It is Jenelle who will drive us down to José's for lessons. It is Jenelle who'll help the beautiful Fay prepare me for our lessons.

But I must say, I think Jenelle is extremely impressed with watching José ride me. The way he trains is pretty special. His method is different to anyone else's. José trains with an 'Ask, don't Tell, Kindness and Patience' approach. It's impressive to watch him in action.

Then comes the big job of my feed! The Blind Chickie babe has to mix up enough feeds to last me two weeks. Each feed has to have my additives as well, all in the one bag. Enough so I have two hard feeds a day.

The Blind Chick goes to all this effort to ensure when the beautiful Fay feeds me each day, all she has to do is add half a cup of linseed oil to a bag of the made-up feed, give it a bit of a shake and voila! Breakfast is ready. Repeat this process for my evening feed.

Then the Blind Chickie babe gets her wonderful husband to load the ute up and the horse float with enough lucerne hay to last me for the two weeks.

I generally get one biscuit of a morning and two biscuits of hay in the evening, but they will adjust this according to my workload.

Then, with winter just around the corner, the Blind Chickie babe goes through my wardrobe of winter woollies. I'm heading for the Southern Highlands where it is notoriously much colder than it is at home in Dubbo.

She pulls out my beautiful moleskin rugs, I have four of these, so she put three aside. She digs out a beautiful warm woollen rug that can go under my top rug, hoping this will be enough. There is also a lovely Weatherbeeta rug there, but it's only a six-foot nine rug, I'm a seven foot. Hmm, maybe the Blind Chick will have to invest in another rug?

She puts my magnetic boots through the wash, so they're nice and clean for our trip. I wear these nearly 24 hours a day, seven days a week. Except for when I'm being ridden when I have my exercise boots on. My Blind Chick is a great believer in these magnetic boots. I am too. They really do help with my circulation, which in turn helps with any limb recovery and repair.

Then she pulls out her tack box and goes through all her grooming gear to make sure it's all clean. She puts some 'No More Knots' mane and tail treatment in one of the holding boxes so my tail is lovely and silky and easy to brush. This is such a cool product. I hate knots in my hair.

Then to make sure I have spares, the Blind Chick packs two sets of clean work boots and at least three clean saddle clothes. She diligently cleans my bridal and saddle and picks up my clean brushes that she's just washed and packed in the tack box.

This is one thing the Blind Chick is fussy about, clean gear, especially in summer. I have a clean cotton rug every day in winter, my heavier moleskin rug is clean and changed once a week. I think the only reason she doesn't change my winter rug every day is that the moleskin rug is heavier and harder on the washing machine. Don't tell Matthew she puts it through the people washing machine! It's imperative that everything is clean that goes through there. Hence why she washes and keeps everything so clean, so it doesn't mess up the family washing machine.

Now you realise with me writing this book there are lots of family secrets that come out. One of these being the Blind Chick using the family washing machine for horsy stuff. It's a big secret okay.

Yippee, everything is packed in the tack box and ready to go in the float and be tied in. All the horse feed is in bins and has been tied in with the hay. Such a big job just generally takes a day and a half, getting everything organise for us to do a road trip.

As soon as Matthew hooks the float on the ute he drives around to the shed and checks each tyres pressure. It's really important that the tyres on the horse float and the ute have enough air in them so we have a safe trip. Before the Blind Chick and Jenelle are ready to go he also checks the oil in the engine, to make sure it is okay.

I think the Blind Chick is incredibly lucky to have Matthew. I remember the first day I saw them together when he brought the Blind Chick to look at me, he held her hand and guided her and told her when to step up, when to step down, when to duck. It was pretty cool. I thought he must love her, a lot.

But keeping in mind way back then I didn't know she was totally blind. I just thought he was a very caring husband. Be he's still doing those same things, looking out for her, making sure she's safe.

Wow! Everything is ready to go the night before we head off down to the Southern Highlands. The Blind Chickie babe dishes up my dinner as well as a little bit more hay than on usual as in the morning I will only have about 1.5 hours to eat my breakfast before we hit the road. It's a six-hour trip down to the Southern Highlands.

Jenelle arrives lovely and early about 7.30am. She comes down to the paddock and gets me, brings me up and then she and the Blind Chick take my top rug off, put it in the tack box, give me a couple of carrots and a big pat and voila! I'm on the float ready to head for the Southern Highlands.

Some people stop and let their horses off on road trips, we don't. The only time we stop is for a wee break for the girls. I prefer to get the travel over and done with as quick as possible. It's quite a nice run from Dubbo down to the Southern Highlands.

When we go out our gate we turn right, travel a little while, then turn left onto the main highway between Sydney and Melbourne. We head off towards Goulburn, after Goulburn it's not long till we're at Jose's in Tallong.

When we arrive, Fay and José's five lovely dogs greet us, all extremely excited. One wants to play ball, another wants a pat and a cuddle, but the girls focus is all about me, getting me unloaded. Jenelle then takes me for a walk and I can have a pick of grass which is rather lovely getting my head down. I walk, eat, and relax for about half an hour before she puts me in my paddock.

My paddock is lovely and spacious. I've got new mates either side of my fence. I love friends. I'm looking forward to seeing my beautiful Fay, she spoils me with carrots and lots of love and hugs.

Jenelle and the Blind Chick organise my feed in the back of the horse float for Fay. It's all stacked so it can be easily accessed. One says 'Morning', one says 'Evening'. In the latter, they just have to add half a cup of linseed oil and it's done. My tack box is taken over to the tack shed and the girls get ready to go.

This is the bit I don't like so much. When the Blind Chick goes something in my heart goes all sort of sore and not so happy. But Fay is there with a big pat and a cuddle and a few treats. This reassures me that I am loved and being looked after here. After a little while I'm okay, but I do miss my Blind Chick.

DAILY DIARY
Introduction

Come join us.
Walk in our shoes.

Welcome to our journey captured here
in our day-to-day diary entries.

BEWARE

training a horse can sometimes be quite repetitious!
So be prepared, some of these daily diary entries
may at first seem repetitious.
What lies behind each of them though,
is working One Step at a Time towards a bigger goal.

7 June

Oopsy!

Feeling Sorry
12 June 2020

Diary entry by Johno

I'm feeling pretty bad, I have a very big confession to make.

Yesterday when I was feeling so spritely and healthy, I did a couple of big leaps in the arena. Why? For no other reason other than I was feeling good. Yes, maybe the Blind Chick had given me a little extra feed, which she has now taken back off me.

So, the Blind Chick had a fall off me!

I feel so bad. It wasn't done intentionally. I was just feeling good and playing. I suppose when you think of someone 18.3hh playing around, it was a big leap.

Needless to say, I'm feeling really bad about what happened. But after the Blind Chick came off Gwen≠ caught me and the Blind Chicks mother-in-law Lee and father-in-law John came up and got her up off the ground. God love her cotton socks, she got straight back on!

She walked me for a bit then did a bit of a trot on both reins. Just lovely soft swinging trot, all done with confidence. Then when she dismounted, she hobbled over and got the lunging cavesson and took me into the round yard. There she gave me a little bit of a lunge to see if I wanted to play anymore. I admit, I did think of doing some more in the beginning, but I soon settled and worked very nicely.

Since then … Matthew, her wonderful husband, took her to the doctor yesterday evening. She's now off to get x-rays today. She's still in quite a bit of pain and can't take weight on the leg. It maybe just some big bruising, but hopefully we'll know today after x-rays. If she needs a scan they'll do that later.

I missed the Blind Chick feeding me this morning. Matthew brought my feed down as the Blind Chick couldn't walk.

I feel so guilty and so bad about what happened, but it wasn't me being naughty. I was just exuberant and playing. Yes, I know that is not an excuse. I'll try much harder to be a good boy. We really did some beautiful work in the arena yesterday.

I hope everybody is safe and well. We are coming into another weekend, so take some time to drop somebody a line, give them a ring. Tell somebody you love them and miss them. Take the time to make somebody's day.

Have a spectacular weekend. Loads of love and hugs, Johno.

P.S: I gave it a lot of thought on whether to share the Blind Chicks fall or not. I decided to, because we're all on this journey together. The good, the bad, the ugly, the warts and the happiness. I thought it was important to share this hiccup we'd had.

Onwards and upwards, all good.

Lots of love, Johno.

Update

Feeling Positive
13 June 2020

Diary entry by Johno

Morning all, I hope you are all having a lovely day. Firstly, an update on how the Blind Chickie babe went yesterday with her x-rays.

The radiographer said he could see no breaks or wee fractures, so that is a good thing. Now they're possibly planning on getting scans to see if there is any tendon damage. That'll happen early next week. I really hope it is deep bruising.

Her wonderful husband Matthew has taken up the job of nurse-maid; lifting her legs in an out of the car, wrapping her knees so they're stabilised, with cotton wool bandage. She is walking around like a peg leg. Naughty Blind Chick, she's supposed to be sitting on the lounge taking it easy!

I must say I did see her out hanging out the clothes, plus I heard she had just made a lovely big pot of chicken and sweet corn soup. So, she must be feeling a little better.

Matthew is also in charge of feeding me at the moment, as Blind Chick will not be able to get all the way down to my stable and back with her white cane, the feed bucket and me wanting to help myself to the feed.

We would also like to thank all our wonderful Facebook friends for their well wishes and concern. Plus thank you for not rubbishing me for feeling a little exuberant and us having a wee accident. We all know things can go wrong with horses.

I have to share with you, the Blind Chick has readjusted my horse feed! She's taken it back to normal. No more extras for a Johno.

Also, it was important to share a little hiccup with the Blind Chick coming off, because this is our story. We are on this journey with all of you and sharing it warts and all. We're so grateful to have you all in our life and the wonderful love and support. We feel so very blessed. Thank you from the bottom of our heart.

We wish everybody a wonderful weekend. Don't forget to make somebody's day, give them a phone call, send a note telling somebody you love them. I have received so much love from our friends on Facebook. We are both very grateful. Have a spectacular day.

Loads of love and hugs, Johno and the Blind Chick.

Naughty Blind Chick

Feeling Grateful
14 June 2020

Diary entry by Johno

We've have had some lovely rain, about 14 mils overnight, which has been wonderful for Matthew's crops. He's growing wheat and barley and a new paddock of lucerne.

Now for some of those beautiful sunny days and the crops will come along well.

Update on the Blind Chickie babe! Well, she has spent another day on the lounge with her leg up. She's got her knees stabilised, very well bandaged, so she doesn't twist it. She still has leg pain when walking, this is under control with some prescription medication.

Matthew has his hands full keeping her off her leg! She wanted to walk to the gate today, but he convinced her she needed to rest it, let it get better. I hear she is planning to make a lovely big pot of home-made pumpkin soup tomorrow.

Also heard by the horsey grapevine that I'm heading off down to my best mate José and Fay's place. Yippee more training, while the Blind Chick convalesces.

I tend to think this is an awesome idea for more than one reason. I get to train with my good mate, the Master of classical dressage, and be spoiled by his beautiful wife Fay. Plus, it also gives the Blind Chick time to not be thinking up ways she can get outside and work with me. She wanted to lunge me this afternoon!

I think the next few days will be spent with the Blind Chick getting horse feeds mixed, and my warm rugs packed for while I'm away.

I'm hope you have had a lovely weekend. I sure have. I have done nothing! I'm very much looking forward to getting back into training though. Have a spectacular week.

Loads of love and hugs, Johno.

Healing From Scotland

Feeling Blessed
16 June 2020

Diary entry by Johno

A very good morning to everybody from a very foggy Macquarie Valley. I think we can call it a Johno in the mist! Even if the Blind Chick could see, she'd have had trouble finding me today, it was a bit of a pea souper.

I was a tad excited this morning. The Blind Chick came down and fed me, it was really lovely. Much slower walking down to my stable than she normally is, but she is moving which is a good thing. I got lots of big pats and lots of carrots.

A massive thank you to our beautiful friend Cathy Price from Wales for doing a healing on the Blind Chicks leg yesterday. It is feeling so much better. She's moving so much better, thank you beautiful.

It's a bit of an exciting day today. The Blind Chick and I are having a visit from one of our beautiful Facebook friends - Maureen from Newcastle. Maureen and her daughter are coming to visit and have afternoon tea. I'm sure they'll also bring me carrots. We're really looking forward to their visit.

Blind Chickie babe has mixed all my feeds for my trip down to José's. She's been going through rugs this morning, working out what is going to be best to take down to the Southern Highlands. It's much colder there than here in Dubbo you know.

Ooops, I nearly forgot to mention the pumpkin soup was a big hit that Blind Chickie babe made. She made it a bit differently than she normally does because she was down a few ingredients. But apparently it turned out really nice, very smooth and tasty.

Quote of the day
"It doesn't matter what you did or where you were...it matters where you are and what you're doing. Get out there! Sing the song in your heart and NEVER let anyone shut you up!!"
Steve Maraboli

I think this quote is very much like the Blind Chick she just gets on with it.

I hope everybody is safe well and warm. I'm wishing you all a wonderful day. Be kind to yourself and tell someone you love them.

Loads of love and hugs, Johno.

Love Who You Are

Feeling Blessed
17 June 2020

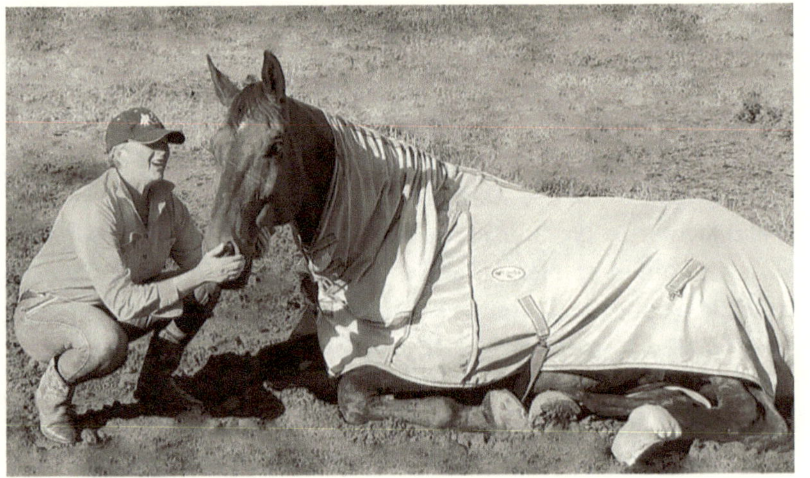

Diary entry by Johno and the Blind Chick

Good morning. I stumbled across this in my travels and thought it was definitely worth sharing. You might like to share it to.

In order to love who you are,

You cannot hate the experiences you've had that shaped you.

Wishing everybody a wonderful day. Be kind to yourself and to others. Smile good morning, it doesn't take much to make a difference.

Sending you loads of love and hugs, Johno and the Blind Chick.

Friends

Feeling Grateful
18 June 2020

Diary entry by Johno

Wow what a spectacular day! The breeze was a little chilly, but the sun has been beautiful. I thought I'd share with you how the visit we had yesterday from a lovely lady called Maureen went.

Maureen is one of our wonderful Facebook friends, and her beautiful daughter-in-law Julie drove her all the way from Newcastle yesterday to come and meet me and the Blind Chick. The Blind Chickie babe did a cuppa tea, biscuits etc, but I know why they really came. They wanted to meet me! They came with carrots and cuddles. It was so lovely to meet the beautiful Maureen and her lovely daughter-in-law Julie.

The Blind Chickie babe even broke out the best china that she was given when she was 21. She had never used it before. After a quick wash of the cups, saucers and plates, the table was all set. She even went to the trouble of cooking Tim Tams and Melting Moments! Ha ha, no, she got those from the shop.

It truly was a lovely time visiting.

After our visit the girls were heading back to Mudgee to a lovely restaurant and an evening in a beautiful motel before heading off to Tenterfield. How cool, a road trip.

Thank you, beautiful Maureen and lovely Julie, for visiting us. It really was a treat and a pleasure to meet you both.

Well, everything is packed in the horse float, warm rugs, and horse feed. There's even been a little bit of maintenance done to the float, sticking down some rubber in where we horses stand. So, the float is all ready to go. The Ranger even has new tyres all-round; safety is the key. We're heading off at 8am in the morning.

I'm hope you've had a wonderful day. Keep safe and well.

Loads of love and hugs, Johno.

I've arrived

Feeling Excited
19 June 2020

Diary entry by Johno

Well, we had a great trip down to the Southern Highlands yesterday. Sorry I didn't do a diary entry yesterday, I was a little off colour when I arrived at Fay and José's. I tend to think that I hadn't had enough cuddles with my lovely Fay.

Not long after the Blind Chick and the girls left, my beautiful Fay saw me pawing and rolling. She was quick to take me for a walk, I was showing signs of colic which concerned her greatly. She rang the Blind Chick and the Blind Chick asked her "please call the vet if you need to". The beautiful Fay took my temperature, checked my heart, and everything was fine. No raised temperature. I think I just wanted some love and attention from the beautiful Fay, the truth be known.

Fay walked me for a little while longer, she let me have a green pick and gave me some carrots, of course. Then she took me back to my paddock and I ate all my dinner. Fay also got up and checked me during the night and I got extra treats. Aren't I a spoiled boy!

I know the Blind Chick is so very grateful to have me down with the amazing José and his beautiful wife Fay, this is my home away from home. I'm loved and looked after as if I belong here. I'm so very grateful, we're both so very grateful the Blind Chick and I.

So, the wonderful José was going to give me some light work to-day, maybe a little lunge and then back into work tomorrow. I'm so looking forward to my training. This is also giving the Blind Chick's leg time to recuperate. Each day she's improving in big leaps and bounds. Gradually she's starting to be able to bend her leg a little, which is great news.

I also heard via the grapevine that the Blind Chick, Jenelle and Gwen called in at family friends, the Stevenson's, and have a lovely night catching up.

The girls have all arrive safely back in Dubbo with pumpkins in hand to make beautiful fresh pumpkin soup! They found a gentleman that grew pumpkins along the road and brought quite a few.

I have also heard via the grapevine that the Blind Chick is missing me already. I'm in the best place, I'm going to be learning with the amazing José. She'll come down and have lessons in a week or so when her leg is up to riding. At this stage I don't think she could lift her foot up to put her foot in the stirrup.

I hope everyone has had a lovely day. Please look after yourself, be kind to others.

Loads of love and hugs, Johnno.

José the Master

José Mendez
ASK and You Shall Receive

Respect for, and partnership with, your horse is key to José's approach to training horses and riders around Australia, the United States and England, writes Jane Camens for an article in HorseVibes magazine.

"Always remember 'ASK'," says one of Australia's master horsemen, José Mendez. The word is emblazoned on his jacket. Below the capitalised letters he has unpacked the meaning: **A**ppreciation, **S**incerity, **K**indness.

José moved to Australia at the age of 19 from southern Spain. Now in his mid-50s, he's worked with horses all his life, starting on his family's property and later, from the age of 12, at the Royal Andalusian School of Equestrian Art in the city of Jerez de la Frontera. The school is famous nowadays for its 'dancing horses' performances, but when José began it was a family business, concerned mainly with supplying horses to men who worked the bulls. Along with full board and the friendship of other student trainers, who are now among Spain's best horsemen, José was pleased to earn the equivalent of about $15 a month. Most of which he sent home to his mother. "The years at the school cemented my skills in the art of classical horsemanship," he says. "It was an essential learning period."

At the age of 19, José took a six-month leave of absence from the school to join his older brother Manolo, in Australia. Manolo had trained at the same school and wanting to see more of the world, took up an offer of a three-year contract with El Caballo Blanco in

Perth. By the time José was invited to join him, El Caballo had a lot more horses and not enough trainers.

"I loved Australia," José says. He also fell in love with Fay, who worked at El Caballo and whom he later married. Australia became José's new home, and now, nearly 40 years later, he and Fay run their own classical riding school, the Mendez Equestrian Centre at Tallong in the Southern Highlands, about one hour's drive south of Sydney. "It had always been my dream to have my own place," he says.

It was a long journey from his arrival in Australia to the amazing reputation he now enjoys. Among the highlights were being selected in 1986 on the beautiful Andalusian, El Caballo Blanco Cadiz, for the World Equestrian Games in Toronto. In the early 1990s he represented Australia three times in international competitions on his magnificent Hanoverian stallion, Leonardo 68.

José has performed in front of thousands of people with different horses. With his soul mate horse Fortuno he performed in the Spanish Opera Carmen in Australia, New Zealand, and Singapore. With the beautiful horse Nevado he performed many times throughout Australia and New Zealand. He gave demonstrations at Equitana in 1999 and 2001 and has featured in numerous television commercials. "Sometimes I'd have to do a quick wardrobe change from dressage tails which I wore to compete in, to my performance Spanish costume, then change quickly back into tails for the rest of the competition," he laughs.

Cupboards in the Mendez home are full of ribbons and prize rugs, testament to the long journey they've taken to arrive where they are today. José rarely shows people these cupboards. There are so many stories in there of events and spectacular horses he's partnered with. He says he doesn't much like standing in front of an applauding crowd, taking credit for something he couldn't have achieved without whichever horse took them to that glory. He prefers to take the horse for a walk and perhaps lie on the grass to bask together with his horse in their shared triumph. "I've been fortunate to work with and own many beautiful horses, and I have loved them all. I look on all horses as my teachers," José says.

He hasn't competed for a while because he's so busy working horses and training riders at his equestrian centre as well as giving clinics all around Australia, travelling regularly to Swan Hill, Geelong, Murwillumbah, the Sunshine Coast, the Gold Coast and Gosford. He has also been travelling twice a year to America to give clinics down the east coast of the United States. "I'm not doing that this year, because I want to focus here," he says. "I have enough work in Australia, which is great."

A typical day for José is to ride (in training) five to eight horses and give between two and four lessons. He would love to find a top-level competition horse again. "I have several possible Grand Prix level horses, but I don't like to predict," he says. I ask him about the importance of his motto: ASK – Appreciation, Sincerity, Kindness. "The horse deserves more respect than most people give them," he says. "They are not machines. They are compassionate beings."

He talks of the need for slow learning, or of not being impatient for the right outcome, because to overload a horse with too much will only confuse him. He speaks of learning the alphabet and how a child must learn each letter one at a time, comparing it to the way a horse needs to be taken gently from one step to the next. He can watch a horse under its rider and see immediately that the horse hasn't been taught the basics and has, for instance, been forced to bend when it's not yet natural for him. Impatience being a trait of this rider (myself), José spent three-quarters of an hour helping me and my little quarter horse learn how to ride a circle correctly. Yes, it's basic, but it was a valuable foundation lesson.

"I can help people understand. Appreciate the horse. Don't just pick up the reins and ride," he says. "You pick them up and say thank you for letting me be on your back. You do this with sincerity. If the horse does something naughty, tap him with the whip to guide him. Horses are never wrong. They only do what they know how to do. When they do something well, give him a pat. Tell him he's a good boy. Treat him with kindness. You will get the reward.

"A horse has a great memory. After the elephant, the horse could be the second. He remembers who it was who punished him and who was kind. The horse can see clearer than we can about many things. The memory is not just the brain. It is stored in the muscle. If it were just in the brain, you could play your training DVDs in the stable and he'd learn. No, he has to feel it in his body. He learns with repetition. He learns rhythm, the paces, commands, and aides. If I ask him to do something in a different way from one day to the next, it's difficult for the horse to understand. You start with rules and repetition, like with little kids learning to paint a picture. They learn to join the dots. You repeat the exercises pretty much every day.

"So, with my circle riding, they can get bigger or smaller, but they must be true circles, done at the same rhythm. We ride around a clock face, aware of where the numbers three, six, nine and twelve are. Without pointers, says José, "It's like walking randomly around the city without landmarks."

Fortunately for Classical Dressage enthusiasts around Australia, José Mendez is there to give us those pointers.

You can contact José and Fay at their centre.
Mendezeqcentre@bigpond.com.au

Smile – It's Infectious

😌 Smile
21 June 2020

Diary entry by Johno

Well, it's definitely a tad cooler down here in the Southern Highlands than in Dubbo, but I'm nicely rugged up and warm. I'm being very spoilt and loved by the beautiful Fay. I hear the Blind Chickie babe's leg is definitely on the improve, she went for a lovely long walk today with great movement and flexibility in her leg, this is awesome news.

I came across something a bit special today and thought we could start our own special pandemic to make people smile and be happy. Have a read and let me know what you think,

Smile
Smiling is infectious, you catch it like the flu.
When someone smiled at me today, I started smiling too.
I passed around the corner and someone saw my grin.
When he smiled, I realized, I'd passed it on to him.
I thought about that smile, then I realized its worth.
A single smile, just like mine could travel round the earth.
So, if you feel a smile begin, don't leave it undetected.
Let's start an epidemic quick and get the world infected!
Spike Milligan

Okay everybody let's be prepared to share let's make a difference let's start the smile pandemic smiling makes us feel good spreads those good vibes around the world

So, José, the Blind Chick and I are starting off the smile, let's see how many other people we can make smile and feel good. Hopefully you've caught it now, you're smiling.

I hope you're all having a wonderful day. Lots of love and hugs, Johno.

The Master Rocks

Feeling Privileged
23 June 2020

Diary entry by Johno

Well, a hearty good morning from José and I from the Southern Highlands. Just a tad chilly here today.

My morning started with a beautiful smile and a carrot from the lovely Fay and my breakfast of course. Then after brekkie Fay came and caught me, gave me a lovely brush and put my saddle, bridle and boots on ready for work with José. I even had a nice rug over my loins to keep me warm when we first started warming up. This was very pleasant as I must say it really is quite brisk down here.

I totally love José's way of warming up. It's so relaxed and encourages me to take the bridle, reach down and stretch my back, stretch my neck and swing through from behind. But no pressure! The invitation is there, and I just take it up willingly because it feels so good.

The amazing 'Ask Don't Tell' approach works so well in training. Well; it definitely works with me! Then we go into a lovely long rein trot, again stretching and swinging through the back. There's massive engagement from behind, I can't help it. This is all just happening naturally because José is not interfering with my body, he's just allowing me to be relaxed and use my body how it's meant to be used. No forcing, no telling.

José then quietly takes up my reins a little, and we do a little bit of lateral work. This is just so easy now. He uses so little leg aid you hardly know he is doing anything, and I am responding to this kindness, so willingly. It's lovely. I can't impress on you enough about this Asking Not Telling approach, it totally rocks out.

José does some lovely work on both reins in the walk and the trot, then we go into the canter. Lovely big, long strides, again relaxed, again on the buckle. He just lets me use my body. Then quietly he takes up the reins and we do a couple of transitions, canter to the walk. I'm getting much better at this.

That wonderful saying 'Less is Best' rings in the Blind Chicks head from her wonderful coach years ago Judy Cubitt. That was one of her favourite sayings. Another she liked was 'Keep It Simple, Stupid'. I think both are great sayings.

The simplicity and ease of the training with José is just lovely. There is just no tension! You have no idea as a horse, how nice it is to be considered, to be invited instead of forced. I have no tension or stress. This is amazing. I know the Blind Chick still trains the old fashion way but she is learning and getting better. Under José's guidance the penny will drop I'm sure.

This is the reason the Blind Chick chose to come to José for his training method. She wanted something different for me, she wanted to train by Asking, not Telling. She wanted a kind way of doing things. She has found this with the amazing José, we are both so very, very grateful.

Here's me going on about my wonderful lesson with José. Yes, I'm very excited. But I better give you an update on the Blind Chick. Well, she went to her doctor last night who was very impressed with her ability to be walking quite regularly. However, there are still problems with something under the kneecap, it's clunking. So Blind Chickie babe is off for an MRI.

It'll be interesting to see how this goes, as the Blind Chickie babe is a little bit claustrophobic. But I'll let you know what the results are as soon as I hear.

I'm wishing everybody a wonderful day. Keep safe, well and warm. Loads and loads of love, hugs and big smiles, Johno.

What's It Like?

 Feeling Empathy
23 June 2020

Prada & the Blind Chick

Diary entry by Johno

Well good morning all from Chile Southern Highlands. I have been giving this one a lot of thought and I have questions for the Blind Chick that may interest you because the answer definitely interests me. I'm wondering, what makes her tick?

My first question to the Blind Chick is about how hard it must be, going blind. Where do you get the energy, the strength, the reason to want to get up of a morning and do something? Wouldn't it be easier to just sit and have things done for you?

Wow! I don't think the Blind Chick likes this question.

"Going blind has not been a choice. Living has been a choice, moving forward has been a choice, my attitude is the choice, my love of life is a choice. I choose to live, I choose to enjoy, I choose to make a difference, and I choose to have a hell of a lot of fun while doing it. Everybody has their cross to bear. It just depends on how you choose to carry it.

I could choose to let being blind be a burden. But I have chosen to make it work for me. Because of my blindness, my Guide Dog and my horse, I have raised millions of dollars for charity. By making my so-called blindness work for me, I tend to try and make an opportunity out of everything that comes into my life. Whether it be positive or whether it be negative.

Going blind has been pretty crappy at times, but I tend to think I have had an amazing opportunity and if there isn't an opportunity in front of me, like if there isn't a light at the end of the tunnel, go down and light the bloody thing yourself.

Life is no dress rehearsal. We are here to give it our best go. So, let's make it work, let's make a difference, let's be happy, let's be united and make a positive impact. It's a little bit like the diary entry Johno did the other day about a smile. Smiling really is contagious, so is being happy and sharing joy, sharing goodwill and good thoughts. They're so contagious. I think this is one of the special reasons that Johno and I have chosen to share our journey. It's because it is special, it's about love, it's about kindness, it's about sharing and having so many beautiful people on this journey with us. All that makes it so very special.

To sum up going blind I tend to think it has made me the person I am. We need to be happy with the person we are. I am happy with who I am and what I represent. It's also important to love yourself for who you are and what you represent. This is so very important. Because if you can't love yourself, you can't love anybody else. Hence, I spend my life sharing love, joy and happiness, and hopefully it is contagious, and it can spread like a pandemic. We need more love and joy in the world.

To sum up Johno's question, has it been hard going blind? Yes, sometimes. But if I was given a deck of cards and asked would I like to draw this card all over again, I would take the life I have. It's pretty terrific and I am extremely happy in the skin I'm in".

Wow, holy cow, what an answer! I wasn't sure what to expect. I knew it would be positive but so determined, so courageous. I will give my next question a lot of thought.

I hope you're having a spectacular day.

Loads of love and hugs, Johno and the Blind Chick with attitude.

P.S: Just a thought. If you think someone needs a little bit of a lift, some awesome encouragement, share this diary entry with them. I think the Blind Chick's message is really important. Love Johno.

Why?

 Feeling Grateful
24 June 2020

Diary entry by Johno and the Blind Chick

I hope everyone is having a lovely day. It's a tad chilly in the Southern Highlands again I hear. We've had some lovely rain at Dubbo.

I thought my question for the Blind Chick yesterday was rather insightful, asking who she is and what makes her tick. I have numerous other questions, but I thought I'd ask her today - What made her go blind.

"Well, I think this one is a reasonably easy question to answer. I have a hereditary disease called Retinitis Pigmentosa.

My mother has the disease, and so does my sister Lizzie. It is carried in our family by the females. My brother Pete doesn't have the disease, he's not a carrier.

The disease is commonly known as tunnel vision. It's a little bit like pulling the middle out of a pen and looking through the wee hole in the centre.

As a young child I was called clumsy, I used to run into table legs, small trees, big trees, I ran into lots of things. Always I had bruises from running into something. Hence the word clumsy.

When I rode my horses though, I rode like the wind. I went everywhere flat out. My horses had two beautiful brown eyes and they looked after me, I felt no difference. It was what it was, the horses taking up the slack. They were my eyes which is what Johno does for me today.

It was very interesting once I started going to school. I must tell you, I hated it with a passion. There were tears every day. All I wanted to do was be at home and be on the horse with my dad mustering.

Then came the day that my dad and mum got a phone call from the Principal. I was in first class and they wanted to talk to my parents. This is serious stuff when your parents get asked to come to the school when the kids only six years old. What has she done my dad and mum thought? What trouble has she got into?

My mum and dad arrived and were asked to take a seat. Quite serious this situation seemed to be. The principal then informed my mum and dad that I had an intellectual disability, and that they needed to find a way to make schooling for me easier because of this disability. This was such a shock to my parents. Hence, they embarked on having me endure lots of tests and then lots more tests.

Finally, someone thought to suggest "Get her eyes checked". Holy cow! The kid can't see real well. Hence, I didn't have an intellectual disability, albeit there are many friends who would probably beg to differ on this. The issue was I couldn't see real well and things really progressed from there.

Being a degenerative disease, things were never that easy at school. I struggled quite a lot. When I read, I see one letter at a time, so my reading skills were never that good, nor my writing skills.

But my saving grace was my horses, and still is my horses.

When I was 19, I went to a Macquarie Street specialist in Sydney who told me my prognosis was I will go totally blind. He suggested I make the best of every day and get on with life, which I have done.

With my riding and dressage, I started off with people wearing white coats and standing at all the letters around the outside of the dressage arena. I would scan and find the people with white coats and ride to the white coat.

Then, being degenerative, my eyesight kept getting worse. Soon I couldn't see the white coats anymore. So, we put big LED lights at the arena letters. I was like a little moth; I flew to the light. This gave me a way to keep riding and competing. I so love dressage.

Then came the day when I couldn't see the LED lights. I couldn't see at all. I could ride at home in the dressage arena, but there was no way I could keep competing. We couldn't think of a way for this to happen, so I had my wonderful coach at the time compete my horse for me. This was devastating. I couldn't cope with the fact I wasn't competing my horse. It was heartbreaking.

After one particular competition that my wonderful friend Yana rode my horse, she did such a good job, but it was not me, I was standing at the sink peeling vegetables for dinner, I was crying. My husband Matthew came along and said a typical male thing, "What are you blubbering about?" All that came out of my mouth was how It should be me riding, I should be competing, I wanted this so bad.

Matthew's words that followed were golden, "Find a way make it happen."

We started with a whole heap of musical instruments Matthew bought home from work. We experimented with which ones I could hear in the arena. A triangle, clack sticks, all the other instruments, but nothing worked better than the human voice.

So, my white coats, the people who stand at the markers around the arena, of which there are eight are called Living Markers. They call the letters as I ride. For instance, if I am heading across the diagonal from F to H, the person I'm riding towards will be calling H, H, H, H, H.

The Living Markers have made the world a difference to me being able to ride a dressage test and keep competing. It's been an absolute blast, and they're always tears, never tears of sadness, absolute tears of joy when the test is finished.

When I ride a test, I'm listening for my Living Markers to call me around the arena. I also count strides for my accuracy. This all happens because of my wonderful friends that believe in me, they help make my dreams come true, and because of the magnificent horse I have underneath me.

Set my goal at the moment is for my beautiful Johno and I to be out competing it won't be tomorrow it won't be next week it will be when it is meant to happen and when we are both ready to go out and compete, I am sure at the moment Johno could do it on his here it's the Blind Chick holding back the team but with our amazing José coaching both of us he will let us know when the time is right

So, I suppose out of all of this, again it has come down to choices. Choosing what you want in your life and how you would like to live your life. Sounds a little bit selfish I suppose. But I'm a firm believer if you want something badly enough, you can make it happen. I'm also a firm believer that dreams do come true. My heavens look at Johno and I! Such a magic dream and such a super journey we are on, we're so very blessed.

Okay I should have said at the beginning it was a two-cuppa diary entry. I hope I haven't bored you to snores. Have a spectacular day and please share this if you think it can help somebody.

I'm sending you loads of love and hugs. Thank you for your friendship and being in our lives. Take care, the Blind Chick.

Corona

Feeling Frustrated
26 June 2020

Diary entry by Johno

Well, jeepers creepers it's so much colder down here in the Southern Highlands than it is in Dubbo. But I'm rugged up and being spoilt. I've been having some awesome training time with the amazing José.

It's been funny, the Blind Chick has been very quiet on the home front. Apparently, she has been to the doctors again, had her MRI, and it wasn't good. There is a fracture in her knee, and she has quite a bit of ligament damage under her kneecap. So, she's off to see an orthopaedic person, I think that is the right word.

But she is managing still to walk and is still doing a couple of trips down to the front gate each day to keep fit. Hopefully coming down to visit next Thursday really looking forward to that. I bet she will want to ride me. It will be a matter of if she can get her leg in the stirrup but we"ll see what the orthopaedic person says.

I hope everybody has a spectacular weekend. Keep warm, keep safe, and be kind to yourself. And don't forget to let somebody you know, you love them. And remember to pass that smile on, it really is contagious. Let's start our own pandemic - spread that smile all around the world.

Loads of love and hugs, Johno.

One Day At A Time

🙂 Feeling Awesome
27 June 2020

Diary entry by Johno

I hope everybody is having a wonderful day. I had a parcel come in the post yesterday and I am now sporting my new extra warm rug specially for the Southern Highlands cold. This one will keep me extra warm.

I hear the Blind Chickie babe has been diligently mixing up my feeds for next week. Apparently, she is coming down to visit, probably Wednesday or Thursday, she will bring my extra feeds down with her, which is wonderful as I think I will be spending another couple of weeks here with the amazing José and beautiful Fay.

She has still not been able to get an appointment with the Orthopaedic person, but I tend to think she would like to think it is going to heal by itself. But who knows … time will tell.

I had a wonderful time training with the amazing José this morning. Every moment I spend in the dressage arena with this amazing man I learn so much. The Blind Chickie babe is going to have so much catching up to do.

I thought I better put up a quote for the day.

Remember those choices we talk about. Keep making good choices.

Quote of the Day

"Although time seems to fly, it never travels faster
than one day at a time.
Each day is a new opportunity to live your life to the fullest.
In each waking day, you will find scores of blessings

and opportunities for positive change.
Do not let your TODAY be stolen by the
unchangeable past or the indefinite future!
Today is a new day!"
Steve Maraboli

Have a wonderful weekend. Remember to be kind, drop somebody a message, let somebody know you love them and care about them, and don't forget to spread the smiles. We want to create a pandemic of smiles. So, keep smiling.

Love and big hugs, Johno.

No Regrets

Feeling Nostalgic
28 June 2020

Diary entry by Johno to the Blind Chick

No regrets Sue Ellen.
No matter how blind, it improved your vision.
No matter how foolish, it made you wiser.
And no matter how generous, it made you more.
Johno

I wrote this for my Blind Chick. She's a bit of okay you know. She has the most amazing strength and determination.

Only three more sleeps and she will be down visiting, I can't wait. I'm loving my lessons with the amazing José and being spoiled by the beautiful Fay.

Do you want to start running a bet on if she rides me? I'd put money on that she will want to be riding. What do you think? She's walking really well, did 6 km today building up strength which is awesome.

I hope you are having a spectacular day. Don't forget those smiles, keep spreading them. We need a pandemic of smiles.

Love always, Johno.

Reflection

🙂 Feeling Awesome
29 June 2020

Diary entry by Johno

Life is just like reading a book.
Hours, days, months, years, just repeat themselves.
Until you turn the page.
Choices - they are all ours to make.
Let's make the choices that are right for us.
Anon

Oops, I nearly forgot to mention the Blind Chickie babe has been very busy out and about getting my first Johno and the Blind Chick book into Horse shops etc and she has been getting a great response she has also been signing them. I'm not quite sure why she is signing them, I wrote the book! But everyone wanted her signature.

Thank you to the lovely people who have already read my book and put a review up. It has been lovely to know that everyone seems to be enjoying it.

In my spare time down here in the Southern Highlands I have been busy writing my next book. Johno and the Blind Chick Mark II, nothing too flash, just the journey of the Blind Chick and I as it continues.

I tend to think the chapter on the Blind Chick coming off me will be an interesting one, don't you? It's all about how guilty I felt, but it was her fault. She shouldn't have given me extra feed because it was cold. But maybe I shouldn't have been naughty. Okay I get it.

Okey-dokey everybody, have a spectacular day. Don't forget about those choices we can make. Let's make good ones, let's make a difference to our life and everybody else's. Share that smile, say good morning, or maybe say I love you. It will make a difference.

Stay safe, stay well. Big hugs and lots of love, Johno.

The Bed That Levitated!

Feeling Fantastic
30 June 2020

Diary entry by Johno

Well, a lovely sunny good morning from the Southern Highlands.

I had a spectacular ride with the amazing José this morning, again working on transitions, softness, suppleness, and relaxation.

I'm so loving this Ask – Don't Tell, this invitation to do something, not being shoved and jammed into a position. Why wouldn't you want to be obliging when someone is asking you so nicely? It's such a different way of doing things. I love it.

Only one more sleep till the Blind Chickie babe gets down here. I'm still running the book on whether she will be riding or not. I put odds on she will want to ride.

Oh, my lordy. What a story I heard this morning, I've got to share it with you. Apparently, the Blind Chick and her wonderful husband Matthew went shopping for a new bed. Well Matthew discussed with the nice young sales lady what they were looking for, and she pointed out a bed she thought might be suitable. So here they are, both of them, laying on the bed. Then Matthew gets up and continues talking to the sales lady.

The Blind Chickie babe is still lying on the bed relaxing, saying how comfortable the bed is and so on, when oh my, the bed started to move! The Blind Chick thought she was hallucinating. The bottom of the bed raised up and the top of the bed was moving too. She was moving! Holy cow did it frighten the hell out of her. Apparently, the sales lady, not knowing the Blind Chick could not see at all, had the controls and was making the electronic bed head rise and the foot rise. The Blind Chick thought she was losing her marbles, her balance and everything else.

Well once Matthew, the sales lady and the Blind Chick had re-assembled themselves from being on the ground laughing at the Blind Chick fearing this levitating bed, they ended up buying the bed. Without the extra buttons though!

The new bed will be here in three weeks apparently.

Keep smiling, keep laughing. Lots of love and hugs, Johno.

8
July

Rhythm, Regularity and Counting Strides

Feeling Grateful
2 July 2020

Diary entry by Johno

Woohoo, what an awesome day!

The wonderful José left working me until the Blind Chickie babe arrived this afternoon with her lovely friend Susan. José and I had an awesome ride, again working on relaxation softness and moving forward. We also worked a lot on transitions and in the background, I could hear the Blind Chickie babe saying to José "awesome transition". She could hear the rhythm and regularity and count the strides of half halt, half halt, half halt and walk. She said it sounded awesome.

Then yes, I won the bet, the Blind Chickie babe had a ride. José and his beautiful wife Fay helped the Blind Chick get on me. With her bad leg it was a lot of quietly and slowly, but guess what? No pain! So, we had a lovely walk for about 25 minutes, just relaxing and enjoying each other's company. It was beautiful.

Blind Chickie babe is hoping to ride me again tomorrow and maybe trot. We'll see how the leg holds up.

Tomorrow is a massive day to organise. We will have a ride first, then the wonderful Jason from Trail Race Saddlery in Tuggerah will be doing another saddle fitting for me. Ooops! I've changed shape again!

Stay happy, stay smiling.

Big hugs and loads of love, Johno.

Saddle Fitting Magic

 Feeling Grateful
2 July 2020

The Blind Chick, Jason from Trail Race Saddlery & I

Diary entry by Johno

Wow what a beautiful morning but the wind was super chilly.

I had a wonderful visit today from the amazing Jason from Trail Race Saddlery in Tuggerah. Jason was at José's to do a saddle fitting for me, I've change shape again!

With all this amazing work José and I are doing, I've changed shape. With this change comes the need to have my saddle re-fitted and to see what Jason thinks is happening with my saddle.

It was apparent quite quickly that Jason was not happy with how my saddle was fitting me right now, so he got another saddle out of his van. Yippee, a lovely Kiefer saddle. This brand happens to be the Blind Chicks favourite, unbeknownst to Jason.

Jason carefully fitted the new saddle to me and was very happy. Then José gave his approval and had a ride in it. José was most impressed with the comfort of the saddle and how it fitted me. I felt wonderful and was moving beautifully. Then it was the Blind Chickie babe's turn to have a wee ride.

She tried doing a little bit of trotting, but her knee hurt too much, so another walk which was wonderful. She was very happy with the saddle. So, the amazing Jason has left this lovely saddle with us to try for a week to see how we go. I'm sure we are going to be happy, but he has also organised for another saddle to be sent down to see if we like it better. What amazing service!

A massive thank you to the wonderful Jason from Trail Race Saddlery. They've been looking after me from day one when the Blind Chicks wonderful husband Matthew brought me for her. Yes, that very first day Jason was there to do my first Saddle Fitting!

So very grateful to Jason and his family from Trail Race Saddlery in Tuggerah. They've always gone above and beyond to make things right for me.

We all know how important it is to have the saddle fitted properly because guess what? We all have the ability to change shape with the correct work. So, don't forget to make sure that your ponies are comfortable.

Lots of love and hugs, Johno.

Plant Seeds of Happiness

Feeling Grateful
4 July 2020

Quote of the Day
"Plant seeds of happiness, hope, success, and love.
It will all come back to you in abundance.
This is the law of nature."
Steve Maraboli

I Just Knew!

Feeling Blessed
5 July 2020

Diary entry to Johno from the Blind Chick

I'm missing you my beautiful friend.

I know you are down with the amazing José Mendez having training, but you are such a part of my life. Getting out of bed this morning I thought oh I must rush down and feed Johno give him some carrots and a pat, but you weren't there.

I so hope the training is going well and you are keeping warm. I'll see you in two weeks but in that time here is my message to you my beautiful friend.

Johno,
My two beautiful brown eyes.
The day you came into my life was life changing.
Right from the time that I met you and stroked your beautiful
neck and went for my first ride, I knew you were the one.
Right from my first ride I knew.
You would always have my back.
I didn't need to see because you were looking out for me with
your two beautiful brown eyes.
Reflection is wonderful, I remember so well the first time that I
rode you.
You carried me with strength and courage and understanding.
You give me courage when my courage waivers
You give me strength when I don't think I can do it

With confidence and courage, you guide me. On the ground or in the saddle.

Sometimes being blind you miss so much, but with you my beautiful Johno I miss nothing.

I think God for your grace and beauty and the day that you came into my life.

We have been together a little over a year now and it has been the most amazing, beautiful period of getting to know each other, growing together, and working as one.

We have great goals you and me. One of which is to do our first dressage test.

Each day we are together this is getting closer.

It will be a proud day, it will be an exciting day, it will be like magic

So, my two beautiful brown eyes you have brought trust, understanding, guidance, and love into my life.

I truly think we were meant to meet and go on our journey together. Our time is made even more special by the fact that we share our journey.

But my two beautiful brown eyes our journey has just begun!

My two beautiful brown eyes you have given me vision when I cannot see.

Goes to show vision is much more than seeing.

To my two beautiful brown eyes I thank you from the bottom of my heart.

Sue-Ellen Lovett

Sue-Ellen

Feeling Fabulous
6 July 2020

© *2CPhotography*

Diary entry by Johno

How amazing is this! My Blind Chick was featured in a Tell All article in Equestrian Life Magazine. Written by Adele Severs it's a cracker of a read. I couldn't resist sharing it with you.

Growing up outside of Mudgee, NSW, Sue-Ellen Lovett was introduced to horses at a young age and rode regularly around the family's 21,00-acre property. At 12 years old, her world changed when she learned that she had inherited retinitis pigmentosa from her mother; she was given a full prognosis from her specialist that she would lose her vision completely and all the abilities that usually go with it.

However, Sue-Ellen wasn't going to let a lack of vision affect her ability to achieve great things. Taking up dressage in 1994 at the age of 35, she rode for Australia at the 1996 Atlanta Paralympics. She then competed at the 1999 World Championships in Denmark, finishing fourth individually and gaining a bronze medal as part of the Australian team, and contested the 2000 Sydney Paralympics. Sue-Ellen's achievements have not gone unrecognised, in 2000 she was made a life member of Equestrian Australia and received the Ministerial Sport Award, and then in 2004 she received the Australian Sports Medal.

Over the years, Sue-Ellen has had to adapt to deteriorating vision. At one point, she was riding with people at each marker with spotlights that they would shine towards her to give her direction. However, about four years ago when even the spotlights became hard to see, she made the switch to what she calls "living markers"; as Sue-Ellen rides the test, the living markers call out their position as she moves towards them.

As well as being a talented dressage rider, Sue-Ellen is an accomplished fundraiser. She has completed an incredible 10 long-distance horse rides, covering 16,000km and raising a phenomenal $3.2 million for organisations such as Guide Dogs NSW, Sydney Paralympian Committee, Riding for the Disabled, Children's Cancer Unit and Lions Save Sight. Her latest ride, in 2018, spanned 800km and raised money for the new Integrated Wellness Centre in the Oncology Department of Dubbo Base Hospital , a cause close to her heart, being a cancer survivor herself.

In more recent years, Sue-Ellen's competitive focus has switched to able-bodied events and training a number of horses to Grand Prix level, including the beautiful Desiderata (aka Desi), who as of last year is now living a blissful retirement in Queensland.

ALONG CAME JOHNO

Just over a year ago, the next chapter in Sue-Ellen's dressage journey began with a horse called Johno; a nine-year-old Hanoverian by the imported stallion Gymnastik Star and bred at Kinnordy Stud. Above budget and more than a six-hour drive away, the partnership between this 18.3 hand giant and his "Blind Chick" very nearly didn't happen. However, some things in life are just meant to be. "Something really, really magical happened with us riding together," recalls Sue-Ellen of that first ride. "He had my back. He was looking after me."

And so the charismatic giant made his way to Dubbo, and a partnership between Johno and Sue-Ellen began. It wasn't long before the horse had his own Facebook page, with Sue-Ellen sharing their journey through Johno's eyes. The page, which can be found under the name 'Johno and The Blind Chick', quickly amassed many enthusiastic social media followers who enjoy reading the pair's training updates from the horse's perspective.

Via the page, Sue-Ellen has given her audience real insight into the partnership between the horse and his rider, and how she works through her training sessions differently as a blind rider. Johno has shared a few helmet-cam videos of their rides together, where Sue-Ellen talks viewers through her thought process. "I generally always start off on the right rein, so the sun is on the left-hand side of my face. Being totally blind, the sun is how I orientate myself in the arena. So, the sun is on the left-hand side of my face, Johno starts to turn through the corner, and now the sun is on the back of my head. I ride across the short side of the arena, and now the sun is on the right side of my face."

"We're about sharing love and joy and happiness."

Over the past year with her gentle giant, Sue-Ellen has also embarked on a new training journey. "I've changed my way of training. I have moved away from the German approach that I've followed my entire career and am now training via a more classical approach with José Mendez. Johno is taking to it like a duck to water. It's been about learning to know when to back off, and to stop over-riding. Instead of 'more', José is saying 'let him relax'. The transformation in

Johno, in his confidence level and softness, is just like magic. When José rides him, you can just hear happiness in the air. I'm slowly learning to bring that to the party!"

As we know, horses always have their ups and downs. Johno's social media chronicles are honest and open, from getting "bitten on the pizzle by a spider", to a little hiccup the other day when he was a little fresh and thought he'd try a couple of leaps in the lead up to a flying change. "At 18.3 hands high … I think I was there for the first leap. And guess what, I didn't bounce!" laughs Sue-Ellen, her sense of humour still intact. Needless to say, Johno admitted his little indiscretion, which left Sue-Ellen with a damaged knee, to his Facebook followers, but not without pointing out that the Blind Chick had perhaps upped his feed too much!

While there have been a few setbacks, Sue-Ellen has been successfully working through them. "Being very honest, I really didn't think it would be as hard as it's been (the training process with a new horse). It's not Johno's height, it's the 'Itty-Bitty Shitty Committee' that gets into your head and undermines you. I needed to find the right trainer for Johno."

Sue-Ellen has successfully trained horses to Grand Prix level before and she's confident she can do it again with Johno, however, this time it will be a different journey. "It's going to be a totally different journey and it's going to be done with softness, kindness - asking and inviting."

Johno is currently training Medium/Advanced. In terms of the future, Sue-Ellen is in no hurry to compete, although she is looking forward to it. "It will happen when it's meant to happen. Once we're at FEI level, Prix St George and Inter I, it's just very comfortable because I know the tests. And then all I have to do with Johno is learn to count the strides …. an 18 3 hands horse has a different number of strides around the arena compared to other horses I've had!" Sue-Ellen hopes to be competing in a year, but she isn't putting any pressure on herself as she may have in the past. She explains that she will enter the competition arena when she and Johno are ready as a partnership, however long that takes.

More recently, Sue-Ellen has been able to add another feather to her cap. As of 31 May, she is a published author! With Johno's Facebook page attracting a dedicated audience, calls for Johno to write a book ensued, leading to the release of "Johno and the Blind Chick – Vision is More Than Seeing". The book shares Sue-Ellen's heartwarming story about love, achievement, overcoming adversity and daring to dream through the eyes of her beloved horse.

Just as Johno's Facebook page is written from his perspective, so is the book. "I didn't write the book about Johno, Johno wrote a book about his journey with a Blind Chick. So, it's very quirky. It also means that Johno can be quite irreverent about the Blind Chick, for example, he'll say she needs to go to the gym and get stronger core muscles!"

Sue-Ellen, who if you haven't guessed by now possesses a great sense of humour and wit, explains that the book follows Johno's view of how things played out, from the moment they met. "The day we arrived; he sees these four people turn up. And there's a fellow holding this girl's hand, who seems very attentive towards the girl … he brings her over to meet him, and he's saying things like, 'Put your hand here, here is his neck'. Johno wonders why this fellow seems to be giving her a lot of information, and observes this girl being guided around, but at this stage he hasn't work out that she's blind … By the end of the first chapter, he's worked it out and says, 'Oh bloody hell, she can't see!'"

Johno's experiences take him from life on the outskirts of Sydney with 150 other horses, to drought-stricken Dubbo and being the one horse that is the centre of attention, something that he really loves.

When it came to writing the book, Sue-Ellen felt that writing through Johno's eyes allowed her to take a step back and not feel as though she was writing about herself. "Through Johno's eyes, I can show vulnerability, whereas it's not so easy to show that when you're talking about yourself. When I've lacked confidence, Johno can touch on that; I can't. It's really hard (writing about yourself), but it's easier for Johno to say, 'The Blind Chick is lacking a little bit of confidence. This is how we're dealing with it'. It has allowed me a different way of putting it that doesn't feel as self-conscious."

Sue-Ellen explains that the writing process for her begins with setting her phone to "dictate" and letting her thoughts, and Johno's, run. 'Johno and the Blind Chick' is very much how Sue-Ellen speaks: warm, funny, and straight from the heart. Once her words are captured, a friend of hers edits them and "puts in full stops and grammar to make it breathe!"

"Writing the book has been really nice in the sense that most people don't reflect on how far they've come with their horse. I think that's been probably the biggest thing for me, is reflecting on how far we've come." Enjoying the process, Sue-Ellen has an autobiography and part two of Johno and the Blind Chick in the making.

For Sue-Ellen, her partnership with Johno has been a different journey; not one without hiccups, but ultimately one that she can only describe as magical. Sharing that journey with others has been part of the fun. "We're about sharing love and joy and happiness. There's just so much negativity in the world and we really need feel-good stories; things that make people feel good and can inspire them."

Referring to the numerous videos and photos of herself and Johno in training that can be found on the Facebook page, she explains that this horse is truly something special. "Check out the Blind Chick's face; the smile does not move when she's on that horse. It just can't be any other way; it just brings such magic and electricity. It's beautiful."

Johno and the Blind Chick is available for purchase at sueellenlovett.com.au or via leading online book outlets such as Amazon. You can also follow the chronicles of Johno and his rider via his Facebook page: 'Johno and The Blind Chick'. **EQ**

Ask, Don't Tell

Feeling Wonderful
8 July 2020

Diary entry by Johno

Wow, a very brisk good morning from the amazing José and I in the Southern Highlands. It is at least 0°C I'm sure!

I am moving and feeling pretty amazing. I have had new dancing shoes put on by the wonderful Farrier Matt Bilderbeck. And guess what? I've never had shoes made from scratch, as in just one piece of steel made into shoes specially to fit me. This is what Matt did. I'm hoping to get some photos for you it was pretty amazing.

The amazing José gave me a couple of days off after my shoeing so I could get used to my new shoes, and I am feeling wonderful.

Now it's time for our training. As per usual we do our lovely calm warm up, lovely big soft walk stretching, little bits of lateral work and changes of direction. I also have my new Kiefer saddle on, so all is wonderful with the world.

I'm using my hindquarters really well, lovely and soft through the back, big swinging walk, awesome use of my shoulders now they can move.

With the amazing way José trains there is absolutely no stress in what we do. Ask, don't tell and be invited to do a movement, so we then quietly go into the trot again lovely big relaxing trot swinging through the back and covering lots of ground.

José then introduces a little bit of lateral work in the trot, then we do a few transitions back to the walk, lovely big, relaxed walk, and then quiet back into the trot. All the time working on my rhythm and regularity, softness and always being asked and invited to do a movement. José asks then quietly puts me into the canter. We do one lap around the arena, then a 20 metre circle, then half halt, half halt, half halt, back to walk, a change of direction and voila! The same on the other rein. Just so soft, just so rhythmical, always asking, not telling.

I am sure to some people this training sounds as if it is the same old, same old, but it's not. Each time it is positively reinforcing Asking Not Telling, positively reinforcing the rhythm and the regularity. Having a new system to do something, this just doesn't happen overnight. You need to work on it and be consistent and persistent, Ask Don't Tell. It's a lot harder than it sounds.

On the Blind Chick front I hear there is a little bit of frustration!

The fracture in her knee is causing her a bit of grief. It's not hurting her to walk but sitting in the saddle does. Why? Because the fracture is at the side of the knee that sits on the saddle. It causes a lot of pain when she rides, so she is not able to ride for a little while longer. She has an appointment on 19 August with the Orthopaedic person. Hopefully, everything will be fine by then.

I must say I feel for her husband Matthew, because I'm sure she is not a happy little camper.

But it takes the time it takes to heal, and hopefully in a couple of weeks, maybe a month, everything will be back too normal. Fingers and toenails crossed for the Blind Chick.

Stay well, stay safe.

Much love and hugs, Johno.

Relax, Soft & Supple

Feeling Fantastic
9 July 2020

Diary entry by Johno

Well, a very hearty good morning from my wonderful trainer José and I in the brisk Southern Highlands.

We are having a quiet chat before we start our ride this morning, talking about what we are going to achieve from this ride, always working on relaxation, softness, and suppleness. Sorry, if it sounds as if I repeat myself, but this is what makes it work so well. It's José inviting me to do something, it rocks. I can't wait for my ride today.

Also, my new shoes that Matt put on the other day are so cool. I feel so light on my feet. Remember today is the start of a new day, it is a blessing, and it is never too late to make changes

Wishing everybody an awesome day. Remember to smile. Let's keep spreading this pandemic of smiles.

Love and hugs, Johno.

A New Dance Partner

Feeling Wonderful
11 July 2020

Diary entry by the Blind Chick

Well, a very good morning from a misty old Southern Highlands. The wind is a bit chilly; I must say. We have the day off today.

So, I thought I might share how the Blind Chick and I ride around the arena. I'll let the Blind Chick explain how she orientates herself in the arena and manages to ride a dressage test.

The Blind Chick uses the sun to orientate herself in the arena and knowing where she is if the sun is on the right side of her face or the back of her head, I would call her a Fairweather Rider unless she has someone with her, she needs to ride when it is sunny so she can be orientated by the sun.

Just for a little exercise … when the sun is out next, walk outside and see if you can orientate yourself in your garden or your back-yard by just using the sun and counting strides, because this is how the Blind Chick rides me and can you imagine learning the strides from a 17 hh horse and then going to an 18.3 hh horse. This requires totally different counting. It is much more difficult to get me through a corner.

Thank you to my amazing two beautiful brown eyes called Johno, who is learning to guide me around the dressage arena.

Being totally blind and taking on a new dance partner has been quite the challenge, one very large stride at a time. We are becoming a solid partnership. I love every ride, every moment I spend with this special horse. Our bond is getting stronger each day, and my confidence is growing.

So, to everyone, never ever stop dreaming and believing that anything is possible. I know deep down in my heart that dreams definitely do come true. But not without a lot of wonderful friends believing in me and helping make my dreams come true. Thank you so much to the people that believe and support me, it is greatly appreciated.

Vision is much more than seeing.

How Long?

😌 Feeling Reflective
12 July 2020

Diary entry by Johno

Good morning, I was asked a very interesting question this morning, a question I'm sure is on a lot of peoples' minds. How long has the Blind Chick been blind?

So, I thought it was a great opportunity to explain the Blind Chick's condition and the deterioration of her sight.

As a wee child the Blind Chick was known to be a clumsy, running into table legs and the like. At no stage did anybody think that she could not see well.

As time progressed still no one was any the wiser. On a horse she rode everywhere flat out. But guess what? The horse has two beautiful brown eyes that saw for her, they always kept her out of trouble. It was when she was on the ground on her own two feet that she ran into lots of things, all the time, hence Miss Clumsy.

When the Blind Chick was in first class at School, the Principal asked her parents to come up to the school. She suggested rather strongly that the Blind Chick had an intellectual disability! Multiple tests were then ordered. Lo and behold, they tested her eyes, and she could hardly see.

Back in those days they didn't realise a lot of things. The Blind Chick's mother was also in the process of losing her sight. She'd lost her driving license because she had been diagnosed with her hereditary disease called Retinitis Pigmentosa.

The disease progresses at a different pace in each person. So, at the age of 12, Sue-Ellen was also diagnosed with Retinitis Pigmentosa.

At the age of 19, a Macquarie Street Eye Specialist said "if you'd like to do something with your life, do it now, as you will not have your sight much longer. So, enjoy what you have, while you have it."

Hence the attitude of making every day count.

As her sight got worse, it also caused other issues. Like how to keep riding, how to keep doing dressage. She went from having big LED lights at the letters where she was like a little white moth riding to the lights to having people standing in white coats at the letters, called Living Markers. Why the change from the LED to Living Markers? Because her sight diminished so much, she couldn't see the lights anymore, but she could hear the people in white coats calling the letters, so she can keep doing her dressage.

When the Blind Chick does Dressage now, she has eight living markers around the arena. They call the letters to her H, H, H or it could be B, B, B, there is continuous calling of the letter which gives The Blind Chick the ability to ride to that sound.

The other thing that happens with the Blind Chick other than her riding is when she sends a message, she dictates into her iPhone. Sometimes the predictive text comes out like gobbledygook, which has the strangest words. But the Blind Chick can't go back and fix these mistakes. So, sorry if in these diary entries some have slipped through.

She has also had six Guide Dogs over a period of 38 years. She retired her last Guide Dog last year, just after Matthew bought me for her.

To explain Retinitis Pigmentosa as best I can, it's like looking down the inside of a pen if you pull the ink bit out. She had no peripheral sight, it just closed totally.

For many years, the Blind Chick had a pin prick of sight, but it wasn't enough to be useful. Now she has no sight at all. She makes use of her hearing and her feelings.

With losing her sight it hasn't all been beer and skittles. It's made it quite difficult for her getting a new horse like me and this has been a major accomplishment. With losing her sight has come a little bit of anxiety, a little bit of nervousness about "can I do it", but as you know the Blind Chick is very stubborn and determined. She will make it happen.

Her favourite saying is: 'Vision is so much more than seeing'.

I hope this all makes sense.

Keep safe.

Loads of love and hugs, Johno.

Just Feel

Feeling Wonderful
13 July 2020

Diary entry by Johno and the Blind Chick

The other day I received a message from one of our lovely Facebook friends Jane, asking how the Blind Chick was able to lunge me, how she knew if I was round and soft and travelling correctly?

Here is the Blind Chicks answer.

"Okay when I am lunging Johno I use a lunging Cavesson. This has been kindly lent to be by José.

One of the things that is quite important when you're lunging is to have the horse straight through the body.

In the walk I have to work quite hard at keeping Johno motivated. He can be quite lazy in the walk and would prefer to stop, often! So, there is a V between my hand going with the lunge rein to the cavesson, and the other side of the V is my hand out holding the lunge whip towards Johno's hindquarters. My arms create the V shape, and this usually creates energy. But I generally have to keep hunting Johno up in the walk.

When he goes into the trot, he is much more animated and forward. In the trot, it is really important that you get the horse to drop his head and swing through the back. The engine is in the backend, so you want the strength coming through from the back. Lovely and soft through the back and a lovely long reaching neck while keeping the horse straight through the body.

As you can imagine anything visual is impossible for me, so I have to rely on listening to Johno's paces. When he is distracted and hollow, his stride is short and choppy. When he is soft and relaxed through the back and stretching through the neck, his trot has air and suspension, and sounds absolutely amazing! With such beautiful rhythm, regularity and cadence, the air in his trot is massive.

Take the time to listen to what your horse is doing. You'll be surprised what you pick up.

In the canter again Johno is quite motivated, but often he wants to drop out of the canter back to the trot. It's so important to keep the rhythm and regularity. He has a lovely big uphill canter, but when he is tense his stride is short and choppy. When he is relaxed, soft through the back, reaching down with his nose and stretching through the back, his canter is a beautiful big uphill, rolling canter. The sound he makes when cantering like this is majestic, it's music to my ears.

For me, lunging is quite the experience, especially after Johno has had a few days off. He is often quite exuberant and very animated. He'll do a little bit of playing and bucking on the lunge. This playing and mucking around is not malicious, it's saying "I'm feeling so good". I personally find it a little daunting as Johno is so large, but he's not doing it to frighten me, he's just playing.

I personally think lunging is a wonderful training tool. If done correctly it's lovely for the horse not to have us on the back interfering".

I hope that explains how I go about lunging.

Stay safe, stay smiling.

Much love, Johno and the Blind Chick.

Dealing With New Challenges

Feeling Appreciated
14 July 2020

Diary entry by Johno and the Blind Chick

I realise with COVID-19 this is an exceedingly difficult time for everyone. We are facing things we've never faced before, and we have no idea of the outcome. But the important thing we have is our wonderful friends.

Together we can make a difference.

So, my challenge to everyone is - let's make a difference today! Let people close to you know you care. Let those you love know you love them. Believe me, such words do make a difference.

Quote of the Day

"One of the most spiritual things you can do is
embrace your humanity.
Connect with those around you today.
Say, "I love you", "I'm sorry", "I appreciate you",
"I'm proud of you". Whatever you're feeling.
Send random texts, write a cute note,
embrace your truth and share it.
Cause a smile today for someone else.
And give plenty of hugs."
Steve Maraboli

Ask - Invite

Feeling Thankful
16 July 2020

Diary entry by Johno

Wow! To say it's been a little chilly down here in the Southern Highlands over the past few days, is an understatement.

I hear they had some lovely rain in Dubbo, over 35 mils. This will be wonderful for Matthew's crops.

My training with the amazing José is going along really nicely. I'm still working on the basics which is what it's all about. Everything is done with kindness, softness and "Ask - Don't Tell". I must sound like a broken record, but it is pretty cool.

I tend to think the Blind Chick is going to have to totally rethink her way of riding. What I'm learning, how I'm being taught is so amazing, it makes me want to please José all the time. Everything is done with such kindness; you're invited to do things. It's so nice not to be jammed up or pushed, shoved, or asked for more forward all the time. I offer or be more forward because I'm given the opportunity to offer it. José's training absolutely rocks!

I also hear the Blind Chickie babe has been doing a lot of reflecting on what she can do better when her knee will allow her to ride again. She's been thinking about what she does when she rides me, and doing lots of listening to the videos Jenelle has done for her of José's lessons, listening for things she can improve on like:
- keeping a better contact with that right rein
- not dropping the right shoulder
- making sure the weight is even in both seat bones
- using her seat to slow me, not her hands

It's amazing what she's picking up from these videos.

It is so wonderful that José when he is giving the Blind Chick lessons talks a lot and gives a lot of information on how to do things. He's not just telling you what to do, he's also telling you how to do it, and how it should feel. He's so different from a lot of coaches that don't give you the information on how it should feel, and how to execute the movement.

I know the Blind Chickie babe has an appointment with the Orthopaedic person on 19 August, so hopefully they we will be able to put some light on her knee and how the fracture is healing.

Keep smiling.

Lots of hugs and much love, Johno.

Listen With Curiosity

Feeling Thankful
17 July 2020

Diary entry by the Blind Chick

I totally love this quote.

Take time to read it and reflect. It's important with our communication between Horse and Rider and also, just between people. It's so true, not everybody listens!

Quote of the Day

"Listen with curiosity. Speak with honesty. Act with integrity.
The greatest problem with communication is
we don't listen to understand. We listen to reply.
When we listen with curiosity, we don't listen
with the intent to reply.
We listen for what's behind the words."
Roy T. Bennett

Great food for thought, don't you think?
Love and hugs, the Blind Chick.

Matthew Is Impressed

Feeling Thankful
18 July 2020

Diary entry from the Blind Chick

We arrived down to the Southern Highlands yesterday to catch up with a beautiful Johno.

With the back of the ute full of wonderful homegrown hay and the Blind Chick's hard feeds. someone was extremely excited to see us. Apparently, he was running around the paddock bucking, pig rooting and having a lovely time when he saw us.

It was so cool; José had left working Johno until we got there. Matthew had not had the privilege of visiting José and Fay's property or seeing the amazing José and Johno strut their stuff. I was so excited to see what Matt thought.

It was interesting. Matthew was spellbound when we left José and Fay's property, he couldn't get over how happy and relaxed Johno was and doing everything with such ease and precision. "He looks so happy, so relaxed and calm."

Isn't that what we all want with our horses? It was so very, very cool

I really enjoyed listening to José and Johno's lesson. I had a great opportunity to sit and chat to José about setting movements up, and even though I'm not riding at the moment because of my knee, being able to listen to what José is saying and listening to Johno's footsteps, is so cool. Listening for the half halt when coming down in transitions in the canter, half halt, half halt, half halt, half halt and walk. You can hear the difference in each stride.

It truly is mazing if you take the time to listen.

Matthew and I have a 5.5 hour drive back to Dubbo this morning. So, we're leaving quite early. Johno is having the day off. I forgot to mention he is so loving his new dancing shoes; they've made the world of difference to how comfortably he is.

Love and hugs, the Blind Chick.

Just Listen

Feeling Grateful
19 July 2020

Diary entry by Johno and the Blind Chick

Good morning, we hope you are having a spectacular day.

The Blind Chick was sent a really interesting question yesterday, saying "Don't you feel bad that you're not riding, don't you feel as if you're missing out?" and I thought this was a really cool question for the Blind Chick to answer.

Like – "What can you really get out of sitting and listening to a lesson when you can't see?"

Hi, Blind Chick here.

Well, I think there is a lot to be said for being able to see and watch something, but when you don't have that option you pick up on a lot of other things. I get this beautiful feeling in the pit of my stomach when things are feeling right. Feelings and hearing are really, really important to me. For example, when we arrived Johno was so excited he was running around the paddock pig rooting and playing. He never does that at home! But he was excited we were there, that ticked boxes for me.

While Matthew was unpacking the ute with all the hay and hard feed, and I organised things inside the horse float for Johno's feed, the beautiful Fay went and caught Johno and took him over to be saddled up.

While I was packing things in the horse float, I heard Johno walk past with Fay quietly speaking to him. Fay then saddled Johno; put his work boots on, gave him a brush and quietly led him over to the dressage arena. José then had a quiet chat with Johno, gave him a pat, walked around the dressage arena on foot, so relaxed and soft. While I didn't see any of this, I heard it. It was comforting inside of me, that everything was so relaxed and how it should be. All was well with the world.

José then mounted and rode Johno in the dressage arena. They just started off on a lovely big, long rein walk. José pointed out to me "Sue I'm holding the buckle, so no connection." The rhythm of his beautiful big, rhythmical, soft walk could be heard as Johno walked around the indoor arena. That's music to my ears.

After a lap or two of the indoor arena, José then quietly took up the rein a little and asked Johno to do on the Quarter Line a leg yield to the left, and then straight forward on the next long side. He did the same thing on the Quarter Line, straight then a leg yield across to the long side each time. This helps softening and suppling his body.

Then a change of rein on the diagonal, José let Johno's nose come out and let him swing through the back, a lovely long rein walk across the diagonal. Matthew commented on the over track of at least 16 inches! Which is pretty cool.

On the other rein José did the same thing, turned on the Quarter Line and a leg yield and then straight round the corner, next Quarter Line straight and then leg yield. All the time you can hear Johno's stride lengthening but it is soft, there is no pounding. You may think a horse that's 18.3hh would have a heavy foot fall. But it's not! He sounds like air on clouds, so soft with beautiful rhythm and regularity.

As each minute went on, I'm just listening, just listening. Listening to the rhythm, the regularity, the softness without tension.

After about 10 minutes of walk José quietly took up the reins and went into the trot. Again, a long rein trot on the buckle, "Sue I'm holding the buckle, letting Johno swing through the back, stretch his neck, use his hindquarters." Those beautiful big powerful hindquarters in the trot straight away had a beautiful rhythm and regularity, but it improved as the session progressed.

Then José would set up an exercise with half pass followed by leg yield, keeping the same rhythm and regularity. As time went on the trot sounded bigger and more powerful, Johno was warming up! It sounded amazing.

José then came back to the walk for a little while, letting Johno relax. Then he quietly took the reins up and invited a walk to canter. The same recipe was applied. A lovely big, long canter, allowing Johno to stretch through the back. Oh, my heavens! It sounded amazing, an on the buckle ground covering big canter. So soft, so bold.

José did a couple of laps of the indoor arena with a lovely long rein, then quietly took up the rein and did a couple of circles, a change of direction and same on the other rein. He did a couple of lovely floating half passes, such beautiful rhythm and regularity. Then he brought him back onto a 20 metre circle and did some canter - walk transitions. This was so cool to listen to. Johno's foot falls, then the half halt, half halt, and walk.

As each minute ticked away you could hear Johno getting more supple, more soft, more uphill. The rhythm and regularity was beautiful. You could set a metronome by him! Then, still trotting José came across the diagonal and invited an extended trot. Oh, my lord! The suspension, the air, I wish I could have seen that. It sounded so majestic, so beautiful.

I also took the opportunity to have a talk with José at length, about the setting up of the movements. We chatted a lot about the transition from the canter to the walk, the half halt, half halt, half halt and walk. No jamming, no shoving, just slow the seat, slow the seat, and walk. I can see it in my mind, I can feel it while I'm sitting here dictating on the iPhone. I can feel what it should look like if that makes sense.

After José rode and we spoke about the session, José gave Johno a lovely big warm down. Then he was taken over and unsaddled, given a lovely big brush, rugged and put back in his paddock after some mini treats.

I wonder if you've ever sat and closed your eyes and listened to your horse in the paddock or listened to someone riding their horse. You can pick up so much from listening. While it will never take the place of seeing, I don't have that luxury. But 'thems the breaks', so I use what I have.

I hope this message made sense. I'd love some feedback. Let me know whether my explanation made sense to you.

I thought I should share this quote again, it's about listening. While it speaks about communication with people, I like it for reminding us about how we communicate with our horses. Listening is so important.

Quote of the Day

"Listen with curiosity. Speak with honesty. Act with integrity.
The greatest problem with communication is
we don't listen to understand. We listen to reply.
When we listen with curiosity,
we don't listen with the intent to reply.
We listen for what's behind the words."
Roy T. Bennett

Have a wonderful day, keep smiling.
Lots of hugs, love, and more hugs, Johno and the Blind Chick.

Just Life

 Feeling Fabulous
20 July 2020

Hectic, Eccles, Blind Chickie Babe & Mudgee

Diary entry by Johno

I thought on this rainy day I'd share with you a little bit about my Blind Chick and her story.

The Blind Chick was born in a lovely country town called Mudgee, her mum and dad Mary and John, lived on a gorgeous farm in the hills around Mudgee called Kaludabah.

The Blind Chicks dad was the Manager of the property. In fact, it was two properties joined together totalling 21,000 acres.

When the Blind Chick was born everything was hunky-dory. As soon as she was old enough like three years old, she worked out if she was far away from the Homestead on a Sunday, she didn't have to go to church! So, she was off around the station from three, but someone always knew where she was on her pony.

At this stage no one had worked out that she had eyesight problems, especially since she spent most of her time on horseback! They have two beautiful brown eyes to see for the blind kid and keep her safe.

No one thought much about the fact that as a little one she spent a lot of time running into table legs, chairs and so on.

The wheels really fell off the car when the Principal at Primary School called her mum and dad up and ask them to come in for a meeting. She had something serious to discuss with them! Mary and John went into the meeting and the Principal proceeded to tell them that their child had an intellectual disability. Wow! Her parents were concerned, where the hell did this come from?

From then a whole heap of tests were done on the kid, tests more tests. Then someone thought to send her to an Optometrist to check her eyes out. Well gee whiskers, guess what? The kid couldn't see much at all!

So needless to say, the Blind Chick didn't like school very much. She definitely wasn't the A Grade student and left school after Year 10. Her mother insisted she do a secretarial course at TAFE which she did, under sufferance. Wow, who would want this Blind Chick as a secretary? Ha ha!

Things cruised along as per usual, the Blind Chick working on the farm with her dad. She was in seventh heaven, every day on her horse mustering, nosing around the hills. It was just perfect, idyllic. Someone wrote the script just for her.

But like most things that are degenerative they sneak up on you, you have no idea. When she was about 19 she went to an Ophthalmologists down in Sydney, Macquarie Street, and he said words you never want to hear. Quite blunt he said "if there is anything you would like to do, do it now. As you will be totally blind very soon." Holy cow Batman! Panic buttons, what do we do now thought the Blind Chick.

What is this degenerative thing? It's a disease called Retinitis Pigmentosa, the Blind Chick's mum Mary has it. It only travels in the girl's side of the family, the Blind Chick's brother Pete doesn't have it, which is wonderful. However, her sister Lizzie does have the disease, but Lizzie has been fortunate as in it hasn't progressed as quickly.

So, the Blind Chick and a mate travelled for a couple years doing itinerate work like picking grapes, tomatoes and farm sitting. Then they went out to a deserted island in the Whitsundays, it was beautiful lots of fun, but then things got serious.

That's when she went into a Blind School at Gilles Plain for rehabilitation and learning how to work with being blind. She was taught how to use a white cane, but her main aim was to get a Guide Dog.

It was 1981 when she received her first Guide Dog, her name was Donna. She was a beautiful German Shepherd Guide Dog, the first and only German Shepherd Guide Dog in Australia! They trialled Donna with the Blind Chick because of her previous experience training sheep dogs and horses. Donna was magnificent.

After the Blind Chick had trained with Donna, she headed back home to Mudgee. On the trip home she had this great idea about how she could thank Guide Dogs NSW for her new found independence and mobility. The tough gig was convincing her dad that it was a good idea! At dinner the next night she sprung it on her dad. Oops, her dad's response was "No bloody way, no way in hell." The Blind Chick followed that with a lot of "But dad …. But dad ….But dad", but her dad's "NO" stayed his answer.

The Blind Chick's idea was to ride a horse from hometown Mudgee to Melbourne in Victoria where they trained the Guide Dogs, a distance of 1,200 km. She had it all planned; six horses, a support truck, support vehicle and a sighted guide. She had everything worked out. All she had to do was ….. convince her dad!

John, the Blind Chick's dad, was a member of the Mudgee Lions Club. Her idea was to get the Lions Club to coordinate it, as most towns have a Lions Club, plus they could do fundraisers etc thought the Blind Chick. Well, John was quite adamant and kept saying no, so she said okay then, I'm going to ask Rotary. Rotary is in opposition to Lions Club in Australia, so the Blind Chick's dad was very quick to change his mind. The very next night the Blind Chicks dad organised for the President of the Mudgee Lions Club, Frank Lowe, to come to dinner. This was the start of the Blind Chicks long distance riding career.

I will just touch on a few of these lengthy rides as there have been 10 of them between 1984 and 2018 transporting the Blind Chick and her entourage of sighted guides, truck drivers, support vehicles and horses to ride over 17,000 km, raising in excess of $3.2 million for charity.

Two of these rides stand out. One was in 1988, Australia's Bicentennial Year. The Blind Chick and her crew rode from Cairns at the top of Australia in Queensland, down to the Gold Coast, a distance of 2,400 km and 56 days in the saddle!

As you can imagine the coordination of these rides is massive. The Blind Chick went through eight sighted riding guides, six truck drivers and numerous other support crew. Most of these people came from her local area of Mudgee.

This ride was to raise money for Riding For The Disabled in Australia. It was a great success and also helped raise a lot of public awareness for Riding For The Disabled.

The other favourite of the Blind Chicks is the ride around her hometown of Mudgee. It was only 700 km, but on that ride, they were raising money to put in three helipads! One at Mudgee, one at Rylstone and one at Gulgong hospital. Each equipped with lighting for helicopters to come in at night plus a fuel pump. This was one very cool ride, when you consider each helipad cost about $150,000!

This one was extra special for the simple reason that it was helping the Blind Chicks hometown. She knew so many people, so many people came and rode with her, it was amazing. At all times she was accompanied by a sighted guide. What a massive job being a sighted guide?

Another of the Blind Chicks favourites was in 1989. This was the year she was diagnosed with cancer! After the third operation she got in contact with the Oncology Unit at Camperdown Children's Hospital and offered to do a ride for Camperdown Children's Hospital. This ride was 1,800 km across central and western New South Wales.

It was truly amazing the money just rolled in. The beautiful people of the Central West were so generous.

The ride started and finished at the Blind Chicks hometown Mudgee. There's something really special about Mudgee. She has never left on any of her rides with under $10,000 already in the bank! What a beautiful generous town with amazing people.

After that ride they went down and presented the cheque to Dr Michael Stevens from the Oncology Unit at Camperdown Children's Hospital. Dr Michael invited the Blind Chick down to meet some of the children. Well, she had tears rolling down her cheeks as she came back up in the lift after meeting all of these amazingly motivated and inspiring children, they all had the most amazing will to live. She turned to Dr Michael Stevens and said "I'll be doing another ride next year."

The next ride was down through southern New South Wales taking in Canberra and finishing at Camperdown Children's Hospital in the middle of Sydney.

Just to drop it in there you, have heard of 'road rage'? Well try riding a horse down Parramatta Road in Sydney at peak hour! There was lots of support, but there were lots of people saying, "Get off the bloody road". Yet again the ride was a total success, made even more successful when they brought all the children out from the Oncology Unit that were able to come out in wheelchairs. They lifted one little girl on to her horse called Mudgee. I tend to think, for her to turn around and do another ride the next day, was such a moving finish to a spectacular ride.

Then in 1996 the Blind Chick was selected to represent Australia in Atlanta at the Paralympic games. Wow what a highlight in anyone's life to be selected to represent their country.

At home she was practising on her Australian Stockhorse called Yarrahapinni Hectic. It was Hectic, Hecco for short, she competed on all over the state most weekends with her dad, even as far as South Australia and Victoria. It was a massive effort to keep up competing.

So, the Blind Chickie babe went to Atlanta, sadly it was really disappointing. The quality of the horses provided for the riders wasn't that good, and while a good craftsman should never blame their tools, these horses were not up to the standard required for such an event. The first horse the Blind Chick was offered, keeping in mind the horses were drawn out of a hat, you didn't take your own horse, unlike the Olympians, was a circus horse! This was hilarious and certainly wasn't going to work.

Time was ticking away; they had four days but only 45 minutes each day to get used to these horses before they rode for their country! Day three was when she still didn't have a horse. Then one of the horses that another country had drawn became available. It had worked really hard and it'd had some time off because of lactic acid build up. So, the Blind Chick got to ride this little chestnut mare.

Being blind the Blind Chick rode in the blind riders' arena which is fenced, unlike most dressage arena is which just have low sides on it. Thank heavens she was in the blind riders' arena in her first test. As they came across the diagonal the mare showed everyone how very spritely she was feeling; she bucked, and bucked and bucked all the way across the diagonal! The Blind Chick was so disappointed at the fact she didn't get a good score for riding that bronc for eight seconds! She didn't come off. My heavens how embarrassing that would have been.

Her best placings in Atlanta were 10th and 11th. Yes, this was disappointing but in the grand scheme of things wow, how many people get to represent their country?

During the time in Atlanta and the Paralympic Games the Blind Chick met many other amazing Paralympians. She spent a lot of time with the wheelchair rugby guys, sitting and listening to their stories, and the wheelchair basketball guys. Wow, such amazing stories of determination, great bloody mindedness, and just make it happen.

After the Paralympics, the Blind Chick was approached by the Honourable Michael Knight to be on the Board of the Sydney Paralympic Games. This was an amazing honour, and she accepted the appointment, taking her place on the Board of Directors of the Sydney Paralympic Games. Wow what a place to be, the Blind Chick was a tad overwhelmed in the beginning.

But I am sure you have picked up by now, that the Blind Chick is a pretty shy type of girl, not! She fitted in straight away but it became apparent very quickly that there was a huge shortfall in the budget to host the Paralympic Games. So, what did the Blind Chick do? Yes, she offered to do a couple more long-distance rides.

Her first ride for the Paralympics was in 1989 - from Melbourne to Sydney. It was awesome to have such an amazing media machine behind her to do this ride. Flyers, faxes, emails and much media going everywhere about the Blind Chick riding from Melbourne to Sydney to raise money for the Paralympic Games.

Keeping in mind while she was on this ride, she was having to keep up her training because she was also shortlisted to compete at the Sydney Paralympic Games.

Not surprisingly the ride from Melbourne to Sydney was a massive success from a publicity and money raising perspective. The ride raised $1.1 million. After the ride all the horses were put on a truck to go home, all except her little mare Mudgee. Sue-Ellen, Mudgee and her Guide Dog Eccles all went up in the lift into Sydney Town Hall, out onto the balcony where the Lord Mayor of Sydney presented the Blind Chick with a beautiful big bunch of flowers as a thank you. It was truly a remarkable day.

That evening the Lord Mayor of Sydney, the Honourable Frank Sartor hosted a dinner reception for 160 seated guests in Sydney Town Hall. There was a beautiful red carpet down the middle of a parquetry floor, down it came the Blind Chick, her horse Mudgee and her Guide Dog Eccles.

The crowd was gobsmacked! The last thing they were expecting in Sydney Town Hall was a horse. It was such a moving experience. What an incredible horse Mudgee was.

This was a very busy time for the Blind Chick as she was also still on the elite squad for the Sydney Paralympic Games, and also pending was the world championships in Denmark in 1999 which she'd been shortlisted for.

In 1999 the Blind Chick was selected to represent Australia in Denmark at the World Equestrian Games. Thankfully at this event the horses the host country provided were amazing, the venue was amazing, the whole experience was ……… yes! Amazing. A truly wonderful experience.

In Denmark, the Blind Chick was really fortunate, out of the hat she drew a beautiful gelding. He was very similar to her stallion Hecco back home, and they got on famously. She was there with some pretty awesome fellow Australian Team members; it was quite a big competition.

Now a couple of special things happened in Denmark. One was the Blind Chick and her beautiful Guide Dog leading the Australian Team in front of the Queen of Denmark, another was the incredible horse spectacular that followed the opening. Oh, my heavens it was all happening. Totally awesome memories I would think.

Then the Blind Chick competed on her beautiful black gelding. Guess what her placings were? Fourth individually and a Bronze medal for Team Australian. Oh, my lord, being ranked fourth in the world, WOW! What a spectacular outcome thanks to the beautiful horse she rode and I'm sure, an amazing support team.

So, the Blind Chick came home sporting a Bronze Medal and being ranked fourth in the world. I tend to think she was pretty chuffed with that.

In that same year 1999 she did another long-distance ride from Brisbane to Sydney, to raise money for the Paralympics, and raise public awareness, inviting all Australians to come and participate, and be part of the best Paralympic Games the world has ever seen.

Then 2000 happened. My heavens what a year! In 2000 the Blind Chick married Matthew and competed at the Sydney Paralympic Games. Holy cow, what are year.

While she didn't get a medal at Sydney, she was so very proud to be representing Australia in Australia. How cool to do what you love in front of your home crowd. It doesn't get any better than that. Her placings were fourth and fifth, so close but I know for a fact she was not disappointed. She was riding a beautiful Australian thoroughbred called Rock of Gibraltar, he was magnificent and gave his all.

So, 2000 was a pretty massive year, the Blind Chick kept competing and working on selection for 2004 Paralympic Games, but then lots of things started going not quite right; her dad got very sick and there was a lot of terrorism happening overseas so she decided to pull back from Paralympic competition and focus holey and solely on able-bodied competition with her beautiful stallion Hecco. She was having a ball under the watchful eye of her coach Judy Cubitt.

This amazing lady had taken the Blind Chick under her wing since about 1995 where they'd met at a state championship for Riding For The Disabled.

During this time the Blind Chick had been through a few Guide Dogs and by 2000 she was onto her third Guide Dog, a creamy Labrador called Eccles.

This Guide Dog was truly amazing. He went with her to the Atlanta Paralympic Games, World Championships in Denmark, the Sydney Paralympic Games, numerous trips to New Zealand and competing all over Australia. Apart from being a well-travelled dog, Eccles was the most amazing Guide Dog. He wore a suit and tie every day, just so incredibly professional.

When he retired, he went and lived with the Blind Chick's coach Judy.

Judy then got quite sick with Parkinson's Disease and gave him to another of the Blind Chicks wonderful coaches, Carolyn Lieutenant. It was with Carolyn that Eccles lived out his life in luxury and love.

I think I will leave it there, in 2000. Yes, there are more stories but they can be another day.

Although this has been a long diary entry, I think the Blind Chick would like me to let you know all this wonderful history. Especially the critical component to all of this, that being it has never ever been a one-man band. Everything the Blind Chick has achieved, everything she's been able to do with the long-distance rides and her competing, has always been possible because of the Team. I know for a fact she is very grateful to the beautiful people who have come and gone in her life, they have helped to achieve so much.

Keep dreaming, keep working on your goals. Dreams do come true.

Lots of love and hugs, Johno and the Blind Chick.

Ride With Me

Feeling Relaxed
21 July 2020

Diary entry by Johno and the Blind Chick

Well, a hearty good morning from the Southern Highlands. It's definitely a little bit crisp here today.

Now the Blind Chick had an idea, she'll listen to some lessons that her friend Jenelle videoed of her and I with the wonderful José. She gets lots of information from José's lessons, but she didn't know how to explain it all to you, what she's doing in the video. So, she thought she might try and just do a little explanation on how she rides around the arena.

Morning all, Blind Chick here.

I'll do my best to explain what happens when I first get on Johno, what I'm feeling and doing. I'll probably miss out on many points, and some of the points might not be correct. This isn't a riding lesson, it's just me trying to explain what I'm doing.

After I mount, I'm taken into the arena, there I put Johno into a long rein walk, generally on the buckle. What I'm feeling at this stage is Johno as he drops his neck and comes up through the back. The further we go, the more swing he's getting, he's loosening up. I'm not asking for anything other than for him to walk forward, be relaxed and enjoy the ride.

We do this exercise of long rein walk for approximately five minutes each side, asking for nothing more than for Johno to drop his head, bring his back up, and swing through from behind. The further we go, the looser he gets and the bigger the walk strides we're getting. It feels like magic.

While we're walking, I'm concentrating on the evenness in my seat bones.

I then quietly take the reins up and as we are approaching the corner, it's inside leg into a steady outside rein. I'm not asking for bend, I'm just asking him to go around the corner, the hind legs following the front legs. We go across the short side, past "C" then next corner, inside leg into a steady outside rein. Then down the long side. Each corner and short side requires the same softness, rhythm and regularity of the long sides. That doesn't change.

After the next long side, we come up the Quarter Line, I keep the softness a little to the right, I put my right leg just behind the girth, and gently squeeze and we do a leg yield, keeping the body lovely and straight, forwards and sideways, forwards and sideways, then we walk straight ahead. With this exercise it's so lovely, I feel the softening in Johno's body. After the first leg yield the walk is often even bigger, and with more swing.

We do the same exercise a couple of times, more on the right rein and then change to the left rein across the diagonal. On the diagonal I allow Johno to have all the rein, I'm holding the buckle. This allows him to stretch and use that powerful hindquarters of his. He can get an over track of up to 18 inches after these exercises, which is pretty good.

Personally, I think the walk is one of the most important gaits, we can accomplish so much in the walk like longitudinal flexion and lateral flexion. You can do lovely leg yields, half pass, walk pirouettes, 10 metre circles winding out and then winding back in. It's such an awesome gait to get the horse supple.

While I'm riding I need to be thinking; is Johno straight, do I have too much bend through the neck, which I am guilty of on the left rein, I really need to keep a more consistent right rein when we are on the left rein. Dah, it's totally different when I am on the right rein. I need a little bit of softness on the right rein, and not so much left rein, still have a constant contact but not as much left rein.

I should be concentrating on having an even weight through both seat bones. I can influence Johno's walk with my seat, pushing him out and slowing him down. Often, I'm in trouble for rushing. I need to address this; I'm so used to pushing and asking for more. I need to allow a Johno to offer this, more 'Ask - Don't Tell'.

I need to be conscious of my right shoulder, it wants to keep dropping, I have to keep it up and back and keep an even weight in both seat bones, so I'm not interfering with Johno's balance.

Apart from all these things that I need to be thinking of, I've got to allow my hands to move backwards and forwards with the movement of his big swinging walk, so I don't inhibit his movement. This is one of our biggest things in the walk, allowing the horse to take your hands. José is always reminding me to keep giving with my hands. We often get caught up with overriding and doing too much.

Apart from all these things, I also need to be listening to my wonderful coach José telling me where I am in the arena, his guidance setting me up for each movement and what we are going to do next.

So, this is my explanation of what I'm doing in the walk. I'm probably doing a lot of other things as well, like possibly overriding, but let me know if this doesn't make sense. Another time I'll attempt to explain to you how I ride the trot and a leg yield.

Thank you so much for your friendship and following the Blind Chick and I. This is such a pretty cool journey. Thank you for making your way through these diary entries. We hope you're enjoying sharing in our adventures.

Wishing everybody a wonderful day. Please keep safe and well.

Loads of love and hugs, Johno and the Blind Chick.

My Diet

Feeling Grateful
22 July 2020

Diary entry by Johno

Wow, a very brisk good morning from the Southern Highlands.

But I suppose I shouldn't be complaining, it is winter for heaven's sake!

Well, we have a remarkably busy morning planned today. José and I have our usual schedule, we should be training mid-morning-ish, but we're also having a visit from the wonderful Jason Phillips from Trail Race Saddlery in Tuggerah, he's rechecking my saddle.

How about that for service! Jason was quite happy with how the saddle was fitting when he was here two weeks ago but he's coming back to make sure I'm comfortable, the saddle is fitting me correctly and that José is happy with it. I know the Blind Chick needs to be happy with it, but at the moment she can't ride. Hopefully, she'll be back in the saddle fingers crossed, legs crossed as well, next week, maybe Wednesday all going well.

I have also noticed that the Blind Chick has changed my feed. She's slowly taking me off all extruded food. Don't ask me, I'm sure she has a reason for this.

I must say I'm loving my new dancing shoes! Thank you so much Matt Bilderbeck for my lovely new shoes. Being a large, tall lad it's critical the shoes are comfortable. Guess what? I'm still pretty impressed they were made specially for me from one piece of straight steel. Whoohoo I'm a lucky lad.

Well, the beautiful Fay has brought my brekkie this morning and a carrot and a pat, plus a beautiful smile. What a way to start the day.

Okay I'll let you know how the saddle fitting goes and my lesson with José

Keep smiling and stay safe.

Love and hugs, Johno.

Distractions

Feeling Fantastic
23 July 2020

Diary entry by Johno

It's a beautiful good morning to you, such a spectacular day in the Southern Highlands.

Today it was so lovely, our wonderful José and I rode in the outdoor arena. The sun was shining, it was such a beautiful day, and we had the most awesome training session.

It was also good to train in a different environment, other than the indoor arena. So many other things to look at and get distracted by! But I must say, I was very intent on listening to José and content in the environment I was in. We did the same things we do in the indoor arena, lots of relaxation. I really enjoy our session.

Oh, change of plan. Jason's rung to say he'll be here next week, not today. So, I'll give you an update on the saddle then. But it's feeling very comfortable.

I must say, I have the most beautiful start to the day. Every morning and every afternoon the beautiful Fay brings me my dinner and my lovely fresh hay with a smile, a carrot and a big pat. I'm feeling very loved down here.

I hear the Blind Chick has been very diligent, listening to a lot of the lessons her friend Jenelle videoed for her of our lessons with José. She's listening intently on things that she can improve on like keeping the right shoulder up, not dropping the right shoulder and keeping a steady right rein when she is on the left rein so I don't bend too much to the left. There's lots and lots for her to think of and be conscious of.

I hear she is also endeavouring to keep fit by walking every day. She had some Reiki healing on her knee yesterday, with her lovely friend Carol. It must be making a difference, Matthew mentioned yesterday that she is moving much more freely. This is a good thing, maybe now she won't need to go to this Orthopaedic person.

Well hoping everybody has a wonderful day. Remember to keep smiling. Spread those smiles.

Love and hugs, have an awesome day, Johno.

Very Blessed

Feeling Thankful
24 July 2020

Diary entry by Johno

I just thought today I'd put it out to the universe. I'm so totally loving my lessons with the amazing José, I'm learning so much, so much kindness, I'm so very happy doing everything that is asked. Again, I must sound like a broken record, Ask Don't Tell, and Invite. It is so very, very cool learning so much. I must say, the Blind Chickie babe has lots of catching up to do!

But I thought I would include this diary entry of the Blind Chick and I having an awesome time just riding, having fun, and playing. I miss her a lot and can't wait till she is down here next week. Hopefully, her knee will allow her to ride. We have so much to achieve together. All of our dreams will come true if we keep working towards them every day.

We would both like to thank all of our wonderful friends on Facebook for sharing in our journey. They're such a part of what is happening. Their encouragement, their love and support are so appreciated. And don't forget - don't ever feel lonely. We are only ever a phone call or a message away. Friendship is very special, and we cherish it. Thank you for being our friend.

From the bottom of my heart, and the Blind Chick's heart, thank you for your friendship.

Thank you for being part of our lives.

Smile Pandemic – Bring It On!

Feeling Fantastic
25 July 2020

Smiles all round! Jose, the Blind Chick, Fay & Me

Diary entry by Johno and the Blind Chick

Well, a beautiful good morning to everyone.

Let's have another go at starting our own pandemic - a pandemic of smiles.

Let's share this all around the world! Please share this diary entry, let people know you care, send them a smile, send them your love.

Smile

Smiling is infectious, you catch it like the flu,
When someone smiled at me today, I started smiling too.
I passed around the corner and someone saw my grin.
When he smiled, I realized, I'd passed it on to him.

I thought about that smile, then I realized its worth.
A single smile, just like mine, could travel around the earth.
So, if you feel a smile begin, don't leave it undetected.
Let's start an epidemic quick and get the world infected!
Spike Milligan

Please share this. Let's start our own pandemic of smiles and give people a reason to smile.

I'm am sending smiles from the Southern Highland and the Blind Chick is sending smiles from Dubbo.

The amazing José and beautiful Fay are sending smiles from the Southern Highlands.

Have a spectacular day, loads of love and hugs, Johno and the Blind Chick.

Basics – The Foundation

Feeling Grateful
28 July 2020

Diary entry by Johno

I hope everybody is safe and well, it's been a little wild and woolly here in the Southern Highlands.

Over the past few days, we've had quite a few storm cells and nasty winds, it's more than a little cold. But thank heavens I have lots of lovely rugs, I'm snug as a bug in a rug.

I had a wonderful training session with the amazing José earlier today. Again, we were just working on those wonderful things called Basics. Lots of transitions within the paces and some canter-walk-canter transitions. I'm getting good at those.

I am feeling so soft and supple and guess what? One more sleep and my Blind Chickie babe will be down. Hopefully her knee will be up for a ride. Fingers, hooves, and toenails crossed.

I heard they've had some wonderful rain in Dubbo, 32 mils I think. This will be great for Matthew's crops, not so good though for the dressage arena! It's still in flood. Thank heavens I'm missing all that wet, wet, wet being here with the amazing José. Here I have the privilege of being trained in his beautiful indoor arena, and when it's sunny we ride in the lovely outside arena. I think the Blind Chick needs to start praying for an indoor arena because every time it rains at home, our arena floods. She could go paddling they've had that much rain.

I came across this great quote and thought it was worth sharing, it's a beauty.

Quote of the Day
"If you want to be happy, do not dwell in the past.
Do not worry about the future.
Focus on living fully in the present."
Roy T. Bennett

Hope everybody is safe and well. Look out for your friends and neighbours.

Loads of love and hugs, Johno.

Just Get On

Feeling Excited
29 July 2020

Diary entry by the Blind Chick

Woohoo! I'm back riding Johno!

I had a lovely ride today, we only walked and trotted and worked on the most basic of things but I loved it. Basics like keeping the outside rein, keeping Johno's neck straight, keeping the rhythm and regularity. Ask, don't tell.

We spent most of the lesson walking, me getting back in the feel of things, keeping that outside rein, keeping the straightness through the body, feeling what was happening underneath me. Johno was such a good boy. José has done such a wonderful job training him. Everything is so easy and flawless, done by one very happy horse.

Okay we only walked and trotted, but that was okay, that was a big achievement for me given I've not been back in the saddle for six weeks. It was rather massive actually. Why? Because when you are totally blind, the importance of doing something day in, day out, having that repetition, is vital. Orientation and confidence soar with repetition day in, day out. We've not had that. This was massive for me. Johno you totally rock, and José the most amazing coach and trainer – THANK YOU.

A massive thank you to José and Fay for looking after Johno, and a big thank you to my friend Susan for doing the filming of Johno and I today. It was just really exciting with my knee having been giving me trouble to just give riding a try. I hadn't been moving very well, but when I got in the saddle everything felt fine! Not quite fine when we did some lateral work, but that will come in time.

I hope everybody is having a wonderful day, mine was totally a ripper of a day. From someone who was thinking they may not ride, to having a lovely ride and enjoying every moment, and that excitement, and that love just bombarding you, it's so amazing.

Love and hugs, the Blind Chick.

Oopsy!

😊 Feeling Excited
31 July 2020

Diary entry by the Blind Chick

Gee whiz, what a spectacular day in the Southern Highlands.

Firstly, we went and picked up some feed for the wonderful Johno from the produce store in Marulan, the staff were amazing and so helpful.

We then headed out to visit the wonderful Johno.

The sun was absolutely beaming down, just such a spectacular day for a ride. The beautiful Fay had Johno out and was saddling him and putting his boots on, getting ready for José to ride Johno first. Then it would be my turn to ride.

It was really interesting. I sat and I listened, and I listened, like a sponge. I try to take in as much as I can and ask lots of questions.

José did a little work in hand with Johno first, getting him to bring his inside hind leg in under him on a small circle on the ground, just lunging. It was interesting listening and the descriptions José was giving as he was doing these exercises and what he was accomplishing by doing this.

I could hear the difference as Johno became more through from behind.

José then mounted up and invited Johno into a lovely big, long walk that was so relaxed on the end of the buckle, Johno was so in the mood today. He just wanted to please big time. Everything José asked, Johno just did, with such ease. They glided through all the movements and the exercises, it sounded amazing. I've got to tell you. You can hardly hear his foot fall! Yes, for a horse that's so big he has the lightest foot fall. When he comes past me, the rhythm and the regularity sounds just beautiful.

José did lots of lovely transitions, some amazing lateral work and beautiful floating half passes. You could hear the suspension in the air and the half passes rhythm and regularity, nothing changed, regardless of what movements they did. Oh, my heavens! I so wish I could see right now.

Then after José had ridden Johno for a while it was my turn. I mounted, loving my new saddle, it's totally awesome as it puts me in such a good position, plus I feel very secure.

Now this wasn't any sort of ground breaking ride. I wasn't doing canter pirouettes or canter half pass. I spent the whole lesson walking, concentrating on my position, concentrating on allowing my hands to move forward as Johno walked, concentrating on when he is on the left rein to keep him straight through the neck, so he doesn't fall out through the shoulder, and twist his withers so he is straight. Concentrating on all the little things that make big differences in the big movements.

Oh, oops! I even managed to walk Johno out over the end of the arena! God love his cotton socks. He will go anywhere I ask him to go. Unbeknown to me I'd walk him halfway over the outside arena edging, then I had a massive panic because I heard the plastic of the arena surrounds and nearly had a kitten or two. José just said, "give him a pat and walk on" and Johno finished walking out, then we went back in. Holy cow! Sometimes it would be lovely to see, and I wouldn't put Johno in these situations. But he coped beautifully God love him.

To be honest walking out of the arena gave me a bit of a shock. I was just totally disorientated, it really highlighted to me how critical me riding every day is. Being able to orientate myself in the rain or know where I am at any given time. Riding in an indoor arena I don't have the sun for guidance, so poor Johno. God love him, he makes up for a lot of my short fallings.

But to be very honest, it was one of the most productive rides I've had for a very long time. Keeping in mind I haven't ridden for six weeks, but just being able to concentrate on the little things; are my seat bones even in the saddle, am I sitting with my shoulders square and not dropping my right shoulder, keep that outside rein when I'm sitting setting up a lateral movement, not too much leg, Ask Don't Tell. It was a lesson that totally rocked. José is just the most amazing coach, and Johno is so patient with me. But oh, my lordy, I have so much catching up to do!

But it was pretty cool, I loved every moment of being back in the saddle. My knee was really excellent today. Mind you I did have a painkiller before I rode, but I think it would've been fine at the walk without it.

Riding tomorrow early at 8 am as then we're heading home to Dubbo. After we ride, Johno will be staying down with the wonderful José and Fay for another few weeks, until I've been to the Orthopaedic Surgeon and find out if there is any real damage in my knee.

Keep a big smile on your face, stay safe, hugs and love a very happy Blind Chick.

8 August

Lost

 Feeling Grateful
1 August 2020

Diary entry by the Blind Chick

Wow what a spectacular day today was, a lovely brisk morning in the Southern Highlands, frosty of course but no wind and spectacular sunshine for most of the day.

We arrived at José and Fay's place nice and early for our 8.30am lesson, the first of three lessons, one each day for the next three days. Johno wasn't that impressed with being brought out of his yard so early, he thought a ride later in the day would have been better.

But he was brought over, saddled up and given a beautiful brush, a couple of carrots, lots of love and attention and taken to the indoor arena.

Now, remember I said it was a frosty morning. Well on frosty mornings condensation gets on the roof of the indoor arena, and it drips down! Only a little bit, like a light rain shower. But, Johno wasn't overly impressed with the drops landing on him as he and José warmed up. Plus, it was quite brisk; so Johno was quite forward and elevated. I must say, I was sitting there listening to them warm up and in my head going; "Wow! How amazing this feels. Wow! Do I want to sit on this ball of energy?" Johno was amazing; big forward movement, soft, flowing, spectacular rhythm and regularity. Everything was bigger than usual.

Well, it was funny in hindsight! José and I were speaking about this after I'd ridden Johno. Jose had been thinking the same thing! "Wow, do I want to put Sue-Ellen on this ball of energy? He is so forward and big, he's not doing anything wrong, just forward and big and Sue-Ellen is struggling with orientation, so riding this Johno is possibly not the best thing. So, guess what happened?

José dismounted, and I got on!

Guess what happened next?

A transformation! A massive transformation in fact. This ball of energy went into Blind Chick mode, he looked after me so well. There were no huge movements anymore, just normal Johno, movements that I'm used to and yes, he was still as soft and flowing with me as he was for Jose. We trained on all our lateral work and transitions in the walk. It was pure bliss.

As you know I'm very honest with what I share with you, it's warts and all.

So here are some of the warts and all on this day I rode.

I was so disorientated not having been in the saddle for six weeks, it was really hard gauging where I was in the arena, and Johno was a little spooky which possibly didn't help the situation. My orientation was terrible, that's no fault of Johno's.

I am convinced that riding at least five days a week is paramount. Because I'm totally blind the orientation of where I am, is lost so quickly. Understanding this will help you understand why after not riding for six weeks, I find it difficult to orientate even in the walk.

But between the amazing José and Johno we got through our first day being back in the saddle. My second day was a little better, the orientation was starting to improve, especially with José calling letters and letting me know where I was all the time. Apart from when I walked Johno out of the arena! Yes, I rode him right over the little arena fence. That was not a good look and it scared the hell out of me. Thankfully Johno just took it in his stride. It goes to show how wonderful he is, he'll go anywhere I ask him to, even over the edge of the arena!

So, after my minor hissy fit, as in 'Oh my god, I've got the front half of my horse over the arena and the back half is still in the arena!' Yes, it's only a little plastic arena edging, but it's enough for many horses to get a good fright if they saw fit to, but Johno didn't. He was absolutely amazing. God love his cotton socks he is such a good boy.

And now we get to my next day's ride, it was so much better. I was feeling so much better with my orientation and feel in the arena. Oh, my heavens, it felt wonderful to have that confidence back again, the knowing sort of where I was and having the amazing José guiding Johno and I all the time.

And again, I'm not pulling punches, I couldn't have had a trot in those first couple of days we had lessons, even if I wanted to. Why? Because I didn't have the confidence or the orientational skills to know where I was to do that safely for Johno or I. But by the Friday with José's guidance and the beautiful Johno looking after me, I could've trotted and cantered. But I didn't. It was more important that I work on my position, my orientation, and all of the little things that are going to make the difference for the bigger things we do later on.

It's not always beer and skittles, it's not always easy, but you find a way to overcome the little hurdles and move forward at the pace you can handle. That's the wonderful thing about José. He didn't push me, he didn't over face me, he was very understanding about the situation. I'm so very grateful to have José as Johno's and my coach. Wow! Johno is just so amazing to ride now. All our movements are done with the softest aid, I ask with the touch of a feather. I have so much to learn and loving every moment of the learning.

As you can imagine, after my ride on Friday I was elated. I'd achieved everything I needed to achieve, and it was all done at the walk! This trip to Jose was a milestone in my riding, my partnership with Johno. I just couldn't believe how much difference three days could make to my confidence and orientation.

But the big thing for me is still consistency. This improvement in three days reinforced how critical me being able to ride at least five days a week is. So, it's onwards and upwards for us. I'll be back to Jose's with Johno again in two weeks for some more training. I can't wait.

A massive thank you to the amazing José for his understanding and his incredible training of my beautiful Johno. To José's beautiful wife Fay, thank you for looking after Johno as if he is her own horse. Johno is so happy, so content, I'm so grateful. I love every moment I get to spend down there with the amazing José and Fay.

A massive thank you to my wonderful friend Susan Cornish for looking after me and for helping with Johno's grooming.

We hope you are having a spectacular day.

Loads of love and hugs, keep safe and well, Johno and the Blind Chick.

👻 Feeling Happy
1 August 2020

Diary entry by the Blind Chick

A very happy birthday to my wonderful horse Johno and all the other beautiful horses in the world.

I hope you get lots of carrots, loads of love.

Have a spectacular day.

Love and hugs the Blind Chick.

Never Under Estimate A Good Walk!

Feeling Grateful
4 August 2020

Diary entry by Johno

Well, a hearty good morning from a very chilly Southern Highlands. It's a little bit nippy this morning and I hear there is a cold front coming through, so it is going to get colder.

But my morning has started beautifully with a happy smile, a carrot, and my brekkie from the wonderful Fay.

I must say I am incredibly happy down here with Fay and José. It's such a wonderful environment, so calm and I'm learning so much.

My lesson today with the amazing José has been awesome.

José did a little bit of work on the ground with me, just getting those hind legs coming through a little more and working on my softness. Everything is done so quietly and calmly. Then he mounts and we go into the arena. We start with lovely big walking, he is holding the reins on the buckle, he's just so relaxed. I must say the odd drip is falling from the roof though, but I will get used to it, I think.

José and I have been doing a lot of work on transitions and making the aids as soft as possible for all lateral work. So today when José asked me for a shoulder-in, or a travers, or a half pass, it was like a feather touching my side. From his request I just brought my shoulder in or my quarters in.

Whatever is being asked, the aid is so soft. The connection through the reins is so light, there's no pulling, no shoving, just a beautiful soft connection. Maybe a little flexion to the left, maybe a little to the right, but everything is so soft and supple.

When the Blind Chick was here last week, we worked a lot on this in the walk. Her first few days were a little bit rocky as she was very disorientated. I guess it must be very difficult being totally blind and not having ridden for six weeks! Getting on and trying to ride around the arena as if you've done it every day isn't easy. There were quite a few times where she got anxious about how unfamiliar it all felt. Imagine being in the dark and not knowing what your surroundings look like. Scary stuff.

But with guidance from the wonderful coach José, she overcome her anxiety quite quickly. José was extremely quick to pick up that the Blind Chick was struggling with orientation and began giving her more information about where she was in the arena than she normally required. He told her whether she was on a Quarter Line, a corner, or going past K and so on. Lots of information to help the Blind Chick sort things out in her head about where she was.

By the Friday things were nearly back to normal again. We only walked but we would've been fine to trot or canter. I totally understand why though, the Blind Chick wanted to work on the set ups of all the movements in the walk first. Getting the feel of the softness, of putting your leg on and asking for a half pass or putting your leg on and asking for a travers and not putting your leg back to far or too hard and getting too much angle. It was so cool. She had the most amazing ride.

I truly think in a horses training that the walk is totally underestimated. You can teach everything at the walk, and you can perfect it at the walk. Then you can move to the trot or the canter. Like teaching the walk pirouette, you can do a couple of strides of walk in the pirouette and then go into the canter and do a couple of strides in the canter, back to the walk, then walk pirouette! It's such a cool gait to teach everything from. There's so much more control of what you are doing with your body, plus I think it gives the horse and rider more time to think.

Before I sign off, I must tell you something funny that happened the other day while the Blind Chick was here. After my training, the wonderful Fay gave me a brush, oh I'm so shiny and I felt so good.

She then put a lovely clean rug on me and put me back in the paddock. Guess what I immediately went and did? Yep, I promptly went and rolled in the dirt. Isn't that what all good horses do?

I hope everybody is safe and well. Please look after yourselves and look out for your neighbours, don't forget to share that smile and have a spectacular day.

Loads of love and hugs Johno.

Secrets

Feeling Grateful
5 August 2020

Diary entry by Johno

Wow, it's a very crisp morning here in the Southern Highlands. Ouch, this cold front is supposed to continue. But my day is brightened by the beautiful Fay bringing me a carrot, a big hug and my breakfast.

I'm definitely looking forward to my session with the amazing José today, going for a ride will definitely warm my body up this morning. I think I may even get to catch up with my lovely friend Emily this morning, she might be visiting her horses, I hope so.

You know, it never ceases to amaze me what the beautiful Fay does for me. She gets me from my paddock, brings me over to the tack up area, give me a big brush, cleans my feet out, puts a lovely clean saddle cloth on me, saddles me up and voila! I'm ready to go. Then a beautiful warm woollen rug is put over the top of me to keep me warm until José is ready to work me. The care is amazing. I'm so grateful to be down here training.

Then I'm led over to the indoor arena, where yes, on these frosty mornings the condensation that's pooled on the roof make droplets land on me! This is most disconcerting for me, I'm guessing also for José, he must get drops down his back.

Once in the indoor arena Jose starts as always with a little bit of groundwork, he takes me for a walk around the arena in hand. Then he turns on the beautiful music and we're ready to dance. He has this amazing sound system which plays beautiful Spanish music while we ride. It is so relaxing, you could be anywhere in the world, it's beautiful.

Okay, you're going to think I'm a broken record, but this warmup totally rocks! In our beautiful long rein walk around the arena, José on the buckle, I'm swinging through from behind and doing a big over track. I would say about 18 inches over tracking, so soft through the body.

After about 10 minutes on a long rein walk José quietly takes the reins up, still in the walk we start doing some lateral work; a little shoulder-in, then down the Quarter Line and a leg yield across to the side. All the time we are working on suppleness and softness, the aids are so light.

After our lovely big warm up in the walk, José asks me to trot, allowing me to stretch down and out with my nose, not jamming me up through the gullet, he lets me stretch and use my hindquarters. This is where my powerhouse is. Jose's warm up recipe allows my back to come up and lets me swing through the back, and it's all done at my pace, no pushing and shoving. I'm giving generously because it feels so good, I want to please.

After five or six minutes with a big flowing trot, José quietly takes up the reins a little, then we start doing a bit of leg yield from the Quarter Line. Some shoulder-in keeping the rhythm and regularity, everything done so softly, the aids are a feather touch, the contact is lovely through the reins. I feel so good.

My reward for the wonderful trot work is, we come back to a walk for a while. We have a relaxing long-rein walk; I'm swinging through my back and feeling wonderful through my whole body. It's still a bit chilly here though, I must say.

Then after about six or eight minutes of the nice big, long walk, José quietly takes the reins up and we do some canter work. He keeps me nice and straight through the neck and body; outside leg back, inside leg on the girth and into the canter. It's a lovely transition forward and uphill, I'm still feeling soft as José canters me around the arena. We are doing transitions within the canter, pushing me out a little, bringing me back a bit, pushing me out a little, bringing me back a bit. All done so subtly and softly you wouldn't know José is doing anything at all, or giving me any aids. Everything is so subtle, Ask - Don't Tell.

José then starts to introduce the half pass. We come down the Centre Line nice and straight and then shoulder-fore, and over we go, beautiful big gliding strides, same rhythm, same regularity, same softness. Nothing changes except we're now going sideways. Pretty cool, I so love this training.

We then do some transitions, canter back to walk, keeping the softness, the rhythm and the regularity. This Ask - Don't Tell is so cool, everything is so easy.

Then José puts me back into the walk. For our warm down we do a couple of walk pirouettes each way, a long rein walk with a little bit of collection, a long rein walk again, but this time with a shoulder-in followed by a travers, with José always working on my softness and suppleness, always inviting me to do the movement with a feather touch.

What a cool ride, and how lucky am I to be training with the amazing José! I think he enjoys training me, I try really hard to please him and I'm learning so much. The Blind Chick has so much catching up to do, but that will happen in time.

When I finished working, I turn my head around to José and he gives me a wee treat and a pat on the forehead, then he dismounts. Oopsie! It's long way down José, don't forget you nearly need a parachute.

Fay was soon with us; she took me to the tie up area and removed all my tack. I was given a quick brush before my winter woollies were put back on, so I don't get cold. I also got some treats from guess who. I'm so lucky that Fay remembers I love carrots, so I get the odd one or two .

Stay safe, stay smiling, love and hugs Johno.

Smell The Roses

Feeling Fantastic
6 August 2020

Diary entry by Johno

Well, they definitely weren't kidding when they said there was a cold snap coming through! Apparently, it was -3°C in Dubbo and I think at least -5°C here in the Southern Highlands. Brrrrrr.

I'm so looking forward to my ride with José this morning, that will certainly warm me up.

I'm also thinking it must be getting close to the time that Matt Bilderbeck our Farrier will be here to put on my dancing shoes. I wonder if he will make them from scratch again.

I also hear on the grapevine that the Blind Chick is bringing my wonderful friend Tanya with her, so I can have another treatment. I can't wait. That girl sure has magic hands.

The Blind Chick and the crew will be down next Wednesday.

According to the weather forecast we're in for a few wet days. I don't mind the rain, but I don't like that cold wind that comes with it. It feels like it's coming off snow. But I'll be all rugged up, so it's all good.

We're all saddled up, off to the dressage arena, I still have the rug on over my saddle keeping me warm, which is lovely. The rug is taken off when José gets on, we start by going for a bit of a walk around the arena. Again! Just the odd drop of condensation falling from the roof.

José takes advantage of our walk in-hand to do a little bit of work with me on the ground. Again, just soft and subtle, asking me to bend and flex, bring that inside hind legs through, getting me to listen. Mind you, I have no problem with the listening, I just love learning.

The wonderful thing about José's way of training is there is no rush and hurry. I know this is a new concept for the Blind Chick, especially as she has spent her life rushing and hurrying, trying to fit in as much as she can with the race against losing her sight. But now there is no rush, as there is no sight anymore! So now, she can relax and enjoy the ride. Which will be great for both of us.

This doesn't mean our goals change. This means we can do it in a much more relaxed way, and I must say, I totally love this Ask - Don't Tell, the not being jammed into the bridle, the not being asked for more, more, more collection, more this, more that. I just give it naturally, it's so easy.

I have a lovely warm up, again a long-rein walk with José on the buckle. José allows me to stretch my head down and my nose out a little, this means I can come through with my hind legs, to bring my back up and swing through the back. Fantastic!

If you look at pictures of me being ridden, you'll notice my lovely neck. I have neck muscles built up evenly on both sides because I'm being ridden softly and correctly.

Also, if you notice José and the Blind Chick never take me behind the vertical, I so appreciate this. Number One, it is quite uncomfortable and interferes with my breathing, Number Two, it's not the correct position for me to be in. It jams me up through the shoulder which means I can't come through from behind. Plus, it also restricts my movement through the back.

After a lovely long-rein walk, José collects the reins a little and we do some lateral work. Lovely and soft big swinging walk followed by my first leg yield. My stride has lengthened by another 2-3 inches, it makes the world of difference.

So now I have longitudinal softness and lateral softness, which is so important. These allow my body to be soft and work correctly.

I'm not surprised that the amazing José has me travelling straighter these days. When I first came here, I wasn't straight through the body. I had a little bit of a twist whenever I was on the left rein and I always had more bend than was needed. Often this was the Blind Chicks fault, but we won't tell her that! The Blind Chick is now much more aware of what to do when we're on the left rein, she needs to keep the right rein and keep me straight and through the neck and the body. This also makes the world a difference to how I travel. It also stops me from falling out through the right shoulder.

Wow I'm still talking, and we haven't even got out of the walk!

Another thing José does is, when we have a change of direction, he does a working walk pirouette. He makes it a little larger than a competition pirouette, keeping my hindlegs marching and the forward movement. This is another great exercise for softening my body and forcing me to listen.

We always do lots of transitions; pushing me out in the walk, on the buckle, then a little bit of collection, a little bit of lateral work, then letting me out again, letting me stretch. After our fantastic warm up routine, I have an awesome over track, it's usually at least 18 inches, which I'm a bit proud of. But then again, I have exceptionally long legs!

Well, we did lots of other very cool things in my lesson, but I'm going to leave sharing those with you for another day. Why? Because I think the walk is possibly the most important gait for learning and establishing things. For me it totally rocks.

I hear we are in for lots of rain over the next few days, so maybe everybody keep rugged up and warm.

I also hear a lot of people are doing it tough. Whether it be the dreaded Covid-19, bush fires, hurricanes, drought, or other things, please take time to look out for each other. Don't forget to drop somebody a line you haven't spoken to in a while. Pick up the phone and make a phone call. Don't forget to tell somebody you love them, and to smile.

Have a spectacular day.

Loads of love and hugs from your mate, Johno.

Dare to Dream

Feeling Grateful
7 August 2020

Diary entry by Johno

Quote of the Day
"To dream of success is to set a goal of where you want to be.
To wake up, take action, and achieve it is
what true success is all about."
Idowu Koyenikan

So, dare to dream!

Let's make those dreams come true.

I would like to share the Blind Chicks and my dream; it is to complete one tiny step at a time. Well in my case, one very large step at a time. We are getting closer to that day, but we're not in a hurry. It will happen when the time is right.

We are blessed to have you along sharing our dream.

Much love, Johno.

Odd Feet

Feeling Excited
9 August 2020

Diary entry by Johno

Well, a very chilly good morning from the Southern Highlands. I hope you are all snug and warm and having a lovely day.

I was so excited my wonderful Farrier Matt Bilderbeck was back at José and Fay's to put new dancing shoes on me on Friday afternoon. Guess what? He made shoes especially for me, just from one flat piece of steel!

It is such an interesting process; the wonderful Matt has put a video of making my shoes which features on our Facebook page. The Blind Chick has listened to it again, and again, and … I don't know how many times! I think she has worn it out.

It explains how my two front feet are different sizes, so Matt has to make the shoes accordingly. He is also correcting my offside front hoof that had a previous injury to it. I tend to swing it a little bit. Matt is correcting this slowly, it's getting better and I am feeling so good in these new shoes, no more pain! It's excellent.

José has noticed how much easier I am moving than when I first started coming down here. José was picking up a little irregularity, this has all gone since Matt started shoeing me and making shoes specially for me. I am so very grateful; I feel so comfortable.

If you would like, have a look at Matt's website or visit him on *Matt Bilderbeck Farriers* on Facebook, lots of awesome information, really interesting stuff.

So, a massive thank you to the wonderful Matt for looking after my hooves and keeping me sound. Remember no hooves, no horse.

I'm having the weekend off, so I can get used to the new shoes, back to work on Monday. Yippee the Blind Chickie babe will be down on Wednesday, I can't wait.

Much love and hugs, Johno.

Tanya Rocks

Feeling Thankful
11 August 2020

Diary entry by Johno

Wow what a very chilly morning from the Southern Highlands. I hope everybody had a lovely weekend and are all safe after the terrible storms on the coast.

I'm feeling fit and well, I have my lovely new shoes on thank you to Matt Bilderbeck. Again, he made my shoes from scratch to fit me, and they are perfect. José is most impressed with how I am moving; I'm getting better because of Matt's corrective shooing. I'm so grateful and so comfortable.

I love these mornings spent with the amazing José. I always enjoy our time training; it's just so consistent and soft, Ask - Don't Tell. I know, I know, I sound like a broken record, but it rocks! Plus, I'm learning so much, and everything is happening so easily. I'm so willing to please given how easy José makes things.

I'm noticing a difference since my diet has changed, no extruded food, which has eliminated some of the not so good oils for inflammation. José has also noticed a difference in me, which is wonderful. I'm feeling really good and looking wonderful, even if I do say so myself.

I hear via the grapevine that the Blind Chickie babe is feeling a little frustrated at the moment. Her knee is improving; she's doing lots of walking. Her appointment with the Orthopaedic Surgeon is next week so fingers crossed, but she is in no pain which is wonderful.

But the frustration level is high, I know she is excited, only one more sleep and she'll be down training with the amazing José and I.

I'm also a bit excited as she is bringing the wonderful Tanya Hind with her. Tanya will give me a treatment while she's down here. Tanya has magic hands; I always feel a million dollars after a treatment.

Today I had an awesome ride with the wonderful José, then a lovely brush down by my beautiful friend Fay, then back to my paddock to relax for the rest for the day.

Much love and hugs, Johno.

Tanya's Story

Tanya's journey into her speciality started over 20 years ago in the natural alternative healing modalities.

She shares her story with us.

At first it was just dabbling with essential oils to treat my daughters temperamental pony mare. Seeking more knowledge into natural medicines and then started using herbs with all our horses.

We then purchased a quarter horse for my daughter to use in all activities of pony club. This horse looked after her and gave her the confidence to go further in her riding career. It is this horse that led me to look further into alternative medicines and modalities, as he came to us with a few biomechanical issues. They included intermittent lameness which swapped from leg to leg, plus he'd had some injuries when he was a yearling. One of the injuries was an injury to his forehead. We were told when it happened, you could almost see the brain.

It soon became apparent that there were underlying issues causing the lameness. We had the horse examined by a vet and x-rays taken. They showed he had spurs on his P1 and P2 joints. It is then that he was started on monthly injections into the joints to relieve pain and hope that this would help with the lameness. This continued for six months and became quite expensive, so once again I started looking for an alternative that would help this horse keep going.

That year I went to Equitana in Melbourne and came across a woman by the name of Maureen Rogers who was demonstrating Craniosacral Therapy on a horse. The improvements that could be seen at the end of her session in the horse that she was treating were amazing. It was then that I realised this is what I had to learn, to help our daughters quarter horse.

It is from this point on that my Craniosacral journey begins. The main centre for training was based in America, so it wasn't possible that I go there. It was about 12 months after I'd seen Maureen at Equitana that she held a course in Queensland. What made it even more beneficial for me was that we got to take a horse of our own to work on. So of course, the quarter horse and I made our way to Queensland to start the craniosacral journey together.

I was hooked from that day forward, and the horse no longer required monthly injections into his joints, just routine craniosacral sessions.

Of course, no one would believe that this very weird therapy could be responsible for the miraculous improvements in the horse, some would call it voodoo. Some of the early enthusiasts wanting to try this therapy on their horses called me the Voodoo Lady.

I didn't mind this, as I admit, Craniosacral Therapy is quite hard to get your head around. So voodoo it was. At this point I started working on horses on weekends and school holidays. Even though I was hooked on the therapy I still wanted to know more about other alternative modalities that were being used in the equine world.

This led me to doing Equine Acupressure and Equine Reiki. You can never have enough tools in your toolbox. After completing the levels with Maureen Rogers, it was some time before she was coming back to Australia, I found another organisation who was doing Equine Craniosacral Courses. Once again, with a thirst for more knowledge in this modality, I started my training with the Upledger Institute in Australia. By completing the levels with Upledger it strengthened my intuitive ability and the techniques that I use today.

Now after 15 years of working on weekends and school holidays with a modality that I'm passionate about and believe in wholeheartedly, I am finally making this my full-time occupation. A good healer is non-judgemental, and compassionate to all that they meet.

This journey has not been easy for me. As you can imagine entering the horse world with voodoo, something that's so out there, and with no manipulation to be seen, horse owners often question how can that possibly work? Even with its results, it's hard to break the old methods of treatments, like the instant fix all injections, drugs, liniment, and bush remedies. I have come to believe that if I only help one horse, then I've achieved making its overall wellbeing better than it was before I entered its life.

I am currently studying Equine Iridology. I'm so excited about the information that the horse's eyes give you. This added modality will enhance my practice. All the modalities I use are non-invasive treatments.

My ultimate goal is to work alongside Vets for a more holistic approach to health and well-being, and to work with trainers of all levels to increase knowledge of Craniosacral Therapy, and how everything in the body is connected, with an aim to improve outcomes for both the horse and rider/owner.

Majestic Guapo

Feeling Grateful
16 August 2020

Diary entry by Johno

Oopsy, I've been neglecting my duties and not recording diary entries regularly. I do apologise. I've had quite a bit on my plate lately.

And I must say the weather hasn't been that flash, a tad wet, windy and quite cold.

But it was really cool, the Blind Chick came down last Wednesday. She had a ride. It was later in the day and very close to dinner, so I was a bit distracted and maybe a tad spooky given the weather was windy, overcast and a bit blustery. This didn't really help the Blind Chicks orientation in the arena.

But she persisted and had an okay ride. I wouldn't say it was one of our better rides, but the problem is, the Blind Chick is not spending enough time in the saddle! So, her ability to orientate is a massive issue. Plus, the knee was a bit sore on Wednesday. So, she didn't ride on Thursday in case she made it worse.

But she did sit and listen to José ride me and learnt a lot more about the movements and what José was doing to get me to do different movements and transitions. The Blind Chick can count the strides and hear the downward transitions. She can tell if it is soft or not, just by the rhythm and regularity. Pretty cool hey.

Then the girls had a lovely picnic lunch with José and Fay and a chance for a catch up. Then the beautiful Tanya Hind with her magic hands, did a Craniosacral treatment on me. Wow it was amazing.

Then after my treatment I was led into one of the beautiful stables at Méndez Equestrian, between two beautiful Andalusian stallions. It was awesome. Guapo, the lovely stallion on my left was picking up on the energy from my treatment, how cool he was yawning and stretching like I was!

For an explanation on what was being done during my treatment Google it. It was so incredible, I felt like a million dollars after the treatment.

After me, Tanya treated the beautiful, imported Andalusian stallion Guapo. His name means Handsome in Spanish. He truly is quite a majestic horse. Guapo also really enjoyed his treatment, lots of yawning and stretching, totally in the moment.

The Blind Chickie babe is off to Orthopaedic Surgeon on Wednesday, so we'll know what is happening with the knee which will be great.

I do hope I've spelt Guapo's name right!

Hugs and lots of love, Johno.

Releasing Tension

Feeling Relaxed
17 August 2020

Diary entry from a relaxed Johno

It's a wintery morning here in the Southern Highlands and the Blind Chickie is due to arrive here this afternoon. Right on time I can see the ute coming up the drive, but hang on, there are three people in it! This is strange as it's typically only two, the Blind Chickie and her driver.

Who is the third person?

As I stretch my neck out to see, oh my lord it's my craniosacral therapist Tanya Hind. It has been some time since my last session, so I hope she is here for me. After the ladies have their meet and greet with José and Fay, I'm saddled up and walked over to the arena where José was so proud to show and explain my progression to the Blind Chickie and Tanya.

I can see the delight on everyone's faces, they're happy with my performance. José and Tanya are having a very in-depth conversation regarding my movement and overall attitude to training. They seem to be on the same channel as each other. I am then unsaddled and popped into one of the stables in between two stallions.

After a short while, everyone came back to my box, what's going on now? Tanya and José entered the stable and I could hear Tanya explaining the Craniosacral Therapy to the group. Oh, I see now I am about to have another session. Yippee I can hear Tanya telling José that she needed to work on my pelvis, as I was brushing my hind legs and my offside was not moving freely.

She explained, by releasing the tension high up in the pelvis where a normal massage cannot reach, this would help these imbalances. She also pointed out the width between my hind hooves was very tiny. I could feel her light touch high up inside my pelvis and then the muscles tendons and fascia started releasing slowly, but surely. It's such a weird but wonderful feeling. So relaxing.

Ha ha, Tanya sure has the touch. Today even José is yawning in the corner of the stable. Powerful stuff this Craniosacral Therapy. Once all this releasing was finished Tanya pointed out the difference in my hind leg position. Blow me down, my hooves are now further apart and positioned nicely under my hip joints. It looks better and I'm happy to report it feels better.

Tanya then moved onto my thoracic sling and withers, they needed to be released. Tanya is very good at following my energy and body rhythms, she's very intuitive and lets this guide her to the areas I need doing. Once again, after this area was released my front hooves were wider apart and my neck, shoulders and withers had become so supple and soft. You can see me going through one of my releases in a video on our Facebook page.

For the finale Tanya did a little bit of work on my head, just to keep me well balanced. I must tell you I feel so relaxed, so do the two stallions either side of me. The whole way through my session they've been taking in the energy as well. They've been yawning and chewing and standing quietly right next to the divider between us. Even in my cranio trance, I could hear all of my on-lookers admiring the changes in my body that they could see. My rugs were put back on and then I was walked back to my paddock. I must tell you; I feel good.

A massive thank you to the wonderful Tanya for my awesome treatment. I'm so grateful and appreciative.

I hope everyone has a spectacular day, loads of love and hugs, keep safe and well Johno.

Sometimes Life Sucks!

🙂 Feeling Blessed
18 August 2020

Diary entry by Johno

These aren't my words, but they are wonderful words of wisdom. Please take time to read and digest them.

Sometimes Life Sucks

Horses break, you fall off, poles come down, events get cancelled, and sometimes it just never stops raining.

There are days you want to scream, cry, shout, hide or just disappear, but people will always come along and cut you down with four little words... "it could be worse."

And all of sudden you feel guilty for letting something "so trivial" affect you, when there are people going through so much more.

So, you shut the feelings down, you push it away and refuse to let it surface because you don't feel you deserve to be disappointed, or upset, or angry, or frustrated.

But as time passes that feeling is still there, it's just silently chipping away at you inside with nowhere to go. The more you ignore it, the worse it feels.

Those feelings of frustration, anger, disappointment, heartbreak... they need to be felt. You can only move on when you are ready to, and if you're still holding onto all those feelings, that will never happen.

One person's worst day might be another person's best. Putting out someone else's light won't make yours shine any brighter.

Be kind, always. People are fighting battles you know nothing about.

Anon

Love and hugs, Johno.

You Never Know What's Around The Corner

Feeling Positive
19 August 2020

Diary entry by Johno

Well, a hearty good morning from the Southern Highlands, I have some news about the Blind Chickie babe's knee.

She has been to the Orthopaedic Surgeon this morning and whoohoo, no surgery is needed! It will still be at least another two, maybe four, months of rehab, the fracture hasn't healed yet, and the tendon damage still needs more time. But all is good, she will keep up her walking. It's important she doesn't have any other setbacks like falling and hurting her knee again. But over-all it's great news.

She won't be able to rush out do heaps of riding all at once, getting back into the saddle will be a gradual, a slow process. She'll be able to get into a new routine, one that allows riding whilst protecting where the fracture is, it sits on the saddle, as soon as she works out how to protect that site. But where there's a will, there's a away.

I hear via the grapevine the Blind Chick and the wonderful Tanya are coming down next Tuesday, they're leaving at 6 am so the Blind Chick can try and get in the saddle a little earlier. I'm very excited as they're coming for four days. This will give the Blind Chick and I time to start rebuilding our relationship and spending time together, I can't wait.

I'm totally loving my time down here with the wonderful José and Fay, but I know my Blind Chick is really missing me and struggling quite a bit at not being able to spend any time in the saddle. This is not a good thing as it affects her confidence level, and her orientation is pretty non-existent at the moment. So, some quality time to-gether will be wonderful.

Quote of the Day
"You never know what's around the corner.
It could be everything. Or it could be nothing.
You keep putting one foot in front of the other, and then
one day you look back, and you've climbed a mountain."
Tom Hiddleston

I'm wishing everybody a wonderful day, keep safe, well and warm. I hear another cold front is coming through with lots of nasty wind, so keep safe.

Loads of love and hugs. Johno.

Will It Work?

Feeling Fantastic
21 August 2020

Diary entry by Johno

Wow, it's a little bit wild, woolly and blinking cold down here. I'm sure this wind is coming off the snow.

I'm so excited I had to share this with you.

After the Blind Chick finished standing and listening to my last Craniosacral treatment with the amazing Tanya Hind working her magic on me, the Blind Chick thought she wanted what I was having.

So, she messaged the wonderful Tanya and booked in a session. A little birdie told me the treatment was absolutely amazing. Apparently, the session was the first time the Blind Chick has been able to lie still for more than two minutes! She's a bit of a wiggly worm, always on the move, always doing everything, anything, to keep moving. But her body was at peace! Best of all her mind was at peace throughout Tanya treating her.

And guess what the Blind Chickie babe did? Lots of yawns, then lots more yawns. A huge amount of releasing and letting go, and letting the energy flow. Oh, my heavens! Ha ha, she didn't paw like I did, and stretch my legs, but she did lay still and absorb all the beautiful positive energy Tanya was working with.

Apparently after her treatment she felt so amazing, the next day she sprung out of bed after having had the best night sleep ever! That great sleep included no pain in her knee, whoohoo. Also, there was another fix. After my Blind Chick's cancer operation, she has had, sorry to be blunt, but constipation issues, yes very basic I know, but gee whiskers, things are working well in that department now. I'm so happy for my Blind Chick, she's on fire, she's feeling amazing.

The other thing which was really special is the Blind Chick could feel the energy Tanya was working with, and then when there was a release where there was a blockage, the Blind Chick said to Tanya "oh wow" as Tanya was saying "and another release" and then there was another big yawn. It was a totally amazing treatment.

Tanya also had a chat to Matthew, the Blind Chick's husband, as he suffers from migraines. Apparently, this treatment is amazing for migraines, tension, shoulder soreness, knee soreness, sore backs, anxiety, you name it. So, both had treatments with the amazing Tanya and both have had awesome results.

Often you go and have a treatment for one thing, and another, and another, and nothing really happens. The improvements are noticeable with the Blind Chick, wow totally amazing, and with myself my body is still releasing, I feel wonderful. Probably the second day I was a little stiff as energy was coming out in my offside hind quarters, but by day three my back, on the top my body had finished getting rid of what was blocked, and I am feeling a million dollars as well.

And apparently my good mate, the beautiful, imported Andalusian stallion Guapo, is feeling amazing as well. All the way through his treatment he was letting everybody know this is totally rocking out, and apparently the relief on his face told the whole story. Tanya said he was just so in the zone, so letting go and releasing all the tightness, an incredible treatment.

I hope you like the picture of the beautiful Tanya and my great mate Guapo.

If you ever get a chance, have a craniosacral treatment, I love them.

Love and hugs from a very relaxed Johno.

So Grateful

Feeling Grateful
21 August 2020

Diary entry by Johno

I hope everyone is having a wonderful day. It's chilly in the Southern Highlands, but guess what? It is winter! Apparently, it's going to get colder though. I am so very grateful the beautiful Fay has put another rug on me to keep me warm. I'm so very lucky and grateful.

Isn't life amazing, full of beautiful people and nice gestures and acts of kindness. Thinking of others, thinking of someone else's horse, and keeping them warm. Thank you, Fay.

But acts of kindness are happening all around us, all the time. But do we take the time to say thank you, or even acknowledge that someone has done something really lovely for us? Sometimes all it takes is a smile.

Now I've had a little bird mention that one of the Blind Chicks beautiful friends has done something very kind and considerate for her. You know how the Blind Chick has a fractured knee, well her lovely friend Janine Turner, affectionately known as Neeni, has a fantastic business called Horse Wear Repairs. Now this beautiful lady has made the Blind Chick a knee guard for her fractured knee, out of lamb's wool and velcro strapping.

This will be great protection when the Blind Chick is in the saddle, because the fracture is right where the stirrup leather strap goes. The pressure on her knee creates lots of pain, so hopefully this knee guard will do the trick. How special is that, this beautiful lady helping the Blind Chick endure less pain. I hear these two girls together are real scalawags, getting up to all sorts of nonsense.

I often hear them giggling on the phone like schoolgirls, I'd love to be a fly on the wall. But our lives, the Blind Chicks and mine, are full of beautiful people always making a difference to our lives. Whether it's someone driving the Blind Chick down to visit me in the Southern Highlands; the amazing José training me and people like Neeni. Keep in mind that I'm ridden by a blind rider, all of these things people do make a significant difference to our lives. We are so very grateful.

And the other amazing thing is our beautiful Facebook friends, you make such a difference to the Blind Chicks and my life on a daily basis. Your love and support, your consideration, it is so gratefully appreciated. Always knowing someone has our back, how very lucky are we.

To all of the beautiful people in our life that make us smile, that make our day, thank you for being part of our life, for sharing our journey, making a smile, being sad when we are sad. Thank you for being on this very special journey with us.

Taboo Subjects!

 Feeling Thoughtful
22 August 2020

Diary entry by Johno and the Blind Chick

This is one of those taboo subjects no one wants to talk about! It's something no one wants to admit they may have. But I'm sure, it happens to all of us.

I'm talking about losing confidence, fear and anxiety.

Whether it is going down to catch my horse, whether it be getting on my horse and having a ride, these things are real in everyday people's lives. For one reason or another some people have lost faith, or they've had a scare and they don't know how to rectify it.

I would like to share with you what the Blind Chick is going through. I think it's easier for me to share, being the third party, than for her as it is pretty hard to admit to losing your confidence. But I think this topic is something that needs to come out of the closet. It is okay, and it will be alright, we just need to find a way.

Two things have happened to the Blind Chick which has not helped with her confidence level. One being her coming off me from a great height when I thought I would like to be a gazelle in the dressage arena! Doing a couple of really big leaps she understandably came out of the saddle from my 18.3hh and damaged her knee on landing. I honestly think this is still in the back of her mind, just a little, the nagging question "Can I trust him, will he do it again?"

The other thing that is probably even bigger than the Blind Chick having a buster off me, is the fact that she is not spending consistent time in the saddle. Not having regular saddle time is very disorientating when she does get to ride. As you can imagine, being totally blind and being disorientated, can be more than a little frightening. So, this has not helped the Blind Chick.

So, let's look at the ways we can make a difference and help her get her confidence back. At this stage with her knee, she can only ride me at a walk. Just being in the saddle is critical for her confidence, even if it's just riding at a walk. Doing all those wonderful movements at the walk, being able to concentrate on her position, that her hands are moving backward and forward with my movement and that she's able to breathe and relax are important confidence building sessions.

The breathing part of the exercise is critical. As you know most people when they are a little bit on edge or frightened, they hold their breath! That shade of blue is not a good look when riding a horse.

Fear is not a bad thing, it's okay to be frightened, it's okay to be anxious. We just need to work out a way to make it manageable. To do this we go - One Step at a Time! One manageable step at a time.

The other thing that will help the Blind Chick is for her to ride in the dressage arena in the sunlight. This allows her to orientate herself by where the sun is on her face, or on her back, or in her face. This is so important when you are totally blind, being able to orientate yourself and know where you are.

It makes a massive difference when her wonderful coach José calls out the letters in the arena, this gives the Blind Chick her orientation, and a feel for where she is. Yes, she could count the strides, but doing that with so much else that she has to think about is too much to expect of her.

So, when the Blind Chick comes down on Tuesday, she'll put the pad on knee to protect it and she will train at a walk. She'll do lateral work in the dressage arena and focus on breathing and giving herself the time to adjust, to get back into the rhythm of my movement. She'll take the time that it takes to do this. There is no rush, no hurry, just walking and remembering to keep breathing.

One of the Blind Chick's coaches years ago said to her "You have nothing to prove!" That's just it, to the Blind Chick this isn't about proving anything, it's about her living her dream and getting back in the saddle, doing what she loves which is riding me. That coach, Carolyn Lieutenant, was so right in saying she had nothing to prove, that it's not about proving. It's about a passion, it's about fulfilling a dream, to live that dream - it's about overcoming a fear.

I think it's good to have a plan, a workable plan, don't be too ambitious, do what you know you can do. Now the Blind Chick knows she can ride, she knows she can canter! But for both to occur with joy, she needs three things. She needs to get orientated, get her confidence back and rebuild the bridges of trust with me.

So, watch this space! Next Tuesday we shall see how our plan comes together.

If you know anyone who is going through the same thing as the Blind Chick, please share this with them, it may help. They're welcome to contact my Blind Chickie babe, they could chat and share what they're going through.

I so hope everyone has enjoyed my babble; I hope it makes sense. Let's see what happens - One Step at a Time!

Quote of the Day
"You never know what's around the corner.
It could be everything. Or it could be nothing.
You keep putting one foot in front of the other,
and then one day you look back and find,
you've climbed a mountain."
Tom Hiddleston

Have a spectacular weekend, keep safe and well, loads of love and hugs, Johno.

The Itty-Bitty Shitty Committee

Feeling Grateful
24 August 2020

Diary entry from the Blind Chick

Well firstly, I would like to thank everybody that sent me a message or comment on Facebook with support and encouragement regarding my lack of confidence. I'm sure with time, this will just be one of the little glitches and hiccups in Johno and my journey.

I've endeavoured to have my phone read me a couple of books that are meant to help you with anxiety, fear and lack of confidence. I must say, these haven't been a massive success! It was a great idea, but I think things need to be put into practice.

I have also been listening to podcasts. I've found the ones by Jane Pike extremely interesting and helpful. I especially love her reference to the Itty-Bitty Shitty Committee! Allowing our bad thoughts to get into our head and direct the way we are thinking isn't ideal. We need to get rid of the Itty-Bitty Shitty Committee. That's the plan.

I've also been busy getting Johno's stable and everything ready for his homecoming. I'll probably change how we get him prepared to ride. Maybe I'll saddle him up down at the stables instead of bringing him up through the garden into the where the tack shed is. I think that would be much safer for all concerned. The change won't be a problem for Johno, I think it just makes it safer for me.

I've been out and had a feel around the dressage arena. Wow, it's blown down with all this wind we've had. I'll pull it apart and maybe see if Matt can drag the arena for me, but we'll need to wait another few day for the water to drain away and it too dry out first.

I'm so looking forward to Johno's homecoming. We're going down tomorrow and putting into practice our plan of One Step at a Time and making everything manageable. I think this will make the world of difference, being able to spend more time with a Johno, creating that lovely bond and relationship we had when I was doing everything with him.

I'm very spoilt with him being down at Fay and José's, he is prepared for me, I just get on and ride. This means I don't get to do any of the preparation work. Maybe I could start doing that this week and see how things go. I think it is very important to have a great relationship on the ground with your horse, this then conveys into the saddle.

As Johno has pointed out, my knee is still not recovered properly, my beautiful friend Neeni has made me a knee guard, but I think between you, me, and the gate post, I truly will only be able to walk, as the pressure on the fracture really does irritate, a lot. So, a walk sounds great to me, it's probably where I need to stay for a bit, while I get orientated

This disorientated stuff is not good, I have no idea where I am in the arena, and it is really quite disconcerting. Not great for the confidence. So, if I can get my orientation skills up and running much better, I'm sure that that my confidence will come back slowly, One Step at a Time.

To give you an idea of what feeling disorientated is like, put on a blindfold and get spun around a couple of times. Then try and find your way from one point of your house to the other. It might be just from the kitchen table to the sink, but it's really difficult that feeling of no direction.

Yippee, just one more sleep! Watch this space and I'll let you know how it feels and what happens. I'm sure Johno will have his version, which might differ a little from mine, but that's what partnerships are all about.

I've been out enjoying the sunshine this morning; I've walked 8 km and will try and do some more walking this afternoon. I need to keep fit.

Hold onto your dreams, love and hugs, the Blind Chick.

Ecstatic Is An Understatement

Feeling Excited
25 August 2020

Diary entry by Johno and the Blind Chick

Oh, my heavens! There's going to be an argument about who puts this diary entry up, me or the Blind Chick!

I think I should go first because I'm the horse and I carry the Blind Chick.

So, the Blind Chickie babe and the wonderful Tanya arrive and come carrying bags. Well guess what? It wasn't bags of food for me, it was lunch for the beautiful Fay and José. But all is not lost.

After they've eaten their lunch, everyone flows out of the house and the beautiful Fay comes to get me. I'm really excited to see the Blind Chick, she is really wrapped to see me. She asked the beautiful Tanya to run her hand over me to check that I am feeling nice, relaxed and all the energy is flowing well in my body.

The wonderful Tanya with her magic hands, homes in on my off-side shoulder and works on me for about 4.5 minutes. Everything just feels so good. Then, I'm saddled, and my boots are put on and I'm taken to the arena.

José takes me for a lovely walk around the arena, him walking with me on the ground, giving me time to have a look around and relax. Then he brings me out of the arena and mounts from the mounting block. We start with a lovely quite warm up, lots of walking for about 15-20 minutes plus a little bit of lateral work. All done with me in a long and low frame, getting me to swing through the back. Tanya is sitting with the Blind Chick observing and describing my movement to her. Tanya mentions how free my walk is, and how soft in the back I am.

We had a lovely warm-up, beautiful big walk strides, lots of lovely trotting then back to the walk again, and some lovely big uphill flowing cantering. I feel wonderful. Then José takes me out to the mounting block and the Blind Chick gets on.

Okay Blind Chickie babe here.

I was so excited about today. I got to spend some quality time on the ground first, just talking to Johno, feeling his body and seeing what he is thinking after José's wonderful ride.

I mounted from the block; it was just like coming home. It felt wonderful to be back in the saddle. I had my knee brace on, and I was looking forward to seeing how that went, as well as just being totally relaxed and remembering to breathe! Heaps of my wonderful Facebook friends reminded me to breathe, hee hee.

Calling how I felt riding today 'ecstatic' - is an understatement!

It felt so wonderful to be back in the saddle, especially as with the knee brace on my knee wasn't hurting. I was totally relaxed. Okay we only walked, but we did some lovely transitions in the walk, we also did shoulder-in, travers, leg yielding and through it all my knee didn't hurt at all. Plus, that Itty-Bitty Shitty Committee had gone on holidays! I had a super ride, no undermining, we felt wonderful. It was where I was meant to be, sitting on my beautiful horse enjoying the ride.

It was as if the universe had done a total transition, everything was in alignment; the rhythm in our walk was wonderful, the rhythm and regularity in a lateral work was just right. The ride was like someone had sprinkled a little bit of magic on us, it felt so good.

A massive thank you to all of our wonderful Facebook friends who encouraged me and gave me ideas like 'don't forget to breath.' Thank you for believing in Johno and I. Thank you from the bottom of our hearts.

After the ride there were lots of pats and cuddles, which Johno to-tally loved. I unsaddled and took his boots off then gave him a beautiful brush. It was like coming home, it was what I was meant to be doing with my beautiful horse.

But none of this would've happened if it wasn't for the amazing José guiding a Johno and I around the arena, giving us instructions on where we were, what we were doing, the position of my hand, keep the outside rein, make sure your hands follow the horse in the walk, all of the amazing things that make a good ride come together. José you are the most amazing coach, thank you for not giving up on me, I'm so very grateful.

I should've told Johno to suggest everybody got a cup of tea before they started this one.

I'm riding again tomorrow, about 11am, I can't wait. I'm so excited, it's as if someone has lifted this amazing big weight from my shoulders. I know we can do this, One Step at a Time. Watch this spot, I'm living in the moment and loving it.

To our wonderful Facebook friends, thank you for believing in us. Have a spectacular evening.

Loads of love and hugs, Johno and the Blind Chick.

The Smile Says it All

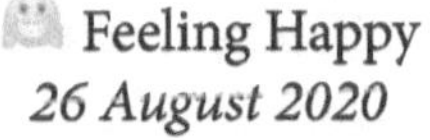 Feeling Happy
26 August 2020

Diary entry by Johno

I think the photos say it all.

The smile has not moved off the Blind Chicks face totally awesome.

Thanks to the amazing José and his patience.

Bring on another lovely lesson.

Keep smiling. Love always, Johno.

Carrots and Cuddles

Feeling Grateful
27 August 2020

Diary entry by Johno

It's a wonderful morning here in the Southern Highlands. What a spectacular day, the sun is shining, and I've just had breakfast, a carrot and a cuddle from the beautiful Fay. Bring on another lovely day.

I apologise I didn't get to do a diary entry last night on how we went yesterday. It was a busy day. Firstly, I had a loose shoe, I must've overstepped. The amazing Matthew the Farrier came and fixed it, he also got shown some of José's horses.

I was saddled up and taken to the dressage arena where the amazing José worked me for about 25 minutes. Just lots of lovely big loose trots; long rein walks, then he collected me up and did some lateral work, some pretty fancy shoulder-in and a couple of walk pirouettes. Just a nice loosen up for the Blind Chick!

The day before the Blind Chick had a ripper of a ride, it was lovely to have her back on board. Yesterday was also really good in the walk, she is very confident. She has time to plan and think about what she's doing. We did a little trotting, but that wasn't as good. The disorientation thing happened a little again, so she stayed on the circle. She tried to keep it a 20 metre circle but it probably ended up looking like an egg with square sides.

I'm sure this disorientation thing will get better with time. In the walk it doesn't bother her as she has time to think. When you're trotting, things happen a little quicker and the movement is different, and you don't have as much time to think. It'll be time in the saddle that helps her.

The wonderful Tanya treated one of Fay's beautiful fillies and oh my heavens! I think she truly enjoyed her craniosacral treatment. She was one very relaxed horse afterwards.

Then Tanya and Fay went down the road and Tanya treated another horse. So, all up it was a very big day for everyone. But it was full of achievements and goal kicking.

Stay true to yourself. With love, Johno.

Tears

Feeling Grateful
28 August 2020

Diary entry by Johno

I hope everyone had a spectacular day yesterday, it was a bit of an epic day with the Blind Chick and me.

As per usual I was saddled up and taken to the arena where José road me, and then it was the Blind Chicks turn.

This is where things get interesting. The Blind Chick was started with a lovely walk, we were both quite relaxed. In the walk the Blind Chick has time to think about what is happening, where she is in the arena and time to prepare for the next movement.

Then, the wheels feel off the cart a little.

With José guiding us around the arena things were going okay, then José said, "Gather the reins and trot on", that's when the melt down sort of happened.

The Blind Chick sort of suddenly felt over faced, overwhelmed, so much to think about keeping the shape of a circle, keeping the softness of the reins, keeping the rhythm and regularity, not having too much neck bend, not rushing. So much to think about. Then the orientation was totally lost in the trot. She didn't have as much time to set things up and work them out.

We did overcome this hurdle, after a few tears. I felt the Blind Chicks frustration, she wants to ride well so badly. But there was so much in her mind she got overwhelmed. I think all she needs to do is concentrate on just enjoying the ride, but it's hard to do that when she's got all these other things whirling around in her head that she has to do.

After the hurdle we went quietly into a trot. It was a nice trot, not big flamboyant or anything like that, it was just a nice quiet trot, keeping good rhythm and regularity, sometimes a little too much inside rein, but we were still moving forward and ……… we were trotting.

Then out of the blue, the wonderful José said, "When you're ready, canter". These words took a little bit of time to sink into the Blind Chick. I think in her head she was saying "no way José", but then voila! The next thing we were cantering. We did a very steady slow canter circle, I really looked after the Blind Chick, I took it so steady and then a transition back to a walk. Wow, what a transition! We fell out of that canter into a walk and she was elated, she had had a canter, so we overcame quite a few gremlins in this ride.

It was so wonderful having José there. Knowing how much José believes in her, I think it made the world a difference to her confidence and helping her believe she can do it.

The anxiety and everything aren't about riding, she knows she can ride. The anxieties are about being lost and working out a way to find herself again, building trust in her ability to orientate again.

As you know it's not trust in me that's her issue, it's trust in herself. She's so worried that she's going to run me into something, but with the eyes on the ground she knows that'll never happen. Especially with those eyes being the wonderful José's.

Once the Blind Chick builds up the trust in herself again, things will improve. Yippee it looks like I'll be going home in a couple of weeks. This will be especially good as the Blind Chick and I can work each day at our place, One Step at a Time.

I'm so very grateful to the amazing José for his patience with both the Blind Chick and me. We are grateful that he accepted to coach us and guide us, we couldn't be in better hands. Plus, the love and support of his beautiful wife Fay, thank you both from the bottom of our heart.

So, all in all a positive visit. The Blind Chickie babe is on her way home on Friday and I'm having the day off, it's has been a big, few days.

With love and hugs, Johno.

10
September

Going Home

Feeling Happy
1 September 2020

Diary entry by Johno

Happy spring everyone. What amazing weather we're having here in the Southern Highlands. It's a sunny and spectacular day.

I have also adapted to my feed change, no extruded food in my diet. I'm doing really well and feeling great.

I'm still being spoilt by the beautiful Fay. Every morning she greets me with a carrot, a cuddle, my breakfast and a beautiful smile. What a way to start the day.

A little bird has told me that the Blind Chick has been very busy getting my stable ready and cleaning out her tack shed for my return home.

Only seven more sleeps and the Blind Chick will be back down here in the Southern Highlands doing some training. Also coming up is I'm due to be shod by the amazing Matt. I wonder if he will make shoes from scratch again. The Blind Chick will speak to Matt about the plans for the future and my feet. Keeping in mind we are 6.5 hours away from Matt. So, this will either mean a trip down to the Southern Highlands every six weeks, or we sort out another option.

The wonderful Tanya Hind is bringing the Blind Chick down and I think she might be going to treat a few more horses in the Southern Highlands. This is very exciting. I always feel amazing after the cranial sacral treatment she gives me.

I hear the Blind Chick has been in the garden. I bet the plants are nervous, especially as she has those secateurs with her. Look out plants. At least it's not Round-Up.

Matthew has dressed the dressage arena and it's looking wonderful. So, things are all ready for my return. The Blind Chick just might be a little bit excited. I also hear I have some new neighbours on the eastern side of my paddock, a mare and a foal have moved in. I look forward to meeting them. Apparently, they are trotters.

Have I told you yet, I'm totally loving my rides with the amazing José? These spring mornings with spectacular sunny days are wonderful. I'm not sure if I'm looking forward to summer, but these sunny days are beautiful.

Lots of smiles, love and hugs, Johno.

Tribute From A Dear Friend

Feeling Grateful
3 September 2020

Diary entry by Johno

Well good morning from a spectacular spring morning here in the Southern Highlands.

I've had a very hearty breakfast, a cuddle, a pat, and a carrot from the beautiful Fay.

I know I've shared this tribute below with you before, it's about the Blind Chick, written by her wonderful friend Bobby Cooper, but we have new friends joining us all the time, so I'd like to share it again. I hope you don't mind.

Sue Ellen

She lives in constant shadows, the darkness of the night,
But strength is her companion in the ever-fading light,
Sue may be blind to others, she is not blind to me,
For I have found her secret, that my friend Sue can see.
Though eyesight may elude her, I have known it from the start,
She doesn't need the eyesight, for Sue sees with her heart.
Her sense of hearing , smell, and touch, are sharpened by her
plight,
Her kind deeds and compassion have kept her from the night.
And no complaints are offered, affliction is her shield,
A knight in shining armour, upon life's battlefield.
We loose our way, we rarely hear the song bird in the tree,

And often we blunder through life with things we will not see.
Her great love for her animals , her courage through each trial,
Her great determination, still leaves me with a smile,
I know that others call her blind, it matters not to me,
For I have found her secret, that my friend Sue can see.
For Sue my hero.
Bob Cooper

Much love, Johno.

Five Sleeps

Feeling Excited
4 September 2020

Diary entry by Johno

Wow what a spectacular day yesterday was, a beautiful sunny day. I had a great ride with the wonderful José, lots of cuddles from the wonderful Fay, carrots and my dinner. Life doesn't get much better.

I even had spare time to have a lie in the sun and enjoy the day.

Well, I hear via the grapevine that the Blind Chick has been extremely busy getting things ready for my homecoming. Anyone would think she was excited about me returning home.

I hear my stable has been gutted and brand-new bedding put in, and in my breeze-way there has been new fresh sand added, which will be lovely under my hooves.

Also, the Blind Chick has had my paddocks mown, the grass is growing like crazy. She might have to put me on a diet when I go home, ha ha.

She has also been recharging the dressage arena marker announcer up, so we must be going to give that a whirl after I've been home for a little bit.

She has also had the round yard sprayed, so maybe she is looking at doing a bit of bareback riding! This will be interesting, she has bought herself a bareback pad, so we'll see how this goes. Mind you, the last time we went bareback the Blind Chick had an absolute ball.

You know she really is a kid at heart, she just wants to play with her pony, brush it, clean its hooves out, make sure its tail has no knots in it, spoil it with lots of carrots, and just take time to enjoy the ride and have special time together.

I think with me being back in the paddock and our spending lots of quality time together, her confidence will come back really quickly. I know this time together will cement our bond even more.

I also hear I have been booked in with the wonderful Tanya Hind for one of her spectacular Craniosacral treatments. I just love them; I always feel so good afterwards. I wonder if the Blind Chick will book herself in as well?

So, five more sleeps and the Blind Chick will be down here in the Southern Highlands having some lessons with our amazing José, then on the Thursday I will have new shoes put on by the awesome Matt Bilderbeck, farrier. On Friday - we're heading home.

Stay safe, stay happy, keep smiling. Loads of love and big hugs, Johno.

Two Sleeps

Feeling Grateful
7 September 2020

Diary entry by Johno

Wow what a spectacular day here in the Southern Highlands, so beautiful.

I had a visit this morning from my wonderful Farrier Matthew Bilderbeck I have new shoes on!

Have had some really wonderful training sessions over the past couple of days with a wonderful coach José. My body is so soft and elastic, I'm so enjoying the rides and learning so much.

Only two more sleeps until the Blind Chick will be here, then I'll be heading home on Friday. As much as I am looking forward to going home with the Blind Chick, I am going to miss all my wonderful friends down here at Fay and José's place.

Being down here instils calmness and confidence. It truly is a beautiful magical place. All the horses are so placid and so happy.

Lots of love and hugs, Johno.

Like A Kid

😊 Feeling Excited
8 September 2020

© *2CPhotography*

Diary entry from the Blind Chick

Well, I guess no one has picked up on how excited I am that Johno is coming home!

One more sleep and we'll be down in the Southern Highlands with Johno, and I'll start getting things organised for him to be returning home.

I'm so very, very grateful to the amazing José Mendez, super coach, for training my beautiful Johno while he has been at Méndez Equestrian Centre.

I know for a fact Johno absolutely loves his rides with José, I'm sure when he comes home to Dubbo, he is going to miss the incredible finesse and ease with which José rides him. I have lots of catching up to do, it will be One Step at a Time.

I'm also so very grateful to José's beautiful wife Fay. Not only for looking after Johno but for giving him love and keeping him looking amazing. I'm so very grateful for the patience, love and support shown by José and Fay.

With fracturing my knee and this ending up with me lacking in confidence, it hasn't been an easy journey for me. I still haven't totally regained my confidence, I've still got a long way to go, but One Step at a Time. I will get there.

I can't wait to have my pony back in the paddock and be able to go down and give him carrots and cuddles and hear him standing at the fence banging the gate to get my attention. So extremely excited.

It's like being a kid at Christmas time. That's how it should feel. Incredibly excited is what this beautiful horse brings to my life, he has me feeling like a kid rushing to get their pony and going for a ride bareback in the round yard. Mind you, I would prefer to be going for a ride down the road! Maybe that is not safe for a blind rider, so the round yard will do.

Going for a ride in the arena with my beautiful Johno I'll try to take a video for my wonderful Facebook friends, showing you what we're doing. This will be one of my first goals when he gets home. I can't wait.

So hopefully all going well I'll do a diary entry when Johno's back next Monday, and we can all go for a ride together on my beautiful big pony.

I'm sure Johno will do a diary entry between now and then, but this one's from me.

I would like to take this moment to thank all our wonderful Facebook friends, your support while I've been going through this confidence issue has been really helpful. It's lovely to have you all with me on this journey, we're all having such a lovely time with Johno.

He totally rocks! Just such a spectacular animal, with so much personality.

Have a really wonderful day. It's been absolutely beautiful here in Dubbo, I think about 24°C with the sun shining, the birds are singing, and spring is definitely here.

Love and hugs, the very excited Blind Chick.

Vertigo Sucks

Feeling Frustrated
9 September 2020

Diary entry by Johno

Well wow, holy cow, where has spring gone? It is freezing here in the Southern Highlands; I think it may snow!

I'm super excited today as the Blind Chick and Tanya should be here very soon.

The Ford Ranger arrived about one-ish but only one person was in it. Guess what? It wasn't the Blind Chick driving, thank heavens. It was the wonderful Tanya. Where is the Blind Chick? What's happening?

Apparently, the Blind Chick is not feeling so good, she is having a bit of vertigo and is quite dizzy and nauseous. So, she has spent the afternoon back at the cottage where they stay when they come down to visit José, Fay and I.

I'm hoping the Blind Chick is feeling much better tomorrow. They will be taking my horse float to get the tyres checked before our big trip home on Friday. So, it will be all hands on deck nice and early, as Tanya has more horses to do Craniosacral treatments on tomorrow.

Tanya was also treating our amazing José this afternoon. I hope he enjoyed the treatment as much as the Blind Chick and I do.

Here's hoping for a nicer day tomorrow and that the Blind Chick is feeling much better

Lots of love and hugs from an extremely excited to be going home Johno.

Spoiling Johno

Feeling Grateful
10 September 2020

Diary entry by Johno

Well good morning, it's all a little bit chilly here in the Southern Highlands. It is quite overcast with a wee breeze. It might even snow!

I caught up briefly with the Blind Chick this morning, her and Tanya were taking the horse float in to have the tyres looked at and get ready for our big trip tomorrow. A little bit of a sad day today as it's my last session with the amazing José, until the next time we're able to come back.

As per usual my training felt fantastic. What a gifted and beautiful rider José is, so very patient and kind. Okay, while he doesn't put up with any crap, he is so full of encouragement. I think he likes riding me, I try my very hardest for him.

It was a little sad this morning, the Blind Chick isn't feeling very flash. She experiences this thing called Vertigo. I heard them say she is also nauseous, so she's back at the cottage in bed. I think this is probably caused by a change in her medication. In any case, something is not quite right. Hopefully she's feeling better soon.

Tanya is here but she's very busy treating horses today, there's quite a line up to do, so that will keep her busy. I'm booked in with the wonderful Tanya on Saturday for a treatment, I can't wait. Especially after my long trip home on Friday it should do me the world of good.

One of the first things the Blind Chick has lined up for me on Saturday is, if the weather is good enough, a beautiful big bath. Then she's getting out the clippers and whooshka! Off goes my mane. It has started re-growing which makes it quite itchy, naughty me is scratching it out but my Blind Chick doesn't like the feel of the bits and pieces, so she will just hog it off again. I have a pretty nice neck, so I'm told, so hogging it off shows it off beautifully.

The Blind Chick will have to get a list of all the wonderful things Fay does to spoil me. Gee whiz I'm going to miss that beautiful smile of a morning, a carrot, a hug and my breakfast.

But I must say, I'm so very grateful to have had the opportunity to be down here training with the amazing José. I've learnt so much and am so very grateful that I've been treated like one of the family, so loved.

So, my next diary entry will be when I get home tomorrow, after our seven hour trip. Hopefully it will be a lovely day for travelling.

I hope everybody you are safe and well. Don't forget if you're lonely or need to chat, drop us a line or give us a ring, I'm always here for a chat.

Loads of love and hugs, Johno.

PS: Today is a special day, it's our countries National day called – Are You Okay Day.

Home At Last

Feeling Fantastic
11 September 2020

Diary entry by Johno

Well, it was quite the drive home, it took longer than planned but we arrived home safely which is good.

We left the wonderful Fay and José's place this morning at about 8.30am, popped in to a service station and Tanya checked the tyres for pressure even though the guys had done that the day before, when we went to the tyre place in Marulan, which is just wonderful so very efficient.

We had a great trip down the highway, there was not a lot of traffic which made our run nice and easy. The countryside looks an absolute picture. There were little baby lambs in the paddock frolicking and playing, it was a beautiful sunny morning. It was so special I wish we could've stopped and watched those lambs, they seemed to be having so much fun.

The closer we drove to Cowra, the more and more fields of gold there were. Beautiful endless paddocks of canola flowers, it looked absolutely spectacular. Lucky those farmers, it looks like they are going to have a bumper season.

We even went past a property that was bailing big round bales of hay. I'm not sure what type of hay it was, but there were certainly lots of big round bales all over the paddock.

The girls then stopped at Eugowra, at a great little lunch spot on a quiet corner. While they were sitting there waiting for their lunch, they caught up with a couple of their mates from Kewdale that we are heading to Forbes, to judge at the big show jumping competition. I hope they all have a wonderful weekend.

Then somehow, we took the wrong turn which added a little more to our trip. No worries, all good, we got home safe and sound.

The Blind Chicks husband Matthew was there to help Tanya and the Blind Chick unload the float and get me to my paddock. Matthew put my rug on, and Tanya took me down to my paddock. Wow my heavens! There was so much green feed around.

Eventually my new neighbours came trotting over. They stayed for a while, had a chat, then they disappeared. The latter distressed me greatly, so I had to run around the paddock like a fruit loop for a while. I wanted my new friends to come back.

I've been told this rather manic behaviour of flipping out when company leaves me, is called Separation Anxiety. I love having neighbours, mind you I do have the beautiful Sophie with the long brown eyelashes on the other side of my paddock, as well as Ben, so it's not as though I don't have mates close by.

I eventually settle down; head down, bum up and eat some lovely long green grass. I know the Blind Chick has put a delicious hard feed and lots of carrots in the tyre feeder for me, but the green grass is winning at the moment. I think she will be a little disappointed in the morning because I won't have eaten all my hard feed.

It was really lovely Matthew made me a nice new tyre feeder. He brought it down to me so the Blind Chick could put my feed in. Then the Blind Chicks wonderful mother-in-law Lee came and said hello. It was lovely to see her, I tend to think she had a lot to do with why Matthew bought me for the Blind Chick. Keep this just between you and I, it being a family secret and all.

Well, it's over and out from Dubbo, I'm back home in my paddock with grass up to my tummy! The Blind Chick will have to watch my waistline, otherwise I will end up looking like a balloon.

I'm sending everybody loads of love and hugs, keep safe and well, Johno.

Music Matters

Feeling Relaxed
13 September 2020

Diary entry by Johno

Oh, my heavens! It is such a beautiful spring day here at home. The Blind Chickie has taken all my rugs off, I can feel the sunshine on my back, it's so nice.

The Blind Chickie has just whispered in my ear that my wonderful Craniosacral Therapist Tanya is coming to visit today. This is perfect timing after my long trip home yesterday. I can't wait, I'll be able to stretch out all of those little niggles from standing all day in the float, which for me at 18 3hh is not the best for the body.

Hmm, Tanya has arrived, but something is going on. The Blind Chickie and Tanya are talking about a speaker and Bluetooth and signal. What are they up to now? What about my treatment?

Then I can hear something like music, but not what you hear from the radio, it's different. "Tibetan singing bowls, pan flutes and the ocean waves" I hear Tanya tell the Blind Chickie.

Oh, my lord! What have I gotten myself, or I should say, what has the Blind Chickie got me into this time? The 'music' starts to play, and Tanya places her hands on me as she normally does, to engage with my energy and body rhythms. This time I lead her to my hind end as it is quite tight and needs that special unwinding that craniosacral work does.

Straight away Tanya has got the spot to place her hands and start working with my body, but I just need to see if those trotters next door are within ear shot. They really need to see and hear what these two women are doing down here. I try my best to keep focus on the paddock, but with this music and energy flowing I just can't. I fall onto what they call a Craniosacral Trance.

All I can do is slow my breathing to take deep breaths. As I hear the ocean waves my head drops lower, then my hips begin to soften, and soften. Oh my! They really are letting go, this time my muscles feel like jelly. I can hear Tanya explaining exactly what I'm feeling to the Blind Chickie, she says she hasn't seen me relax quite this much before. They are just so delighted with this result, and I tell you …. so am I! It feels so good.

Now the music changes, I hear something like a bell chiming on and off. Tanya has moved up to check the flow in my nuchal ligament, I'm falling into a deeper state of tranquillity. Oh wow! I stay in this state for about 10 minutes or so, just moving my energy to places within my body that require a hand to relax, then just as quickly as I fell into this state, I'm out, back with the girls and still standing next to the Blind Chickie just as I was before!

What just happened was amazing. I didn't know at first why the music was on, but now I think its purpose was to add a calming effect. It certainly did that. The pan flutes and musical mix had me totally chilled.

Well ladies, I can honestly say that your little experiment today has definitely worked.

Aagh, where are they? I still cannot see those trotters next door. Why are they never here when I have something important to show them!

Well, the green grass is calling me now, so I will leave today's update here and catch up with you again very soon.

Loads of love and hugs, Johno.

My Routine

Feeling Fantastic
14 September 2020

Diary entry by Johno

Okay where can we move to where it is spring all year-round? This weather is spectacular; a beautiful sunny morning, the birds are chirping, and the grass is growing. It doesn't get much better than this.

The Blind Chickie babe came down about 7am to feed me with a carrot and a smile. She took my top rug off, I don't need it now but because it is still a little chilly of a night I do need it then.

I had about 2.5 hours to eat my breakfast and have a relax before the lovely Gwen and the Blind Chickie babe come to get me for work. When the girls bought me in to the saddling up area I was tied up, then given a beautiful big brush. Gwen did a lovely job on my tail and got all those nasty knots out.

Then I heard this weird little motor going. Oopsy! There goes my mane.

I had been diligently growing my mane while I was at José and Fay's. It was up to about 4.5 inches of beautiful mane, which I was diligently rubbing out because it was itchy! So, the Blind Chick hogged it all off, but I still have a lovely forelock.

Mind you I have a spectacular neck that can support not having a mane. Having it hogged gives me lovely definition, I think. And I don't think the Blind Chick left any scrappy bits, so it should look very neat and tidy.

I was then given another big brush to get all that loose hair off, saddled up and taken out to the round yard. I had the lunging cavesson on, so I knew I was going to the round yard to be worked, but I did notice the Blind Chick had her helmet in her hand and my bridle! I thought I might have been going for a ride after I worked in the round yard.

Well things were a little hairy when we started off, I was definitely distracted by my mates the trotters next-door. They were doing a bit of running around which distracted me, so I sort of acted a little bit like a fruit loop! Slowly but surely though, I settled into the rhythm, the regularity and the routine and only intermittently acted like a fruit loop looking for my mates. Overall, it was a good session.

When I finished my work in the round yard, I thought the Blind Chick might have been going to put the bridle on so we could go for a ride, but not today! Maybe tomorrow she said. Maybe I won't be as distracted and I'll be back in the routine of working well again at home, and not worrying about my mates the trotters.

The girls then took me back into the tack shed, unsaddled me and gave me a lovely big bath. Wow, did I have some dirt and sweat in my coat! I feel much better now, fresh as a daisy.

They also put a lovely brand-new rug on me. It's just a cotton rug with mesh in the sides for ventilation. It's very comfortable I must say.

I was then taken to my paddock and given a biscuit of hay and a couple of carrots for being a good boy.

I must share with you something I noticed while having my bath. There are some gorgeous king parrots nesting in the pine tree beside my tack shed, I can't wait till the babies come out, they are such very pretty birds.

Gwen noticed one of the king parrots in the Paulownia tree while I was having my bath and mentioned how very beautiful they were. I must see if I can get Matthew to take a photo of one of them for you, they're just so very pretty. The little wrens and finches in the garden have been chirping all morning. They know it is spring, everybody is cleaning house and so happy.

I hope everyone is having a lovely afternoon. I'm having a very relaxing afternoon in my paddock eating grass and my lovely biscuit of lucerne hay.

At the moment my good mates the trotters are standing in the corner chatting to me. I guess they'll go for a wander later this afternoon. That's when I'll run around like a fruit loop for a little bit, and then put my head down and eat more grass.

Stay safe. Loads of love and hugs, Johno.

My Moments

🙂 Feeling Wonderful
15 September 2020

Diary entry by Johno

Wow! Bring on this glorious spring weather, it's another spectacular day here. Don't you just love this time of the year?

Well, the Blind Chick had me ready when Gwen arrived today, she was in a little bit of a time restriction as the Blind Chickie babe is off to have her haircut.

So, keeping in mind my fruit loop moments from yesterday, I am endeavouring to do better today. Gwen leads me out to the dressage arena and into the round yard, here I am quite settled and happy. No! Then those trotters move, well I need to do a bit of a fruit loop whinny, and I think I need to probably prance when I could be walking. I'm sure this isn't very pleasant for the Blind Chick as she has no idea what I'm doing or why I'm being a fool. She gets some feedback from Gwen what the trotters are doing, but I'm sure it's not good for the Blind Chick, it must be scary.

You will all be very proud of me today. I only had one and a half fruit loop moments today. I had another little worrisome moment when I saw one of the trotters moving away, but then quickly I came back to being a very good boy and working very hard. My Blind Chickie babe was quite proud of me, even mentioning to Gwen how much of an improvement on yesterday my work ethic was.

If the trotters weren't there, you know there wouldn't be an issue! It's just because they are, and I want to know what they're doing. In other words… I'm a busy body!

One of our wonderful friends Norma from Canada suggested getting me a donkey, as a mate. I could bond with the donkey and not be worried about the trotters. It's definitely food for thought, I'm not sure what I think about getting a donkey though.

But a mate would make a difference, but it is another mouth to feed and another hassle for the Blind Chick, two separate horses when feeding etc. But I'm sure with time I will improve, I'll worry less about the trotters. I haven't been home a full week yet, so maybe in another week I should be heaps better.

But I'm not making any guarantees!

Well back in my paddock enjoying this beautiful sunshine the guys across the river are busy cutting a paddock of oats. It smells lovely.

Stay safe, love and hugs, Johno.

Back In The Saddle

Feeling Grateful
16 September 2020

Diary entry by Johno

Well, it's another spectacular morning here on the Macquarie River. This weather is totally awesome. My heavens, doesn't spring rock!

Everyone will be very pleased with me today. The Blind Chick had me ready when Gwen arrived this morning. We went up to the round yard and did some lunging and guess what? I didn't have a fruit loop moment. Okay I did do a couple of whinnies, but no fruit loop moments. I'm definitely putting my best hoof forward this morning.

I did some lovely lunging at the walk and the trot, a couple of changes of direction and transitions. I was only distracted a couple of times by my mates the trotters, but I am doing my best to concentrate on the Blind Chick.

Now I did notice she had her riding helmet with her again today, plus my bridle and her top boots on! So, I thought she might have a ride. It was quite windy though and she doesn't generally ride when it's very windy.

But guess what? The Blind Chick is back on board! Okay, we only walked and did a little bit of trot on both reins; we were in the round yard. But it was One Step at a Time - no racing, no hurrying. She did it! I don't think the smile moved off her face, she was very proud of herself.

Mind you I was very proud of her. Confidence is one of those very fragile things, which is hard to keep track of. She did really well, I'm so very proud of my Blind Chick.

She tried her very hardest to get the video camera to work on the phone, but she didn't quite know how to do it. I'll get her to do a video of us going for a ride together. She so wanted to take you all for a ride this morning, but we will endeavour to get our technology sorted for tomorrow, so she can do a proper update of us riding together and taking you for a ride.

Also, I forgot to mention, since I've been home there has been at least two times that Matthew has come down and put my night rug on. This is rather lovely. Plus, he brings me down a carrot. I just stand patiently while he puts my rug on, I think he likes being part of what is happening and seeing how he is the one who brought me for the Blind Chick, it's so nice that he is such an active part of the Team.

Mind you, he does like stirring up the Blind Chick. He keeps asking her how his horse is going! Ha ha.

Well, I have had a lovely bath, got a clean rug on and I am now back in my paddock grazing and enjoying this beautiful sunshine.

I hope everyone is safe. Loads of love and hugs, Johno and a very happy Blind Chick.

Colic – It's A Pain In The Belly

 Feeling Relaxed
17 September 2020

Diary entry by Johno

Wow what a spectacular morning and what a sleepless night!

I was a bit of a fruit loop last night, those trotters kept coming and going and I kept running around. I was also being a bit loopy this morning before the Blind Chickie babe came down to feed me and to take off my top rug. I was a tad sweaty.

After giving me my carrot, the Blind Chick felt under my bottom rug, oops! Saturated with sweat. I don't think she was overly impressed, mind you she did hear me running around last night and this morning from her bedroom.

So, she returned about 9 am with my halter and a carrot, of course, caught me and we went down to the yard where I generally get saddled up. She got the grooming gear out and was grooming me and just having a chat. Then she started doing some work with me getting my attention back on her. Every time I wanted to go walk and look at the trotters, she would put her hand on my poll and asked me to put my head down and relax.

This process went on for about a good half an hour, also every time I was distracted. She'd put her hand on my poll, gently pushing my head down, and asking me for my attention back on her. By the end of it, I was so much more relaxed and listening to the Blind Chick, plus getting lots of good scratches and pats. I'm not really a slow learner, I just get distracted easily, ha ha.

When Gwen arrived, the Blind Chick said we would go out and do some work in the round yard, which was great. So, we went out and everybody will be so impressed with me today, I didn't have even one fruit loop session! I was such a good boy. I walked around nice and relaxed for about half an hour, not one moment of distraction. I know the Blind Chick was most impressed.

Then she thought she'd take me for a walk in the dressage arena. Now this could've gone terribly wrong, the Blind Chick and I just in the dressage arena by ourselves! Gwen was sitting outside. But the Blind Chick trusted me, and I was a very good boy.

It was just the time for relaxation and keeping my mind on the job. Every time I wanted to pop my head up and look at the trotters, the Blind Chick would gently put her hand on my poll and I would drop it, re-concentrate and just keep walking. This process worked a treat. By the end of it I was so very relaxed and in the zone.

I know it would've been lovely for her to be on my back, but today we accomplished a lot more on the ground, I think. Rebuilding that trust!

I was then given a couple of carrots, lots more scratches, and given a lovely bath and a brand-new rug. So, I'm now squeaky clean.

I hope everyone is having a lovely day. It's been a very relaxing day for the Blind Chick and I. Today we kicked some goals just being together and enjoying the time.

Love and hugs to you. And don't forget to smile, Johno.

Attitude Is A Choice

Feeling Thankful
18 September 2020

© 2CPhotography

Diary entry by Johno

Good morning from the Macquarie River. It's a bit of a bleak day today; overcast and windy, but definitely not cold. I think we're going to get rain on Sunday.

Because it is windy and overcast the Blind Chickie babe won't be riding today. Instead, she'll be doing some ground work with me, which will be good. I enjoy the time we spend together.

I really love this quote about choices. Ha ha, I should remember it and not choose to be a fruit loop. What do you think?

Quote of the Day
"Attitude is a choice.
Happiness is a choice.
Optimism is a choice.
Kindness is a choice.
Giving is a choice.
Respect is a choice.
Whatever choice you make, makes you.
Choose wisely."
Roy T. Bennett

Thank You

Feeling Happy
19 September 2020

Diary entry by Johno

Well good morning, it's a funny old day today here today. A little overcast, but still very warm and pleasant. I'm still suffering from a couple of fruit loop moments, worrying about the next-door neighbours, but I think I'm getting better.

Well, the Blind Chick and Matthew were away early this morning. Matthew had Fire Brigade things to do later in the day, so they were up and gone to get the shopping done. They came home with lots of lovely plants so the Blind Chickie babe has spent the morning in the garden.

I must say the garden does look rather lovely, lots of beautiful flowers and lots of lovely little wrens in the bushes. The sounds are amazing early of a morning.

I would like to thank all our wonderful Facebook friends for following us and being part of our journey.

Loads of love and hugs, Johno.

As One

🙂 Feeling Blessed
20 September 2020

Diary entry by Johno

Well, it is a little bit of a soggy old day here on the Macquarie River, but the rain has been fantastic. We had 14 mils this morning and it's still showering on and off.

Well, I put it out there to our wonderful friends on Facebook what you would like to know about and one of our lovely friends Sky asked – "how the Blind Chick catches me and prepares me for the day's work?" So, I thought I'd share this with you today.

Firstly, the Blind Chick shouldn't be doing anything with me by herself anymore, because it might be dangerous with her being totally blind and my Equine Shivers, but sometimes, we sneak and do stuff together. Don't tell anyone, I don't want to get her into trouble.

The Blind Chick still feeds me by herself and all that sort of thing, but anything involving taking me out of my paddock and so forth she is accompanied by her friend Gwen.

To catch me the Blind Chick comes into my paddock, with a carrot of course, and stands and listens to where I might be standing. Now if I was a bad pony, I could hold my breath and stand totally still, she wouldn't know where I was! But I love the company of the Blind Chick plus the fact she possibly has a carrot, so I will go and seek her out. She puts my halter on and takes me down to the stable.

When we're in my paddock and the Blind Chick has the halter on me, I guide her around like a Guide Dog. She puts the lead-rope in her left hand and her right hand on my neck. I guide her through the gate, up to the tack shed where she ground ties me.

She then removes my rugs and gives me a big brush. Keeping in mind the Blind Chick is totally blind so she feels her way around. Often, I get the odd head butt because she runs into my head! I love my brushes and the Blind Chick feels my body all over, she feels for blemishes, swelling or heat. Her feel is her way of keeping an eye on what's happening with my body. She is also feeling for my waistline, I have an abundance of lovely green grass. So far so good with the waistline.

Now before the Blind Chick catches me, she's got my saddle, bridle, and everything ready to put on me hanging on the tie up rail.

So, if someone wanted to play a trick on the Blind Chick, they just have to move things around a bit! Being blind you'd notice she is very repetitious on where she put things, and how she puts them. This is so she always knows where things are.

When she picks up my saddle cloth, she feels it all over to make sure there are no birrs or bugs stuck to it, then gently places it on my back. She then picks up the saddle, feels where the saddle cloth is and gently settles the saddle on my back.

The Blind Chick then gently cinches up my girth, just a little at a time, not squeezing my tummy too much, too hard, or too quickly.

She then gets my work boots and feels inside them before putting them on my legs. Before putting them on me she feels my legs to make sure there are no burrs, dirt, or anything on my legs. This should have been brushed off when she brushed me though.

So now I'm saddled up, boots on, it's time for my bridle. The Blind Chick getting the bridle can often be an issue. It ends up upside down, inside out! It doesn't take much for things to get confusing when you can't see, but eventually we get the bridle on.

Some of the things that can go wrong when saddling up are if the Blind Chick has put the saddle cloth on the wrong way. Not upside down because it has beautiful lamb's wool underneath, back to front. A lot of times and when she goes to do the girth up there are no keepers to put the girth points through, these hold the saddle cloth secure. Such times are often the cause of great frustration for the Blind Chick.

After I'm all saddled up and ready to go, two things can happen: her lovely friend Gwen can lead me up to the arena and the Blind Chick follows with the white cane or the Blind Chick takes my reins in her left hand, puts her right hand on my neck and I quietly guide her out through my paddock, through the garden, to the dressage arena.

This has not happened a lot since I've been home, keeping in mind I've only been home a week and two days. Mainly because with my friends the trotters and the antics of their coming and going, generally it's been Gwen leading me. But give us another week and I'll be back guiding the Blind Chick to the dressage arena again.

It is a big responsibility guiding the Blind Chick. I have to be conscious of not running her into the garden and through the pine trees, we have to go out into the other side of the garden, out towards the dressage arena. Yes, there is a path we follow all the time, it took me about six months to learn this routine. I am very, very good at it at the moment, yes there is a little distraction because there's a bit of grass around, but it doesn't take much to get me back on task.

So, when I guide the Blind Chick to the dressage arena, I know she is putting a hell of a lot of trust in me, I'm being her eyes! It is really important that I don't shy, or have any fruit loop moments. If I did, this would do two things: firstly, it would disorientate her and secondly it'd give her a terrible fright.

Once we get out to the dressage arena, I line myself up with the mounting block so the Blind Chick can mount and have a lovely ride.

Wow, I should've suggested you grab a cuppa! This is a bit of a long one. I might draw breath now. I so hope this all makes sense.

Loads of love and hugs, Johno.

Determination

 Feeling Grateful
21 September 2020

Prada, the Blind Chick & Matthew
© 2CPhotography

Diary entry by Johno

Good morning from a drizzly Macquarie River. We had a few more showers overnight, I can hear the grass growing.

The dressage arena is flooded which means I probably won't get worked, yippee a day off. One of our wonderful friends yesterday asked why the Blind Chick doesn't have a Guide Dog anymore. That got me thinking. Let me fill in a few of the gaps and tell you about her Guide Dogs.

The Blind Chick received her first Guide Dog in 1981. She was quite young when she received her first Guide Dog.

Her first Guide Dog was a beautiful German Shepherd called Donna; she was the first German Shepherd Guide Dog in Australia. The Blind Chick was selected to partner with Donna because of her having trained many working sheep dogs and training horses. They thought that that might be a good match as German shepherds are extremely intelligent.

This was truly a match made in heaven. All the Blind Chick had to do was think something, and Donna did it! They were an awesome pair; they worked so diligently and well together. But Donna was not to be in the Blind Chicks life for long. Tragically Donna got cancer and died only four years into their working life together.

Because the Blind Chick had had a Guide Dog, she knew the independence and mobility that came with such a partnership. She desperately wanted another Guide Dog, so she trained in Victoria at the Guide Dog training school with a lovely little Guide Dog called Tara. She was a very sweet dog but I don't think her and the Blind Chick ever bonded as well as the Blind Chick and Donna. Losing Donna left a hole in her heart, but Tara was a good Guide Dog nevertheless.

Tara retired when she was about 11.5 years old, which is quite old for a Guide Dog.

The Blind Chickie babe then went to Melbourne and trained again with another Guide Dog, his name was Eccles.

Eccles was the most professional Guide Dog ever. Together they travelled the world, they did so much together. They travel to New Zealand four times, one of those to compete in a trans-Tasman competition with horses.

Eccles also went to Atlanta in 1996 where the Blind Chick competed in the Paralympic Games. He then took her to Denmark in 1999 for the World Championships where she won a Bronze Medal and was Ranked Fourth in the World. Then came the 2000 Paralympic Games where Eccles yet again did his superstar best.

When Eccles retired, he went and lived with the Blind Chick's amazing coach, Judy Cubitt. When Judy could no longer look after Eccles, he went to another of the Blind Chick's wonderful coaches, Carolyn Lieutenant. It was with Carolyn that he lived out his life.

After Eccles retired, she then received a lovely chocolate Labrador called Jag. Jag was a pretty cool Guide Dog, not as diligent as Eccles, but still fantastic. When Jag retired, she gave him to some friends. It was really sad though, as she never found out how Jag's retirement went. After she gave him to them, they sort of lost touch.

After Jag retired, she then had a lovely Guide Dog called Prada. Prada lived up to his name in every way, he was classy and a great worker. The Blind Chick did lots of speaking engagements with Prada and to lots of social engagements, he was a real socialite. Like all of the Blind Chicks Guide Dogs, Prada had great manners and always would always divert his head if people attempted to pat him. He knew he was not to be patted while he was in harness.

The last Guide Dog in the Blind Chicks life was a little black Labrador called Armani. Armani was a bit of a dag. He was an incredibly happy dog with quite a good work ethic, but he would've been happy to just play in the garden.

And then came Johno! I'm the biggest of the Guide Dogs, well Guide horses really.

The Blind Chick retired Amani in April last year. I think for numerous reasons with being totally blind, it was difficult going shopping and as it was, she would have to get someone to drive her in from the farm to go shopping, so she needed assistance in any case. So, once she had someone she could rely on and take her shopping, it was easier and much more fun to take that sighted guide person to buy whatever was needed and get descriptions from them.

But I know the Blind Chick is ever so grateful for the independence and mobility that Guide Dogs gave her over 38 years. During that time, she travelled the world and raised millions of dollars. None of this would've been possible if not for the independence her Guide Dogs gave her.

I hope this puts some light on the Guide Dogs that have been in the Blind Chicks life.

Loads of love and hugs, Johno.

Jelly Snakes

Feeling Relaxed
22 September 2020

Me, a delicious jelly snake & The Blind Chick

Diary entry by Johno

Well, what a spectacular day! Over the past two days we have had 28.5 mils of rain, I can hear the grass growing.

The Blind Chickie babe was terribly worried last night as they'd forecast gale force weather warnings - with hail! She was so worried for me, but thank heavens we only got some lovely rain and no catastrophic weather conditions, definitely no hail. That would've been terrible.

Needless to say, the dressage arena is in flood once again. I didn't work today as the Blind Chickie babe and Matthew went to look at some farm machinery in a lovely little town about an hour and a half from here, called Dunedoo.

After they'd had a look they went back to Dunedoo and had lunch. Matthew took a photo of the silos that had been painted by a local artist Peter Mortimore, of the famous racehorse Winks her jockey Huey Bowman and Trainer Chris Waller. Huey was a local from Dunedoo that rode to fame. I thought you might be interested in a little bit of local knowledge … well nearly local.

I'm thinking I might put in a picture of the Blind Chick's garden at some stage. It's looking spectacular. I get to wake up to a beautiful garden on the southern side of my paddock every day, and on the northern side of my paddock is the beautiful Macquarie River, with amazing birdlife. I can watch the swans and the pelicans floating by, and hear the cockatoos and kookaburras early in the morning, heralding in the new day.

So hence I have spent a pretty stress-free day hanging with my mates the trotters and relaxing in the grass and having a lie down doesn't get any better than that.

I hope everybody is having a spectacular day. Keep safe and well. Loads of love and hugs, Johno.

PS: Matt took a sneaky shot of the Blind Chick feeding me a jelly snake. Yum, they're delicious.

12 Days

Feeling Thankful
23 September 2020

Diary entry by Johno

Well, another beautiful day of spring and you know what? I can hear the grass grow, also the weeds!

Okay super-duper amazing news, I have settled down! No more fruit loop moments when the trotters leave! I've been home now for 12 days and I have also eaten all my breakfast and dinner for the last four days. So, I'm feeling quite pleased with myself.

Okay I home so everything should be better, but when I left, I didn't have these three young trotters next door running backwards and forwards and distracting me. All I wanted to do was go play with them. Well now I watch them go frolic in the paddock and go over to the other side of the paddock, and it doesn't bother me.

So needless to say, there is one very happy Blind Chickie babe who is quite impressed with me. Okay it didn't happen overnight, but it did happen. I've settled back in, I'm very relaxed and very happy, glad to be home and not being distracted by the trotters anymore.

Blind Chickie babe just did some work with me in the paddock today, she was going out lunching with the girls.

But again, I was totally concentrating on the Blind Chick and not concerned where the trotters were or what was going on anywhere else. It's so good to be home.

I suppose there is a message in this, one that's no different to the Blind Chick's knee healing – Give It The Time It Takes! You can't hurry these things. I needed to settle down and get back into the groove of things. The Blind Chick needed to give her knee time to heal, which is rather wonderful as now she has no pain, her knee is totally mended.

Quote of the day
"Courage doesn't always roar.
Sometimes courage is the little voice at the
end of the day that says, I'll try again tomorrow."
Mary Anne Radmacher

Have a wonderful day. I hope everyone is safe and well. Loads of love and hugs, Johno.

Johno In The Mist

Feeling Wonderful
25 September 2020

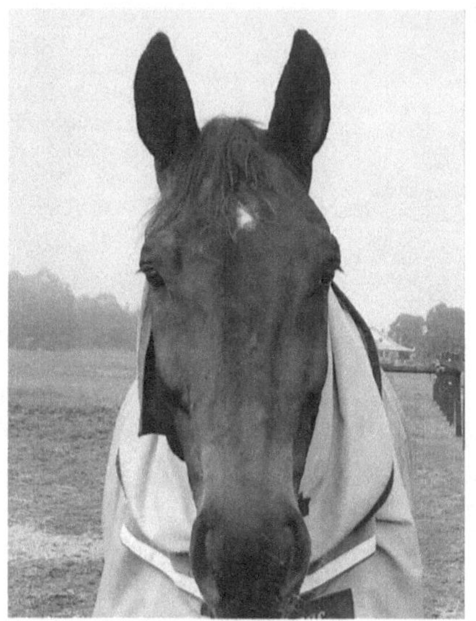

Diary entry by Johno

Well, a very foggy good morning from the Macquarie River. It wasn't 'Gorillas in the Mist' here this morning, it was 'Johno in the Mist'.

But I must say it did clear to an absolutely perfect spring day, and wow was it a busy day!

I suppose with the fog the Blind Chick didn't have to worry about looking for me, because she can't see! So, she didn't even know it was foggy when she came down to feed me about 7am.

She then went back in and had breakfast, and then next thing I see her heading off towards the dressage arena with a shovel. Holy cow, what is she going to do with the shovel?

Wow, I got to inspect her great work when we went out to the round yard for me to be worked. Because the dressage arena was in flood there was a lot of water around, so she'd been busy digging a trench to help it flow away. When her lovely friend Gwen arrived, she helped finish it off and I could tell where the highpoints were in the trench to drain the dressage arena. Whoohoo, the girls did a great job.

So, after having a quick look at their handiwork, I had a great session training in the round yard, lunging. It was especially awesome because …. not one fruit loop moment! Yes, good lad me, my full attention was on the Blind Chick the whole time. It was great, some lovely transitions, big flowing trot and lots of stretching.

After my round yard work out, I went and inspected the arena. Not bad, maybe needs a little bit more channelling done to get rid of the rest of the water, but a job well done. I was then taken back in and given a lovely big brush, clean rug put on, and a lovely big biscuit of hay. The rest of the day was mine to enjoy.

Then the Blind Chickie babe and Gwen were off to town to do a little bit of shopping. Then Gwen was dropping the Blind Chick at her friend Janelle's at Waterville Park for lunch. Apparently, the girls had a super lunch, mind you I've never heard of them not having a super lunch!

So, the Blind Chickie babe got home a little later than normal, hence this diary entry was a bit late getting done. Tomorrow, Friday, we're expecting pretty appalling weather; gale force winds etc, so I'm having the day off.

And then on Saturday whoohoo my wonderful friend Tanya who does the Craniosacral work is coming to give me a treatment. She's going to use the music again, which was so cool. It was called Frequency Healing Music, I just loved it.

I'm wishing everybody a lovely day, loads of love and hugs, keep safe and well, Johno and the Blind Chickie babe.

The Amazing Waterville Park Team
Janelle & Jacqueline

Janelle, Me & Jacq

Janelle Waters, Jacq Benn and Ming Thompson are the quorum and team members of Waterville Park Show Jumping Team. We have been together for 15 years, training, working horses and attending shows and jumping competitions.

Nell is a Professional Show Jump Rider, who has had 50 years' experience. Nell has trained horses and competed them from the beginning to World Cup Standard. She won a World Cup in early 2000! Since then, she has had many wins and placings with a variety of horses.

Jacq and Ming are the proud owners of the current show jumping team. We both attend all the shows, work hard, and laugh a lot!

Nell and Jacq have been assisting Sue Ellen for approximately 5 years. We started with Desiderata, where Sue Ellen rode at a variety of dressage events. Now we are assisting Sue Ellen with Johno.

Our current roles are Nell as trainer and coach, Johno needs some ground training to help Sue-Ellen get back in the saddle and cope with Johno's temperamental changes due to Shivers. Jacq as the coordinator, caller of C and minister for everything!

Together, we look forward to the road back for Johno and Sue Ellen's partnership, and many happy rides together!

Family Fun

☺ Feeling Awesome
26 September 2020

Diary entry by Johno

Well, it's a freezing good morning from the Macquarie River. It's only 7°C at the moment and the wind chill factor would have to be zero, it is absolutely freezing.

Oh, I just have to give you a report on the dressage arena. It has much less water in there now but wait for it …. there is actually NO dressage arena surround anymore! The big winds last night blew all the pieces everywhere, it's like fiddle sticks. Matthew said he would help the Blind Chick put it up again later today, but maybe they'll leave it for a couple of days while this wind is so gusty.

The Blind Chick was most excited yesterday, she had some family call in and visit. Her beautiful Auntie Nancy, Nancy's sister Jennifer and cousins Pete and Pammy. Matthew even came home from work and brought some delicious cakes.

Jen and Pammy came down to visit me, and for a big pat and cuddle while the Blind Chickie babe took Auntie Nancy for a look around the garden. What was really interesting was what they call my Blind Chickie babe. They don't call her Sue-Ellen, they call her Suey!

Apparently, all her family call her that. I thought it was a bit cute.

While the girls are out visiting me and Auntie Nancy and the Blind Chick are in the garden, Pete and Matt organised afternoon tea. It was so lovely to catch up with everybody, the Blind Chick was so excited.

Auntie Nancy and Jennifer are the Blind Chicks fathers' sisters. They are very special in her heart.

They also took some copies of our book home. Jen was going to send some to the Blind Chick's Auntie Dal in New Zealand, so that was really cool. There was lots of laughter about me writing Johno and the Blind Chick, they all love our Facebook page, which is awesome.

Well Blind Chickie babe is inside making a big pot of soup for a cold winter's day ahead, and Matthew is out training with the Rural Fire Service. So, he will be home later this afternoon.

Meanwhile I'm trying to find somewhere out of the wind! This is terrible. What happened to our beautiful spring weather? No matter, apparently it is going to be 30°C on Friday.

I hope you are safe and well. Please keep warm on this chilly morning. Sending you loads of love and hugs, Johno.

Dressage Arena In Flight

😊 Feeling Wonderful
27 September 2020

Diary entry by Johno

Oh, my heavens, what a wild and woolly afternoon we had yesterday! Very big winds; lots of rain, loads of hail and a great deal of noisy thunder and lightning. It was really quite a frightening afternoon.

With all the hail coming down it was horrible; it was hitting me in the head! The Blind Chick had put my good rain sheet on, so that protected my body, and I stood under the tree and put my head down and bum to the hail.

I was really concerned for Matthew's wheat and barley crops he has in. I'm not sure if any got damaged, but the hail stones were large enough to sting when they hit you.

The Blind Chickie babe has been outside to check the dressage arena. Oops! It's blown away! So, it looks like she and Gwen have a big job this morning. There is also a fair bit of water in the round yard. The Blind Chickie babe was putting in a channel but it doesn't look like that helped much. She might have to get Gwen's eyes on the job.

Thankfully it's an absolutely spectacular day here today. I think the forecast is another little shower, but the sun is shining, and I can hear the grass growing.

Looking forward to going out and doing some light work with the Blind Chick and Gwen, possibly not in the round yard, maybe in the dressage arena in hand.

I hope everyone has a lovely day. Stay dry, stay warm. Loads of love and hugs, Johno.

Playing In Puddles

😊 Feeling Blessed
28 September 2020

LEFT: Charlie, the Blind Chick, Me
RIGHT: Jackie, Me & the Blind Chick

Diary entry by Johno

Wow what a spectacular day! The sun is shining, the grass is growing, and the Blind Chick is down at the stables doing some groundwork with me.

I've had a few days off because of the yucky weather and the dressage arena being flooded. So, the Blind Chickie babe is going to lunge me today.

I had an awesome session in the round yard, mind you I kept falling out of the canter. Yes, that's just being lazy and probably because I could make the Blind Chick work a little harder. I did some really good work at the trot; lovely big, long strides, swinging through the back, my neck stretching down, and my powerful hindquarters working very hard.

My wonderful friends Jackie and Charlie came out to watch me work. They're from Sydney and are friends of *Johno and the Blind Chick*. Jackie has been a friend of Sue Ellen's for a very long time. How nice, Jackie just finished reading my first book yesterday, she said she enjoyed it, how cool. I think the Blind Chick's sister-in-law Mel is also going to read it.

I'm hoping you have a lovely day. It is spectacular here. Loads of love and hugs, keep smiling, Johno.

So Happy

Feeling Blessed
29 September 2020

Diary entry by Johno

Good morning, what a spectacular morning here in Dubbo. It's going to be 20°C and a beautiful day.

The Blind Chickie babe came down to catch me and get me ready for some work. I noticed she had the lunging gear with her, so I thought nothing more about it. By the time Gwen got here, the Blind Chick had me all saddled up and ready to go with my work boots and lunging gear on.

We went out to the round yard and did some awesome work; some lovely transitions from the canter back to the trot, some very big bold canters, and lovely big swinging trot.

Now it was very remiss of me, I didn't notice anything else. Then the next thing that happens is I see the Blind Chick putting her helmet on! Yes, I'd noticed earlier that she was wearing her top boots, but I didn't put two and two together. Oops, sorry. Then I'm walking the Blind Chick out of the round yard up to the mounting block. Voila, we're in the arena walking around.

Woohoo! This is so cool. Blind Chickie babe is back on board. We're walking and trotting, doing changes of rein, it feels wonderful. You can guess what happened to my Blind Chick. Yes, smile did not move off her face. In fact, I think she's still smiling!

She didn't ride me for our usual 20-30 minutes; she did 15 minutes of quality work. I had already worked in the round yard, so it was all good, a big success all round. The Blind Chick is so happy, so am I.

Yippee the Blind Chickie babe is back on board - One Step at a Time.

Quote of the day
"You never know what's around the corner.
It could be everything. Or it could be nothing.
You keep putting one foot in front of the other,
and then one day you look back and you've climbed a mountain."
Tom Hiddleston

So never give up on those dreams beautiful people, remember it is just One Step at a Time, we can make them come true.

Loads of love and hugs from Johno and a super duper happy Blind Chick.

The Itty Bitty Shitty Committee

Feeling Grateful
29 September 2020

Diary entry by the Blind Chick

Well, it has turned out to be a pretty spectacular day. I went down and caught my handsome Johno, gave him a brush and did quite a bit of ground work with him. I worked at keeping his attention on me. I hadn't decided if I would ride or not. Why not?

It really is hard to explain to people about confidence, how it can be so debilitating it can make you or break you.

That Itty Bitty Shitty Committee that can get in your head and undermine you, and make you think you can't do things. Some days it takes away my being positive and having all these goals; that I'm going to ride. But then, when the time comes to ride, it's easy to make an excuse not to do it today. There were no excuses, Johno was just perfect doing the ground work. I knew it was the time to get back on.

As I put my foot in the stirrup, I had no butterflies, I was not afraid, I wasn't thinking bad thoughts. When I eased my seat into the saddle and breathed out, it was like being home. It was right where I was meant to be.

Now I'm not saying everything is hunky-dory and it will all be perfect again tomorrow, because it may not be! But we took the first step today on our One Step at a Time coming back. The smile has not moved off my face. I am so very grateful for my beautiful Johno and his patience.

To my lovely friend Gwen who comes and helps me with Johno each day, she is my eyes, her patience is so greatly appreciated. There is no pressure, there is no expectation, she is there solely for a Johno and I. But she is incredibly supportive and encouraging. We're very grateful for Gwen's help.

But the biggest thank you goes to my beautiful Johno, all 18.3hh of majestic horse with two beautiful brown eyes. In my eyes, he had my back. Today he felt extra spectacular. I am so very, very grateful.

Please don't stop believing in your dreams. If you want it badly enough just remember - One Step at a Time, it will happen. Johno and I still have a long way to go, it's a big journey. We have lots to do, but we are having fun doing it.

I hope everybody has had a lovely day. I'm still smiling like a busted watermelon. I'm so, so proud of my beautiful Johno for having my back. I'm sending everyone loads of love, hugs and big smiles. Take care, the Blind Chick.

You're Not Alone!

🐾 Feeling Grateful
30 September 2020

Diary entry by the Blind Chick

Wow firstly I would like to thank everybody for their encouragement and for being so pleased for me being back in the saddle.

I believe this confidence thing isn't talked about enough. I think so many people suffer from it and feel as if there is no way out.

We feel alone, we feel helpless, we feel as if we are the only one that is going through it, and we can't see the light at the end of the tunnel. When you want something so desperately you can keep giving yourself a hard time and bashing yourself up – asking yourself the 'why can't I do it?' It leaves you feeling hollow inside.

I personally think it's important to share the journey Johno and I are on because this journey to regain my confidence is exactly what is happening with us at the moment. After having my unceremonious dismount off Johno about four months ago, that really shook me up and severely dinted my confidence. I think the main thing that caused the dint was the ongoing time out of the saddle for the knee injury rehab.

I think the best place to start for rebuilding the confidence is - One Step at a Time. Start doing lots of ground work, building the confidence up literally from the ground up, which you can take through to the saddle when you're ready. Like we did yesterday.

Yesterday was kind of magic. When I think about it, I know I've had quite a bit of magic happen in my life, but yesterday in particular magic happened. I didn't go out with the intention of riding, I did some lovely ground work, then we went to the round yard and he did amazing work. It just seems right to get back in the saddle. I rode for no more than 15 minutes; take the time it takes! That's all I needed to do, to have the effect on my confidence.

Let me share with you the feelings I had when I put my foot in the stirrup. There was no anxiety, there was no 'what ifs.' The Itty Bitty Shitty Committee had gone on holidays!

I lifted myself up over the saddle and eased myself into the saddle, as I did, I breathed out. Sitting there felt like I was home, this is where I was meant to be. Then realising my stirrups were too long, we took them up and I continued to just sit quietly, no fuss, no hurry, no bother. Then we walked into the dressage arena and both of us did a beautiful big breath out, and off we went.

We started off on the right rein, the sun beaming on the left side of my face, it felt so nice. Johno's beautiful big walk underneath me, him swinging through the back, no tension, I had a nice loose rein. We did our warm up at a walk on both reins, then we had a couple of thoughts about doing some trot work. But I thought 'No', let's do a bit more walking.

And then it just happened! I shorten the reins; gave a little squeeze and said, "trot on" and Johno just trotted on around the arena. We did a couple of circles, some transitions back to the walk, just little steps - One Step at a Time.

But I also think one of the big things about our successful ride was there were No Expectations! No pressure! I didn't have it in my head that I was definitely going to ride, it just snuck up on me and all of a sudden, I was sitting in the saddle, where I was meant to be.

I also think it is really, really important when you are rebuilding your confidence, to have someone around you who believes in you and your beautiful horse. They encourage you and enable you to do things. I am so incredibly grateful that Gwen is helping me. Just having someone positive there, someone that believes in me but adds no pressure, no pressure at all.

Also, I'll just put it out there to the universe, if someone wants to chat or have a sounding board, I'm a good listener. I have quite a few of our wonderful Facebook friends that I talk with via Messenger about confidence, about rebuilding, about getting back on the horse. I'm always here. It often helps sharing the issue.

I'm so very grateful for our wonderful Facebook friends who always support Johno and I, and encourage us, and believe in us. Thank you from the bottom of my heart, you all make such a difference.

Okay, I probably don't talk nearly as much as a Johno. I should've suggested getting a cuppa, but thank you for reading these words, they're from the heart. I think they're important to share.

Have a lovely day. Johno I and I are having today off, it's raining here, but hopefully sunny tomorrow. So, we'll be back outside working on the ground if it's too wet to ride. It doesn't matter, One Step at a Time, heading towards our goal.

Loads of love and hugs, the Blind Chick.

11
October

The Blind Chick On Fire

Feeling Fantastic
1 October 2020

Diary entry by Johno

Well, what a beautiful day. It's over 20°C the sun is shining, and we have a light breeze. It doesn't get any better than this.

Definitely so, especially in comparison to yesterday which was a bit of a yucky wet day. Yet we only got about two mils out of it, it was quite cold and windy.

The good thing about not getting a lot of rain is the arena wasn't in flood, which is awesome.

Well Blind Chickie was on fire this morning. She came down to my paddock quite early, took me down and had me saddled up in no time at all. Then I walked her up to the gate.

She was a little early today as she was expecting someone to come and help her do some gardening, so she wanted to get the horse work over so she could get the arena sprayed. There were quite a few weeds coming up I must say.

Matthew led me out to the arena and the Blind Chick lunged me for a little while on the left rein and on the right. We did some lovely walk, trot and canter work then our wonderful friend Gwen arrived.

The Blind Chick then put my bridle on, and I lead her through to the mounting block, she mounted, and we were back in the arena again. We had an awesome ride and guess what? Today she cantered.

In the walk we did some lovely lateral work on both reins and then quietly into the trot. I think she gave it a fair bit of thought before she cantered but we were coming round having done half a circle and then sat up tall, breathed in, outside leg back and canter!

We also did a couple of canter circles, a transition back to the trot, a walk, a change of rein and another canter. It was lovely, it was so easy. I admit, I did think of dropping out of the canter, but the Blind Chickie babe had the confidence to ride me forward, and keep me going which was awesome.

So, another successful day in the arena. I'm so very proud of my Blind Chick. She really did a great job today. After our ride I was given a bath, a lovely clean rug and some beautiful homegrown lucerne hay. Plus, lots of carrots! I think the Blind Chick was a bit proud of me.

So, I hope everyone had a lovely day, keep safe and well, loads of love and hugs Johno and the Blind Chickie babe.

Panic! I Slept In

Feeling Grateful
2 October 2020

Diary entry by Johno and the Blind Chick

Well guess what? I slept in this morning! The Blind Chick was in a bit of a panic when she came down to feed me as she couldn't find me, plus I didn't meet her as she came in the gate for a cuddle and a carrot.

So, off she goes, tapping away with her cane to my usual haunts, down through my breezeway into the next paddock - still not a Johno! All the time she's calling out to me, "Johno, Johno."

Oopsy! I hear the Blind Chick calling me. I was sound asleep, flat out lying in the lovely soft dirt. When she heard me, she stood back and waited for me to stand up. She gave me a carrot and then I followed her up to my feed. Oh, my heavens, I slept in! It was such a beautiful morning.

But it gets better! The Blind Chickie babe came down about 9am, gave me a brush, got all the knots out of my tail, had a cuddle and a chat, and left me with the halter on! No work boots, no saddle, nothing else! Then the Blind Chick asked me to lead her up to the gate leading out of my yard.

There was no Gwen there, no Matthew to help, so I guided her up to the gate. She opened the gate and I proceeded to guide her through the garden, through the pine trees, out through the next garden, out nearly to the dressage arena and then …. the wonderful Gwen arrived.

The girls stood and had a chat for a while, then I continued my way guiding the Blind Chick out to the dressage arena. We just had a leisurely walk around the arena for about half an hour. It was so nice and so relaxing. I guided the Blind Chick all the time by myself. After our walk, I guided her back through the garden, through the pine trees and stopped in one of the gardens and had a carrot. Then I walked her home, down to the stable where she put my rug on and my fly veil and gave me a beautiful big biscuit of hay. I'm now relaxing in my paddock. What a cool day.

This is all about confidence building. How much trust the Blind Chick has in me, letting me guide her all the way out nearly to the dressage arena, without anyone here to help. It was so cool, so much trust.

What an absolutely awesome day! I know the Blind Chick is enormously proud of me, I'm a great guide horse.

Oh, by the way thought I might mention those trotters were there, but I didn't take any notice of them. I was totally focused on my Blind Chick.

I hope everyone is having a spectacular day. Loads of love and hugs, keep safe and well. Take care, Johno and one mighty happy Blind Chickie babe.

I Can't Control It

 Feeling Relaxed
4 October 2020

Diary entry by a very relaxed Johno

Today was a little warmer than usual. I hope it isn't a sign of a very hot summer.

My day started out with the lovely Blind Chick giving me a little bit of a pamper session. When this was finished my favourite Craniosacral Therapist arrived.

The Blind Chickie filled Tanya in on the past few weeks - she told her about me being a total Wally when I can't see the trotters who live in the paddock next to me. I was a little ashamed of my antics but as soon as Tanya put her hands on me, she understood why I was acting this way.

Thank goodness for her intuition with these sorts of things. To begin with, I just couldn't control the anxiety. So, Tanya has to change tactics with my treatment today. She could feel what was going on and then without even a harsh word she worked with me and my energy to bring me back to down to earth.

I could hear Tanya explaining to the Blind Chickie that she was working with my nervous system to help me to switch off the flight mode button. Oh my! It was hard work for me today, but such a relief by the end of my session.

Now the other amazing thing about my session today is that Tanya worked all of her magic without even having to touch me! This was especially great because I just couldn't handle having her touch me today, even as gentle as her touch is, my nerves where enlightened so much that my head felt like it wanted to explode.

But just like all our other sessions that we've had, she had me melting like butter in the end.

So, there you go folks! This lady sure does have magic, not only in her hands but in the energy surrounding her as well.

A massive thank you to the wonderful Tanya. I feel so relaxed. I have to say I feel much better than I've felt. Before this session I felt like I had a headache and was all wound up.

So, I will be having Sunday off and taking time to relax and chill out.

I hope everybody is having a lovely day, keep safe and well, relax. Loads of love and hugs, Johnno.

The New Me

🤍 Feeling Loved
6 October 2020

The Blind Chick & Me

Diary entry by Johno

Well, you wouldn't guess what has happened today by default!

I have the day off. They are busy doing roadwork on the road into where I live. There are graders, there are vibrating rollers and water trucks! Hogan's Ghost, it's all happening.

So, Gwen and the Blind Chick spent a bit of time with me doing some ground work and Gwen gave me a nice massage, which was lovely. Now I'm just relaxing. I think I may even have tomorrow off as the Blind Chick and Matthew are off to Mudgee to visit her mum.

The Blind Chick is also working on giving me some different herbs to help stop my anxiety in the paddock when the trotters leave. I'm being extremely good when I'm working, but I'm running myself to a frazzle when the trotters leave. I know it's silly, it's stressing me out and giving me a headache. But I don't know how to stop it.

I think I might be a little bit obsessive, compulsive! Once I start, I can't stop running around like a fruit loop. I suppose anxiety and horses are little bit like anxiety and people. We have to work out how to manage it best.

Lovely weather here now, it's a balmy 29°C and quite humid. I think they're forecasting another change coming through for Thursday, possibly a bit more rain.

Quote of the day
"Don't confuse poor decision-making with destiny.
Own your mistakes. It's ok; we all make them.
Learn from them so they can empower you!"
Steve Maraboli

I hope everyone is having a lovely day, loads of love and hugs, Johno.

Flower Time

♥ Feeling Loved
9 October 2020

Diary entry by Johno

Wow what a spectacular morning. We've had a couple of days of light rain, I think five mils in the rain gauge, which has brightened everything up. I must say the garden smells absolutely beautiful.

The jasmine is out in flower, so are the orange blossoms and lemon blossoms plus the Paulownia is just about to flower. Even the Indian Bean tree is nearly ready to flower. Wow! I can't wait till it flowers, it smells beautiful. It would make a lovely perfume. The Blind Chick loves perfume.

I have had a lovely morning with the Blind Chick. She came down and gave me a nice massage, put a clean rug on me and gave me a brush. Then we had a wee walk around the paddock. Just special time together, just the two of us.

I heard the Blind Chick having a very interesting conversation about me to a lovely young lady called Mickie Magan. Mickie is my Equine Herbalist, it was quite interesting listening to Mickie and the Blind Chick chatting. They discussed my fruit loop moments, how much water I drink, what additives were in my diet and what my diet was. Oh, my heavens, they were on the phone for at least an hour and a half. And it was all about me!

So, the wonderful Mickie is going to make up two tonics for me: one for my gut health which I think is really important because everything stems from the gut, if my gut is unhappy then I'm unhappy, and the other one will be herbs. I'm so looking forward to my new treatment.

Hopefully this may still my mind and let it rest, so I'm not so anxious and having fruit loop moments when the trotters go away. I know in my heart they're coming back you know, but I still have to run around like a fruit loop! Hopefully my new tonic will do the job.

A big thank you to Mickie Magan Equine Herbalist for her patience with the Blind Chick. The Blind Chick had so much information to give her, including all the things she has tried, that haven't worked. She needed to cover all the bases. Thank you, gorgeous lady.

I hear they are still doing work on the road, and from what Matthew says it is looking pretty good. Hopefully they'll finish it today and it'll be already for Gwen to come out on Monday for us to go to work with the Blind Chick.

Oh, my heavens! I have to mention the Blind Chick has a new friend. A beautiful bird called a king parrot. He follows her around the garden whistling, a lot. Such a very pretty bird.

When the Blind Chick sits on the veranda, talking on her phone, the little bird sits opposite her chirping away to itself and having a chat as well. It's really cute. The Blind Chick is also feeding it on the veranda. I think the birds are loving the seed.

I hoping everyone has a lovely day. What a spectacular time of the year. Stay well, loads of love and hugs, Johno.

Happy Birthday Blind Chickie Babe

🩶 Feeling Loved
12 October 2020

Just hanging out together
© 2CPhotography

Diary entry by Johno

Wishing my Blind Chick, a very happy birthday.
I'm so grateful to be on this journey together.
Lots of love, Johno.

A Perfect Day

🙂 Feeling Blessed
13 October 2020

Diary entry by the Blind Chick

A massive thank you to everybody who sent me birthday wishes yesterday. Thank you from the bottom of my heart.

I had the most wonderful day surrounded by beautiful friends and family, and this beautiful horse of mine. Having him in my life is like having a birthday every day. I feel so very blessed.

Again, thank you for making my day so special.

Loads of love and hugs, I hope everyone is well, take care, the Blind Chick.

Bucking & Fruit Loop Moments

Feeling Fantastic
14 October 2020

Diary entry by Johno

Well, I knew it would have to come to an end, my days off! That is not withstanding birthdays, weekends and Blind Chickie babe and Matthew doing trips to Mudgee. So back in work today.

I was given a lovely big brush and Gwen led me out to the round yard. I started off in a nice walk, then not being asked to trot by the Blind Chick, but doing this myself, she let me keep trotting. Then oops! You know those fruit loop moments we talk of? I sort of had one of those moments. I went a little bit too fast then did quite a bit of bucking. I was feeling really good, plus I was a little distracted because I was watching for my mates the trotters. But mainly I think it was the fact that I haven't been worked for four days. I was just feeling so good I had to have some Oopsy. Yes, it was not what I should be doing, I know.

I eventually settled down and did some lovely work on the right rein. Then the Blind Chick put me on the left rein. Well, the guys that have been doing the road up came and picked up some equipment, so I thought that was a good reason to have another one of those fruit loop moments. As if I haven't seen a car before and a trailer. Yes, really and truly! But boys will be boys, I had one of those moments.

But it was really cool. The Blind Chick got Gwen to ask the guys in the vehicle to stop while the Blind Chick got me under control. She got me to stand, to lower my head and just relax while the vehicle went past.

Then we just got back to the business at hand. I settled down and did some lovely work. I know fruit loop moments are unacceptable behaviour, but I hadn't been worked and it's spring and I'm feeling really good. Yes, I know none of these are an excuse, but other than that I was a really good boy.

Then I was given a lovely bath with wool wash. Gwen said I have lovely dapples all through my coat. I'm lovely and shiny now. The wash was greatly appreciated as I was quite itchy, I was a bit sweaty from being a duffer.

I am working on being much better behaved tomorrow when the Blind Chick works me. I did hear her mention to Gwen that she was really glad she wasn't riding me when I was bucking! So was I.

I hope everyone is having a lovely day. This spectacular spring weather is magnificent, I can't believe the beautiful scents in the garden. It is so nice to walk through the garden, plus it looks very pretty.

Quote of the Day
"Even if you cannot change all the people around you,
you can change the people you choose to be around.
Life is too short to waste your time on people who don't
respect, appreciate, and value you.
Spend your life with people who make you smile,
laugh, and feel loved."
Roy T. Bennett

I hope everybody is having a lovely day, loads of love and hugs, Johno.

Because Of You

Feeling Grateful
17 October 2020

Lucky Us
© 2CPhotography

Diary entry from the Blind Chick to Johno

Because of you Johno
– dedicated to Johno

Because of you Johno,
You give me vision when I am blind.

Because of you Johno,
I have independence and unconditional love.

Because of you Johno,
I have two beautiful brown eyes that see for me.

Because of you Johno,
I have a heart full of goals and dreams that are being fulfilled.

Because of you Johno,
I have unconditional love and love unconditionally.

Because of you Johno,
I live in his eyes. I am not judged for who I am, what I am, or
what I do or what I say.
He's just happy with who I am.

Because of you Johno,
I am never alone, and I always have a heart full of love.
Because of you Johno when I ride you, I have wings.
You don't care that I am blind, you have my back, you keep me
safe.

Because of you Johno,
I awake every morning and can't wait to be greeted at the gate
by your beautiful soft muzzle saying hello, with a cuddle and a
carrot of course.

Because of you Johno,
You have brought so much joy to my life. We have big goals, we
have big dreams, we have each other. I am so grateful for the
day that you came into my life. I'm so grateful for my husband
Matthew buying you for me. I am one very very lucky girl.

Because of you Johno,
You make my dreams come true. I love you to the moon and
back. You make me smile from deep inside; you fill every day
with joy. I am so grateful, so humble to the horse that you are,
and for our friendship and unconditional love. We are so lucky.
You are my Forever Horse.
I am here for you through the good and the bad.

I will endeavour to give you the best quality of life that I can.
It's all pretty simple you know, thank you for just being you Johno.
These words are for you Johno.
I can't thank you enough for being the beautiful horse that you are.
Your mate, the Blind Chick.

Zoned Out

Feeling Relaxed
18 October 2020

Diary entry by Johno

It's Saturday again! Oh my, this week has just flown by. I guess this is what happens when things in your daily life get busier and busier. I can hear some chatter going on up near the house, it's the Blind Chickie and Tanya deep in conversation as they make their way down to me.

Mmmm, they're going over my health status at the moment. The Blind Chickie is letting Tanya know what I've been doing since the last session. Just to remind you, I had a very, very bad headache last time she was here, and she had to work off body as it was just too hard for me to have hands on with the way my nervous system was sparking and pulsing through my body.

Today I don't feel so anxious about any touching. If I do get upset about something, I know Tanya will sense it and let our energies blend. She'll help me gently through it.

You see, I have a lot of things going on within my nervous system that makes some things hard, but these Craniosacral sessions really help to diffuse my underlying issues.

Well today's session was quite difficult at times. Throughout it, Tanya let the Blind Chickie know exactly what was going on, that she could feel the frustration I was holding within the tissues of my body. At one point it all just released and oh it just felt amazing!

There was a bit of a struggle, that was when Tanya was trying to rebalance my facial nerves that run either side of my face under my eyes, and horizontally to my nasal bones. With a little bit of time and patience they did balance, and my eyes even rolled a few times which according to Tanya, this apparently is a very good thing!

The really strange thing that happened during my session, something I haven't done prior, was I got a very itchy hind end! This took a lot of rubbing on the wall of the stable before it subsided. This really shows how much things are connected within the body, especially the nervous system.

I also did a lot of moving about today, with my back legs stretching awkwardly quite a lot during this session as well. I must tell you I sure am lucky to have someone here in Dubbo that can help me with all of this cranial work. It helps me stay as coordinated as possible.

Till my next diary entry, love to all, Johnno.

I Have Equine Shivers!

 Feeling Determined
19 October 2020

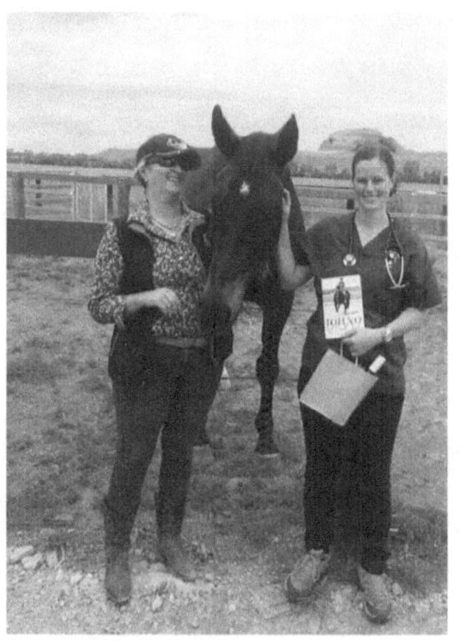

The Blind Chicke babe, my good self & Superstar Dr Sarah Gough

Diary entry by Johno

I hope that everyone is well and has had a lovely day.

Not sure if you will remember me saying that it is such a privilege to be sharing our journey with our beautiful Facebook friends and with all the ups and the downs and the fact that it's not all beer and skittles!

We have had a remarkably interesting couple of days. Yesterday the Blind Chicks good friend Jenelle Waters, and Gwen Ryan who helps the Blind Chick each day, we all went on a road trip to Scone to the amazing facilities at the Hunter Equine Centre.

Our wonderful friend Robyn Buddle organised for us to visit the beautiful Dr Sarah Gough (Veterinarian) there at the Hunter Equine Centre.

Since Matthew brought me for the Blind Chick, things really haven't been quite right. I have had major problems backing up and with this has also come my anxiety which has all gotten worse over the past one year and seven months.

I have previously been to two other lovely Vets Dr Jo and our wonderful Vet here in Dubbo Dr. Don Crosby and they both diagnosed me with the same condition, so we thought we would go down to the Hunter Equine Centre and see what the wonderful Dr Sarah had to say about my condition.

Keeping in mind I was diagnosed well over a year ago, but the degeneration has been rather significant and so has been my anxiety and hypersensitivity.

The wonderful Dr. Sarah and her lovely veterinary assistant put me through all these different exercises like backing me up, walking me in small circles etc.

Some things were really difficult. Walking in a small circle was very difficult and I really have no control over my hind legs which is a bit scary and when I try to back up, I have really weird spasm movements with my hind legs.

Dr Sarah diagnosed me with a degenerative neurological condition called Equine Shivers - and degenerate it has.

This is not affected when the Blind Chick walks with me, trots with me and canters but my ability to back up is extremely hard because my brain doesn't connect very well with my hind legs. I struggle.

If my brain can be still and if I stop worrying so much, then I can back a little - maybe One Step at a Time with one leg. But this is really frustrating because I don't know what my hind legs are doing, and this was very apparent.

When Dr Sarah put me onto small circles, the Blind Chick noticed how there was no rhythm or regularity to my steps. It was pointed out to her that my legs were moving randomly.

So, after getting the same diagnosis again, we spoke with Dr Sarah about my anxiety and my hypersensitivity. What can we do?

There is going to be a massive team effort, with the wonderful Dr Sarah who is going to be consulting with vets in England and America that specialise in the field of Equine Shivers.

They will be speaking to different vets about my neurological condition of Equine Shivers, my hypersensitivity, and my anxiety. All the things that trigger my anxiety, like the day the Blind Chick came off me, will be discussed.

I've never caused a rider to dismount ceremonially before. For some reason I reacted to something and it was a big reaction, the Blind Chick came off! There have been numerous other trigger factors when she's lunging me, or when I'm in the paddock. So, we need to find a way to settle my brain. This is why we're working closely with the lovely Mickie Magan, Equine Herbalist.

This is quite an amazing team! I'm so grateful that they are all looking out for my health and my well-being.

On the home front we have a wonderful local vet Dr Don Crosby looking after me here in Dubbo. Don came out the other day and did a diagnosis. The Blind Chick is working very closely with Dr Don and Dr Sarah with regards to how we move forward from here.

This is why the Blind Chick has not been spending a lot of time in the saddle and has been spending time lunging me. We don't want me to have a fruit loop moment when the Blind Chick is on me.

While we are organising my brain and my anxiety to be less reactive, the Blind Chick will continue to lunge me and do ground work. I would say that she will be back on again very soon, but it is One Step at a Time and the Blind Chick possibly should've been the one doing this post but she cries every time she talks about it. She is very lucky that she has the wonderful support of her lovely husband Matthew, and her beautiful mother-in-law who is always there for her with a cuddle and support for the Blind Chick. I know she appreciates it so much!

So, we really had to share what was happening in my life at the moment because this is a part of our journey, and it's a part of our learning opportunity to educate people about Equine Shivers, getting vet checks and helping other people and vets to know what Equine Shivers is.

I will keep you in the loop with what is happening with me and the Blind Chick and how I am coping mentally as well as how we intend to move forward with our amazing team.

So, a few very big thank you's to our beautiful friend Robyn Buddle for doing so much research and for organising with the lovely Dr. Bridget at the Hunter Equine Centre.

To the amazing Dr. Sarah Gough for her patience and for putting up with the Blind Chicks tears - I think it is exasperation of not knowing where to go or what to do.

Dr. Sarah is positive about contacting the experts who do the research on this condition to find out if there are any novel treatments being investigated.

Keep in mind that it is a degenerative condition and it is neurological. It is not curable but they will try their best to positively manage it.

To our amazing veterinarian Don Crosby at Dubbo, his patience with the Blind Chick is amazing and his guidance is so much appreciated. So grateful to have such an amazing vet right at our doorstep.

To the wonderful Mickie Magan, Horse herbalist thank you and it is so cool to be working on one thing at a time and that's what we need to do with everything - to address things one at a time and work on improving them.

Also, a massive thank you to Tanya Hind who is our wonderful Craniosacral Therapist who works her magic, thank you!

To the Blind Chicks amazing friend Jenelle Waters she was there the day I got picked up and she drove me home and we always have a great relationship and I know she looks out for that Blind Chick all the time. Blind Chickie babe is very lucky to have such a lovely friend.

To our beautiful friend Gwen Ryan who is here daily supporting me and picking up the pieces when the wheels fall off the cart and for supporting the Blind Chick. Thanks Gwen you rock! You are one hell of a lovely lady!

And thank you to the Blind Chick for loving me and caring enough to want to make a difference. We are on this journey for one reason or another, but we are meant to be together and it is so lovely to have the Blind Chick in my corner, trying to sort stuff out for me so I can have a good quality of life and not always be so anxious and worried. I know my Blind Chick loves me very much!

So, I'm sure this is not what people were expecting. I do apologise, I'd just like to keep sharing our journey of moving forward. I know the Blind Chick believes in miracles and making dreams come true, so we are going to make this happen together with our amazing team.

A massive thank you to our beautiful Facebook friends for always being there for us over the past nineteen months. We so appreciate your love and support and belief in us. So, keep us in your prayers. We believe in magic and miracles and making things happen. Okay, they can't fix the Equine Shivers, but we can manage it.

Sorry for the long post but I think it's definitely worth a read and please share. I think it is really important for people to know about Equine Shivers and I will put a little post down the bottom that will describe the difference between shivers and Stringhalt.

PS: So, at the moment, we're just sorting some stuff out. I don't think it will ever be possible as I cannot back up correctly so maybe doing a dressage test competitively will be out as well, but time will tell but here is a description of shivers which I think is very interesting.

Equine Shivers is a chronic neuromuscular condition which is believed to be a defect in the region of the brain called the cerebellum. The cerebellum controls muscular activity.

With Shivers, the hindlimb is brought up and to the side in a spasmodic state.

Stringhalt it is brought up high and then almost stamps down suddenly, quite forcibly and noisily. Sometimes the hind is brought up so high it hits the horse underneath his tummy and can also even reach forward towards the forelimb.

It's also presents at trot sometimes, where Shivers does not.

With Shivers, stepping backwards is often affected and in more severe cases, moving forwards can also be affected. The tail can also elevate.

You can find out more information about Equine Shivers on this web link -> https://bit.ly/3hmis57.

So, I hope everybody is safe and well and I hope you've had a lovely day. Loads of love and hugs, Johno

Love Is All We Need

Feeling Grateful
20 October 2020

Diary entry by Johno

Well good afternoon. This is a massive thank you to all of our wonderful Facebook friends for their outpouring of love and support for my diary entry yesterday letting you know - I had the degenerative neurological condition Equine Shivers.

If love alone could cure this hideous condition, I would've been cured yesterday. I'm so grateful for all the support and love.

I'm just putting it out there to our Facebook friends, do you know anybody who has a horse with Equine Shivers? Or do you have a horse that has Equine Shivers? If so, how did they/you treat it? I would love people to share their knowledge. I know the Blind Chick would appreciate the feedback.

I'm so very grateful to the amazing Dr Sara from Hunter Equine. Some of my blood tests have come back, my Selenium level is good, we're waiting to see what the Vitamin E level is, as well as a lot of other tests results that they're running.

Dr Sara even took some of my tail hair so they could do DNA tests on!

I'm really looking forward to hearing what the vets have to say when Dr Sarah talks to the other veterinarians in England and America about my Equine Shivers.

So needless to say, at the moment I'm not being worked, but not for the reason you think. I've thrown a shoe. But hopefully this will be rectified by the end of the week.

We are hoping with my call for help that we can get some information on this degenerative neurological condition, Equine Shivers. We'll share this information, letting people know about it. So many people have no idea what it is.

Without the correct diagnosis you could think it was stringhalt or maybe a locking patella. We'd appreciate any input. I'm waiting for my herbs to arrive so we can see how they go with my anxiety. One Step at a Time seems to be the way to go. We're addressing one thing at a time and seeing if we can make a difference.

I hope everyone is having a lovely day. It's spectacular here today beautiful spring weather. Mind you, the flies are so very annoying and sticky. But I have my fly veil on, fly spray and lovely mesh rug. But they're still annoying.

Have a spectacular day. Loads of love and hugs, Johno.

Dr Sarah Is A Superstar

Diary entry from Dr Sarah Gough – the amazing vet who confirmed my Equine Shivers diagnosis.

<u>Dr. Sarah Gough BVSc/BVetBio (Hons I), DipECEIM</u>
European and Australian Specialist in Equine Internal Medicine.

Position: Internal medicine specialist and head of hospital and intensive care unit, Hunter Equine Centre

Background

After completing her degree in Veterinary Science Sarah completed an internship in medicine, surgery and reproduction of horses followed by a hospital registrar position at the University teaching hospital of Charles Sturt University, Wagga Wagga Australia.

During this period, she developed an interest in internal medicine and as such undertook a residency in Equine Internal Medicine through the European College of Equine Internal Medicine to become a specialist in internal medicine. During her years of training both in Australia and in the United Kingdom Sarah has treated many horses with a variety of neurological diseases, including horses with Equine Shivers.

Equine Shivers is a chronic neuromuscular disease that results in a progressive movement disorder that primarily affects the hindlimbs although in severe cases it can also affect the forelimbs. Although the exact cause remains unknown it is thought to be associated with dysfunction of specific cells in the cerebellum of the brain called Purkinje cells.

The movement disorder is characterised by intermittent muscle fasciculations of the hindlimb muscles and tail, and a sudden elevation of the hindlimb into an outwardly flexed and spastic position (hyperflexed abduction), which is then held suspended for several seconds or longer before being rapidly returned to the ground. This is often accompanied by muscle fasciculations of the tailhead.

While the "upward and outward" flexed position or "hyperflexion" is the most common, some horses may instead display a rigidly extended hindlimb or "hyperextension" in which the hindlimb is placed further backward during backwards walking, with both the hock and stifle joints hyperextended. The forelimbs may also be extended during backing, resulting in a saw-horse stance.

This sudden hyperflexion or hyperextension is often elicited by walking backwards, or sudden directional or gait changes, such as suddenly turning left or right from a straight position or moving from a standstill to a walk. In addition, and often where the signs are first noted, shivering is often triggered by manual lifting of the limb, such as to pick the feet out or lifting the leg for the farrier. Importantly, stress or excitement may exacerbate the clinical signs, and anecdotally anxiety may increase the speed at which the condition progresses. It may affect one or both hindlimbs, as well as the forelimbs in more severe cases.

While it is less commonly seen in modern times, this disease was quite common in the days of heavy horses being used for industry, as it is a condition that primarily affects Warmblood and draught breed horses, although other breeds, including light breeds can also be affected. Both males and females can be affected, although geldings are three times more likely to be affected. Sadly, this condition is progressive, with most horses beginning to show signs by 5 years of age with severity of signs increasing over time.

Diagnosis of Equine Shivers involves confirmation of the specific characteristics of the abnormal movement by an experienced veterinarian, as well as ruling out other potential causes of abnormal limb movement such as osteoarthritis, generalised musculoskeletal pain and other neurological dysfunctions.

Unfortunately, once diagnosed there is no specific treatment for Shivers, and management of the condition revolves around maintaining fitness, encouraging movement (stabling is not recommended) and ensuring there are adequate levels of vitamin E in the diet.

However, irrespective of management this condition is progressive, albeit at a variable rate, and ultimately in many cases results in euthanasia due to poor quality of life.

Physiotherapies such as massage may be beneficial when increasing the workload, particularly in horses that become tight or stiff behind during periods of rest. Minimising stress and anxiety is also important, as the condition is likely exacerbated by stress/anxiety.

Sadly, Johno has been diagnosed with Equine Shivers, and unfortunately his clinical progression in the past 18 months has been rapid.

Sue-Ellen and Johno came to me in September 2020 for confirmation of his diagnosis and guidance on managing Johno. In addition to the clinical signs of Shivers which make movement intermittently extremely difficult for Johno, he also suffers from extreme anxiety, a condition which often goes hand in hand with Shivers.

During periods of stress Johno's shivering signs are extreme, which further enhances his anxiety, creating a vicious cycle of inability to move and anxiety. As Johno has good levels of vitamin E and his diet is already optimised with a low carbohydrate balance our approach to managing Johno has been centred around reducing his anxiety to slow the progression of the disease and prolong his quality of life.

Chemical anxiolytics such as Valium and acepromazine can be beneficial, however long-term use is not without risk. As such, we have been balancing the use of these drugs when necessary with other means of managing his anxiety attacks. For Johno, supplementation with an amino acid called tryptophan has also been beneficial. This is a critical amino acid in the synthesis of serotonin and melanin and has had a calming effect on Johno. However, it is not a "silver bullet" for Johno's condition; in fact, Johno's condition is dynamic and changing almost on a daily basis.

Consequently, this necessitates variation in his therapeutic programme day by day, week by week and month by month, in a bid to prolong his quality of life and reduce the rate of progression of his shivering.

Sue-Ellen and Johno bravely fight this condition day in, day out. They desperately hope that there will be a breakthrough in treatment for the condition before it is too late for Johno.

Unfortunately, despite me contacting experts in the field of equine neurology throughout the United Kingdom and North America, including some of the major research institutes in neuromuscular diseases, there are currently no advances in treatment on the horizon, although work continues in this area.

It may be wishful thinking that a treatment will become available for such a degenerative neurological disease, however we can only hope.

In the interim, we continue to adjust Johno's therapeutic regimen to maintain him in as calm a state as possible to slow down the progression of his clinical signs.

I'm A Celebrity

Feeling Excited
21 October 2020

Thunder Paws

Diary entry by Johno

We had a nice early brekkie, some carrots and my herbal tonic prepared by the beautiful Mickie Magan, I was ready for a relaxing day.

Well apparently, not so relaxing! I noticed the Blind Chickie babe was up cleaning my bridle earlier, and we've already done some ground work together. She informs me that we are doing an interview with the beautiful Amy from Channel 9 News!

How exciting! She would like to talk about my book called *Johno and the Blind Chick.*

But I have never done a TV appearance! I have to get my hair done, my nails, make up ….. well maybe just put some fly spray on and the Blind Chick will give me a brush! That sounds about it. I'm so looking forward to my new experience of being on TV. I wonder what questions they'll ask the Blind Chick?

Amy follows me on Facebook, which is really cool, so she knows all about my Equine Shivers and is interested in our journey with that as well, so it should be good.

I suppose you want to know how I'm going with my next book. Well, I've had a lot going on lately, so I've not done a lot with it. Yes, I better get myself into gear and keep writing.

I think I'll get the Blind Chick to put my bling bridle on, I should look pretty sexy. I'll also have to watch out that pretty cat doesn't steal the show.

"Tonight, we bring you the heart-warming story of one Dubbo local and the horse who's given her hope... and a fresh pair of eyes."

This is how they are going to start the TV segment about me and my Blind Chickie. How cool!

Okay, well I hope everyone is having a lovely day, I'll let you know what it's like being a TV star for three minutes! Loads of love and hugs Johno.

Amazing Troy

Feeling Frustrated
22 October 2020

Diary entry by Johno

Well, a much lower key day today. No film crews, just the Blind Chick and I and a visit from my wonderful Farrier Troy.

I thought I would share with you what it's like to be shod, with me having the condition Equine Shivers. Keep in mind, this is a degenerative neurological condition which typically starts by affecting only the hind legs. Well with me, it affects all four legs. Troy showed so much patience with me this morning, getting me to relax while he was putting my shoes on.

I'm not sure exactly how to explain this, but the messages aren't getting through to my legs from my brain. So, when Troy goes to pick up my foot it doesn't quite register, so I can be a little bit resistant. It can be quite hard for me and today it was really difficult in the front two hooves.

Once Troy had my two front shoes on, he then moved to my near side hind leg. This leg has always been a problem, ever since I came into the Blind Chicks life. Quite a few people thought I had a locking patella, but no! I had shivers. When Troy goes to pick up my hind leg again, what happens is the messages not getting through from my brain and I don't know what to do. I jerk my leg up and then it spasms out behind me quite quickly, and I try to jerk my leg out of Troy's hand. Again, his patients is so appreciated.

So, Troy dressed my hoof and heated my shoes in the gas fire, but it's really hard for me to hold my leg up. I really don't quite know what I'm doing with my leg, it's so very, very frustrating. Eventually Troy gets the shoe on my near side hind hoof.

When he was doing my off-side hind, after he put my hoof down, the Blind Chick took me for a walk. Every time after Troy did something, whether he went back to shape the shoe or do something else, every time the Blind Chick walked me, she kept me moving forward. When Troy came back it was much easier for me to lift my offside hind leg. So, for future reference every time after Troy has done something with my hoof the Blind Chick will walk me and keep me moving while he is not doing my shoeing.

It's just a matter of finding a way to manage this hideous thing that is getting worse! Find a way that I can have less stress while being shod.

After my shoeing, I'm moving really well. Troy has shortened up my toes so I break over easier and earlier, this will put less stress on my tendons. The Blind Chick had a feel of my hooves and mentioned how amazing they felt.

So Troy was really happy with how my hooves came up, especially since I'd lost my near side front shoe and had worn that hoof back quite a bit. But all is good. I have new dancing shoes on so look out

One of the things that's important for horses with Equine Shivers is to be kept in light work. So, I'm pretty sure the Blind Chickie babe will have me in the round yard tomorrow to do a bit of quiet lunging. I would possibly say just at the walk while I get used to my new shoes.

Well, I don't know what everyone else is up to this afternoon, I am having a relaxing day in the beautiful spring sun. I hope you are all safe and well, loads of love and hugs, Johno.

Journalists, Jokes & Cheeky Me

Feeling Excited
24 October 2020

Diary entry by Johno

What a wonderful soggy good morning to all. It is raining here in Dubbo but it's rather pleasant. We've had a couple of showers go through last night, heavy ones. I'm not sure how much rain was in the rain gauge.

I thought I should give you an update on my 30 seconds of being a TV Star and my news interview with Channel 9. Well make up was easy - fly spray a good brush, and of course my bling bridle.

It was so cool, Matthew was able to get time off work and come home and be part of the Team, as he is the one that brought me for the Blind Chick. So, the TV people arrived, two beautiful young ladies; Journalist Amy Clements and Bree McCullagh was the lovely lady behind the camera.

Oh, my heavens! There are lots of bloopers to go on the floor in the Channel 9 cutting studio. There was lots of laughter, it was just so much fun. I think the funniest part was when beautiful Amy was trying to do the closing of the story and she was holding me, I kept trying to pull the buttons off her double-breasted jacket! She just could not stop laughing. She'd get three words into the sentence and giggle and giggle. Everyone was in raptures.

So, all in all, being a movie star was pretty cool. My 30 seconds of being a famous pony was lots of fun.

We will possibly do an update tomorrow. We've been speaking with the beautiful Dr Sarah from Hunter Equine, she has had updates from England and America, so I'll share these with you tomorrow.

Needless to say, it's raining, so I have the day off, whoohoo!

I hope everyone is safe and well. Have a spectacular day, loads of love and hugs, Johno.

Technology Rocks

Feeling Relaxed
25 October 2020

Diary entry by Johno

What a spectacular spring day. It's a little overcast 16°C. We just had 20 mils of beautiful rain.

Matthew has bailed his lucerne hay and had it all in the shed just before the rain came. Perfect timing! The lucerne is coming along beautifully.

I've had a lovely, pleasant surprise today. Just a little after lunch, Matthew and the Blind Chick came down and Matthew caught me and took me for a lovely walk around the inside of the dressage arena. He then took me outside where I had a lovely graze on all the lush grass. It was so cool hanging with Matt and the Blind Chick.

It was really cool and a little bit funny the Blind Chick was videoing Matt and I having a relaxing time together. She had to show Matt what she had videoed to make sure she had us in the picture. Technology is amazing. Her phone talks to her, telling her what to do so she does indeed capture the right images in the frame!

I must say I'm feeling pretty chilled and happy with myself today. I hope everyone is having a lovely day and you are all safe and well. Loads of love and hugs, Johno.

Herbs & Healing

Feeling Grateful
27 October 2020

Diary entry by Johno

The sun is out, hip-hip hurray! Plus, we had some beautiful rain, about 24 mls I think. Everything is still very soggy though.

But guess what? While it was pouring down rain on Saturday, the Blind Chick was out doing channels in the dressage arena and ….. the dressage arena is not in flood! How about that. The Blind Chick is very excited. Yes, it's still a little soggy underfoot, but that's okay. It's better than being a lake.

And the other thing is, I'm feeling much more chilled. I attribute this to probably a couple of things that are happening in my life at the moment. I'm on the amazing herb tonic made by the wonderful Mickie Magan, Equine Herbalist and I truly think they are taking the edge off my anxiety. I've been on them a week and one day, I'm sure it's helping.

The other very special thing that happened on the weekend was I had a treatment from a very special friend Cathy Price, from Wales. She did a healing on me and the next day I just felt really chilled. So, all of this wonderful love and caring is definitely making a difference. Little by little I think my mind is calming, thank heavens.

And I have had the pleasure of another amazing lady who has come into my life, the wonderful Jennifer Pearce. Jennifer does kinesiology and is a Reiki Master. Oh, my heavens! So many other wonderful things she brings to the party. So, Jennifer did a kinesiology session on me the other day, with the Blind Chick listening. I think the Blind Chick was totally blown away. It was quite an awakening for her.

This session was another long distance one as Jennifer lives in Victoria. Wow, so many amazingly talented beautiful people out there. I am so grateful that they are wanting to help me. We are starting to move forward, but it only one little step at a time. But that's all we need! Okay we can't cure the Shivers, but we can manage it and make my life better.

I'm so incredibly grateful to these beautiful people helping make a difference to my life, so very grateful. And I must say after my new shoes going on, I feel very, very comfortable. Gwen even mentioned that I seemed to be moving out with more confidence and a longer stride, which is pretty cool. Thank you Troy for being so patient with me. You truly are a wonderful Farrier, we're so grateful.

Well, this rain has been beautiful, but the weeds are going crazy! The Blind Chickie babe was in the garden for a little bit doing some weeding this morning, after she came back from checking the dressage arena. Whoohoo it's not in flood.

I'll do an update from the wonderful Dr Sarah from Hunter Equine sometime this week. We are just waiting for a couple more test results to come through.

I hope everyone has a wonderful day. I think the Blind Chick and Gwen are going to take me for a walk around outside the dressage arena. I might even get a pick of grass which will be lovely. We're just slowly testing the field as far as how my anxiety goes. When I'm away from those trotters all seems to be on track - One Step at a Time.

So have a wonderful day everyone. I hope you are safe and well, loads of love and hugs, Johno.

Hail Stones

Feeling Ouch
29 October 2020

Diary entry by Johno

Oh, my heavens! What a wild and woolly afternoon we had yesterday. We had very big winds, lots of rain, and even hail and a lot of thunder and lightning! It was really quite a frightening afternoon.

With all the hail coming down it was horrible. It was hitting me in the head! The Blind Chick had put my good rain sheet on, so that protected my body. I stood under the tree and put my head down and bum to the hail.

I was really concerned for Matthew's wheat and barley crops. He's not sure if its damaged or if the hail has knocked the seeds out. The hailstones were large enough to sting when they hit you.

The Blind Chickie babe has been out to check the dressage arena. Oh, my heavens! It's been blown away. So, it looks like her and Gwen have a job this morning. There has also been a fair bit of water in the round yard. The Blind Chickie babe was putting in a channel to take the water away but I don't think she has had much luck draining the round yard, not like she did so well with the dressage arena. She might have to get Gwen's eyes on the job.

It is an absolutely spectacular day here today. I think they have forecast another little shower, but the sun is shining, and I can hear the grass growing.

I'm looking forward to going out and doing some light work with the Blind Chick and Gwen. Probably not in the round yard, maybe in the dressage arena, just in-hand.

I hope everyone has a lovely day, loads of love and hugs, Johno.

Moments

Feeling Happy
30 October 2020

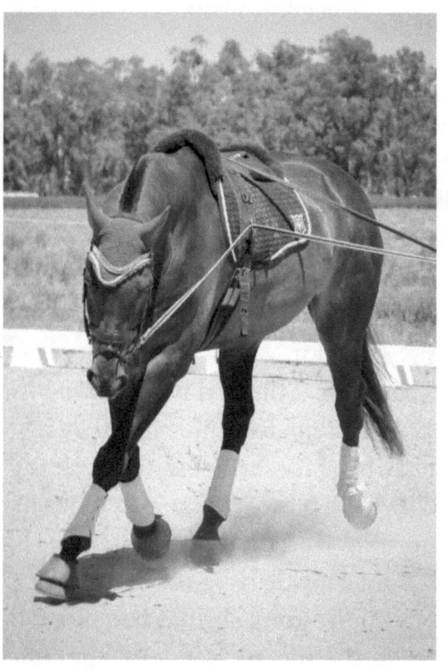

© 2CPhotography

Diary entry by Johno

What a funny old day it is today. It's overcast, I think we might have a storm brewing. The flies are very sticky, and the wind is just starting to pick up, but it's a very pleasant day for working.

And work we did. We were going to do some work in the round yard, but it was still a bit soggy on that southern side where Gwen and the Blind Chick had put in some channels to drain the water, so maybe next week in the round yard. Mind you, they are forecasting more rain.

So, we did some pretty handy work in the dressage arena. Firstly, a lovely big 15 minute warmup in the walk. I started off just tracking up, by the end of my session I would have had a beautiful big over track, plus I was relaxing and swinging through the back. We then did some lovely trot and canter work and after the canter I was tracking up even more instead of me being a bit lazy and not using my hindquarters.

I had a couple of my moments. While we were lunging a big white cockatoo flew out of the crop, I thought that was worth maybe half a fruit loop moment, and then all of a sudden, I thought of my buddies in the paddock.

Well, that was probably worth nearly having a fruit loop moment. So, I had a couple of moments of not quite paying attention to the Blind Chick, but I very quickly came back to her and we did some lovely work. I know she was very proud of me today.

I hope everybody is safe and well and wishing you all a wonderful day, lots of love and hugs, Johno.

12
November

Surprising Moments

Feeling Fantastic
2 November 2020

Diary entry by Johno

Good morning all. It's another spectacular spring day here on the Macquarie River. I had a lovely relaxing weekend.

I noticed this morning the Blind Chickie babe has been doing domestic goddess duties before Gwen arrives.

Well, I must say, we had a great session in the round yard today. It was awesome all of the water had dried up and it was quite nice surface to work on. I have to tell you the Blind Chickie babe was pretty proud of me today. I had my full concentration on her, except for a couple of moments when I wanted to pick the pretty blue bells in the round yard.

I was a little more relaxed on the right rein than on the left today. I did some wonderful transitions from the canter to the trot, and my walk was lovely with a big over track. I was so relaxed today and whoohoo, no fruit loop moments.

On the way back to the tack shed I stopped and checked out Matthew's wheat crop, it seems to be coming along really well. I think he might be going to strip the barley in the next couple of weeks or see if it is dry enough at least. How exciting. I have not seen the Header going before, so this should be a new experience for me. Apparently, the Header is a big red machine, it strips the grain.

So, all in all a pretty awesome day, and I know the Blind Chick was pretty chuffed with how I worked, so we will see how things go tomorrow.

I am spending the afternoon kicking back, relaxing in my paddock.

I hope you're safe and well, have a spectacular day. Loads of love and hugs, Johno.

Over Track

Feeling Happy
4 November 2020

Diary entry by Johno

Wow, what a spectacular day and what fun we had in the dressage arena today.

I must say I do prefer to be lunged in the dressage arena than in the round yard. Okay it is a 20 metre round yard, but in the dressage arena you have even more space to stretch out. I had a great session this morning, lots of wonderful transitions, nice big bold trot and a lovely big walk with a massive over track.

It's so cool having Gwen there for the Blind Chick. She tells me if I am tracking up, if I am not tracking up, if I'm gawking, which I'm not! I'm being very good. The medication is working a treat.

This is my third day on a medication we're trialling. It's working beautifully, I'm much less stressed. Hence, I'm feeling much better within myself. Okay the Shivers is not going away, but without all the anxiety it won't be as bad …… I am hoping!

So, everyone is pretty happy, the Blind Chick in particular is loving the fact that when we go out to work I'm not having a fruit loop moment. Okay it's taking medication to not have a fruit loop moment, but that is probably the way the rest of my life is going to be. I will have to be looked after all the time like I am. Yes, that makes me a bit high maintenance I guess. But if it takes medication to make my life a better quality of life, so be it.

They're forecasting rain for tomorrow. I think there are quite a few farmers around here that would rather it not rain. There are crops to be stripped. But nature will do what nature will do. Maybe if it rains,

I'll get the day off! Mind you I don't mind working. In fact I quite enjoy it.

Hope everybody is having a lovely day. I've been put into a new paddock with lots of lovely green grass, so it's head down bum up grazing for me today.

Stay safe and well, loads of love and hugs, Johno.

Cute

☺ Feeling Blessed
5 November 2020

Diary entry by Johno

Well good morning, it's a bit soggy here on the Macquarie River. We've had some lovely showers, I'm not sure how much rain is in the rain gauge.

Needless to say, I have the day off whoohoo. I think I'll spend my day grazing and chatting to my mate next door. The main aim is to do as little as possible.

I thought I'd share a pretty cool picture with you. The Blind Chicks wonderful mother-in-law Lee found this photo on the internet. I like the photo of me when I was a tiny wee little baby. I think I might even have been for sale, but I thought you might like to see a baby picture of me, I think they are few and far between.

Well, so far, my new medication is going really well. It is only temporary at the moment, costing a fortune but hopefully Dr Sarah will have the new medication we are going to trial for a couple of months in the mail early next week. It will be interesting to see how it goes, I'll let you know. But I think it is one of those things that I will be on for life, but them's the breaks. If the new meds give me a good quality of life and allow the Blind Chick to be safe, taking them for the rest of my life is what I'll do.

Have a wonderful day, stay safe and well. Loads of love and hugs, Johno.

Swinging

😊 Feeling Wonderful
6 November 2020

Diary entry by Johno

Wow what a spectacular day! We had some lovely rain, 8 mils, I can hear the grass growing. Today is an amazing 24°C with the sun shining and a light breeze. It's beautiful.

And guess what? We had an amazing day in the dressage arena today. The Blind Chickie babe is still not riding so we did lunging and working through the process of me getting used to my new medication. The work was super.

We started off with a 10 minute relaxing walk in the dressage arena. Gwen mentioned to the Blind Chick that my over track was about 16 maybe 18 inches! I was swinging through the back and I was sure using my hindquarters. I was so relaxed it felt so good, then we went into a quiet trot.

We did lots of amazing transitions from the trot to the walk, walk back to the trot, trot to canter, canter back to the trot, all done with me listening carefully to the Blind Chick. My transitions were really sharp. Okay, sometimes I was a little slow coming back from the trot to the walk, but it got better as time went on.

On the lunge the Blind Chick wound me into a smaller circle, probably a 10 metre, in the canter. I did a few circles, then she wound me out then wound me back in again. Then she asked for a trot transition. Wow! We did some pretty cool stuff today. I was so engaged and coming through from behind. What a great session in the dressage arena.

I also got to do a couple of walk to canters. Now these were very cool, and very uphill. I haven't quite mastered being on the lunge and doing a sharp canter back to walk transition. I just need to sit a little more in my canter and slow the canter, slow the canter, sit, slow the canter, and walk. But we'll get there.

Well as you can see, I had a pretty awesome time in the dressage arena today with the Blind Chick. I'm so grateful for this medication, it's totally changing our lives.

I hope you're having a spectacular day and you're safe and well. Have a wonderful weekend. Loads of love and hugs, Johno.

On The Aids

Feeling Happy
10 November 2020

Diary entry by Johno

Well good morning. What a spectacular day here on the Macquarie River relaxing with my trotter mates next door.

Well, I have to share with you what happened yesterday. The Blind Chickie babe and Gwen took me out to the dressage arena and we did some awesome work. Oh, my heavens, I was doing the most amazing transitions; trot to walk on command and then trotting on doing lovely small canter circles. The Blind Chick would ask me to slow the canter, slow the canter, slow the canter and trot on. The transitions were lovely. The Blind Chick was chuffed. Wow, this medication is working so well.

So, just a little background about my current medication. What I'm being given at the moment is a fill-in because my proper medication coming from Dr Sarah hasn't arrived yet. I'll let you know when I start this new one and we can see how we are travelling.

The Blind Chick is still assessing how I'm going because although she'd like to start riding me, she's not going to put herself in any situation where she can't cope. She needs to know the medication is working and I'm not about to have a stressful moment.

As you know my stressful moments can be brought on by anything. It could be a bird taking off in the paddock, anything that triggers my brain to have a little relapse of anxiety, tension and stress. These triggers can be random and a little bit silly, but the medication so far is working really well.

I also think the current medication is costing the Blind Chick and arm and a leg, so it's really not sustainable. She is looking forward to the medication coming from Dr Sarah Gough.

I'm looking forward to another lovely day doing some good work in the dressage arena. It's nice not to be in the round yard. I get though that this choice of where we work is a trust thing. When I'm not having such big anxiety attacks, the Blind Chick is confident working me on the lunge in the dressage arena. Which I like very much. That space gives me so much more room to work.

So hopefully we will have another wonderful day training.

Have a great day, love and hugs Johno

Banned Substances Suck

Feeling Determined
11 November 2020

Diary entry by Johno

Wow the weather is warming up and the flies are getting worse!

My Blind Chickie babe is having to put fly spray on me twice today, but they are still annoying the hell out of me. I have a fly veil on plus a mesh rug, but I think I need to be in an air-conditioned room. Well maybe not that, that'd be pretty boring.

We had a pretty spectacular day in the dressage arena today. We just went for a walk, 25 minutes on each side and okay they weren't circles, they were great big eggs. It was so very relaxing and extra wonderful as instead of starting on the near side, Blind Chickie babe started me off on the offside! Fantastic, as this is my better side. So right from the get-go, I was walking out with a massive over track. What a way to start a work session!

Just a quick note to thank everybody for all the love and support and yes, the current medication is totally rocking out, it's working. My new medication from Dr Sarah Gough of Hunter Equine in Scone, will be arriving in the next few days. I'll keep you in the loop.

On the home front there have been a few reality checks with me and this medication. I think me doing competition is now out of the question! Why? Because I can't compete if I'm taking medication that is swappable, it's a banned substance.

We need to be realistic on how we move forward. The Blind Chickie babe and I are going to keep up our training and we'll find another way to be out in public. I'm not sure how we will do this, or how we will come to you. We may do displays at competitions! Who knows? What we do know is that being on the medication will not allow me to compete, legally.

I know we are going down this track of trying to find the right medication for me because it is the only track we have left. I need this medication to manage my anxiety and tension. Without it I have these times of anxiety and not being able to cope. Plus, I get a headache. It's not good at all. I want things to continue just how they are at the moment - One Step at a Time and the Blind Chickie babe and I enjoying each other.

So we will keep you in the loop. While it seems that competition is probably out of the question, watch this space. We have plans!

I know this is going to be sad for quite a few people, to know we're not able to compete, but since we've started *Johno and the Blind Chick* we've been honest with all of you, and that honesty will continue.

This doesn't mean *Johno and the Blind Chick* are finishing their journey, this is just a new chapter. We need to reinvent ourselves and how we can move forward not competing but still doing what we love doing. Firstly, we need to get the Blind Chick back in the saddle, well no not really. What first needs to happen, is getting my brain settled, then the Blind Chick back in the saddle. From there we can move forward.

We can't lose sight of the fact that I have a neurological degenerative condition called Equine Shivers! It is degenerating. In the last 17 months it has markedly worsened. But we will find a way to manage it and keep moving forward. I'm doing some spectacular work on the lunge and we will continue to build on this. The Blind Chickie babe will be back in the saddle hopefully very soon.

I would like to thank everybody for their love and support, and we are just doing what we love doing. The Blind Chickie babe is enjoying her pony and her pony is enjoying being with the Blind Chick. Together we will move forward - One Step at a Time, at our pace. We have some exciting things in front of us which we'll share with you in the next few weeks, so thank you.

Have a spectacular day and lovely evening. We hope you are well. Loads of love and hugs, Johno and his Blind Chickie babe.

Sushi Train Fun

Feeling Grateful
13 November 2020

Diary entry by Johno

I hope everybody has had a lovely couple of days. The last two days we've had thunderstorms and a little bit of rain, but not enough to flood the arena which is so good.

But this means because of the rain, I've not had to work!

I've been having a lovely time in my paddock, but I do have some exciting news. I started my new medication this morning! This is very exciting; I'll keep you updated on how I am travelling.

Before the rains, the Blind Chick has been having a lovely time with her wonderful husband Matthew. She's been spending quite a bit of time of an afternoon in the header stripping barley.

It was a very slow job as the rain had the barley quite water logged which means a lot of it was nearly lying on the ground. So, Matthew had to travel very slowly with the header to get the crop stripped.

And then today the Blind Chick took her very good friend Jackie Cantrall out for lunch for Jackie's birthday. They went to the sushi train in town. Apparently, this is one of their favourite places to go, then they went to a lovely wine bar and had a couple of champagnes to celebrate. It sounded like the Blind Chick had a lovely afternoon.

I hope you have a wonderful weekend. I probably won't be doing too much until Monday while the Blind Chick assesses how my medication is going. Stay tuned, we'll keep you in the loop.

Have a spectacular weekend. Keep safe and well. Lots of love and hugs, Johno.

Harvest Time

Feeling Optimistic
17 November 2020

Diary entry by Johno

What a spectacular morning here on the Macquarie River. It's just a little bit cooler than yesterday's 39°C, wow what a stinker. I think today is going to be 31°C.

I had a great day training with the Blind Chick yesterday. We trained in the dressage arena again, on the lunge. I had a couple of little moments yesterday just not quite paying attention, but all was good.

Wow today is so much nicer weather for working. Mind you we worked at 8 am. We did a 40 minute session, all at the walk. It was nice, I only had one major fruit loop moment. That was because my friends were coming over from the paddock next door and I could see them. I momentarily forgot what I was doing with my lunging and had my moment or two of whinnying and being a bit of a duffer. Then I settled down again, after the Blind Chick got my attention.

Today is my fourth day on my new medication. I think these things take time to work so we'll be patient and review how it's going in 3 to 4 weeks. The Blind Chick is still not confident she could ride me without me having one of my moments. Fingers crossed this medication works.

Things were busy here on the farm. Matthew was up incredibly early raking the lucerne hay. I'd say he'll be bailing in a few days, which will be really good weather to be making bales.

I'm sorry my diary entries aren't full of really interesting stuff at the moment. Hopefully, this medication works so the Blind Chickie babe can be back in the saddle. At the moment she's monitoring how I'm coping on this new medication. As per usual, it's one day at a time.

I hope you are safe and well. Have a spectacular day. Lots of love and hugs, Johno

Take The Time It Takes

Feeling Time Is the Secret
23 November 2020

Diary entry by Johno

Well, it's a very overcast good morning from the Macquarie River. We had a few light showers overnight and are expecting a top of 34°C today. It's going to be very steamy and muggy.

I apologise for not making many diary entries lately. Things aren't changing much; I'm still trialling my medication, working some days, not others and partially working Sundays. I think time is the secret. We need time to build up this new medication in my system. Fingers crossed.

I did have a highlight over the weekend though. The wonderful Tanya Hind my Craniosacral Therapist came and gave me a treatment. Wow it was totally amazing! I felt absolutely wonderful afterwards. My headache is gone. Tanya said you could see by the look in my eyes that I was so much more at ease. Thank you so much, beautiful lady.

The Blind Chickie babe has been busy of late, spending quite a bit of time with Matthew in the header stripping the wheat. Yesterday they were busy stripping the wheat and a few light scuds of rain came through. This meant there were two vehicles to bring back from down in the paddock. "How was this going to happen?" Matthew jokingly said to the Blind Chick, "You drive the Ranger home and I'll take the tractor." I think he may have regretted that idea.

Hilarious! So yes, the Blind Chick got in the Ranger and started driving. Before pressing the accelerator, she rang Matthew and put her phone on loudspeaker, Matthew was behind her in the tractor. He guided her the half a kilometre drive home. I think the Blind Chick was as nervous as hell and Matthew may have been as scared as hell, but everything went perfectly.

Matthew said, "a little right", "a little more right", "a little left" and voila! They were back home with no dints or scratches! I think the Blind Chick was very relieved to get back in the passenger seat, but it must have been fun. I think she enjoyed it.

So, it goes to prove there is more than one way to skin a cat! That's not a nice saying, but there is more than one way to achieve a job. Who'd have thought the Blind Chick would've been able to drive the ute home?

Okay, I've been on my medication now for 11 days. This has been a very interesting experiment. We've possibly got another month to go. The Blind Chick is logging all my reactions; when I have them, how I have them, and so on for Dr Sarah our wonderful veterinarian at Hunter Equine Scone.

Because I had my treatment with the wonderful Tanya yesterday, I've got today off so my treatment can keep doing its good stuff.

I just saw the Blind Chickie babe out on the veranda, she's been out feeding the beautiful kookaburras. They come and eat meat out of her hand, they're such amazing birds.

We hope you are having a wonderful day, keep safe and well. Loads of love and hugs, Johno and his Blind Chick.

Call The Vet – Now!

Feeling Grateful
24 November 2020

Diary entry by Johno

Well, I must say, I feel as if I have a bit of a hangover!

Yesterday late evening I ended up with a bout of colic. Without a doubt this is a really painful thing to go through. Your tummy hurts: you want to paw the ground but at the same time, you want to roll! It really isn't a good situation. I feel pretty crappy.

But then enter the Blind Chick who is always listening for something different going on in my paddock. She heard me pawing.

Then she heard me rolling, then more pawing. Then she hit the panic button! She was out in my paddock in a flash. I must admit I really was a little bit frantic with the pain and not listening. But I did hear her calling for Matthew to come and help as she didn't know where I was, nor what I was doing. So, Matthew came down and caught me.

Oh, my heavens there was a fair bit of tension in the air. I think the Blind Chick was very aware that I was in lots of pain and Matthew kept saying "no he's fine now, he's fine." But no! I wasn't fine, I felt terrible. So, while Matthew was catching me, the Blind Chickie babe was busy ringing her wonderful Dubbo vet.

Dr Don Crosby also has a team of awesome vets if he's not available. The first point of contact was the beautiful Wendy. Wendy looks after the Blind Chick and I, so when the Blind Chick rang and Wendy answered the phone, the Blind Chick was struggling to even put a sentence together because she was so distressed for me. Wendy said, "It's okay, I have it in hand, someone is on the way."

Wendy rang back within one minute letting the Blind Chick she had Killian on his way.

Killian had treated me before; the Blind Chick has lots of faith in Killian's ability. While they waited for Killian to arrive the Blind Chick and Matthew kept walking me. They wouldn't let me roll, even though I desperately wanted to roll. I wanted my tummy ache to go away so badly, I was really distressed. Consequently, there was a fair bit of tension between the Blind Chick and Matthew. I think that was mainly because of their concern for me.

While the Blind Chick was waiting for Killian to arrive, she rang Dr Sarah my veterinarian in Scone who is managing my Shivers medication. The Blind Chick wanted to make sure the medication wouldn't react with what I was going to be given for the colic. Lots of information passed from one vet to another.

When Killian arrived, he gave Matthew and the Blind Chick directions on what he was going to do. So, Matthew brought me up into the garden and I was given quite a few injections. One to calm the pain in my tummy, one to sedate me. Killian was so in control and amazing. All the time he was busy doing what he needed to do he let the Blind Chick know what he was doing. After he listened for gut sounds, he gave me a dose of paraffin. Then he cleaned out a lot of poo. I had quite a bit, not compacted, but it was sitting there not going anywhere, so he cleaned it out. He was so informative and kept telling the Blind Chick everything he was doing, which she so appreciated. I think she was pretty stressed out.

So, this morning I am definitely a little bit groggy and doey. I think the Blind Chick is just going to take me out for a walk with Gwen around the dressage arena. Then maybe I'll have a pick of some grass before getting a bath as I am filthy after all my rolling yesterday. Then I'll get a clean rug on me and the day off. Hopefully, no more colic!

A massive thank you to the wonderful Wendy for organising a vet so quickly. We're so grateful, we appreciate having such amazing vets in Dubbo. Thank you, Dr Don Crosby and the amazing Killian

I hope you have had an awesome day. I look forward to a wonderful day and being a lot less groggy. Loads of love and hugs Johno

Desensitisation

😎 Feeling Relaxed
25 November 2020

It's only a plastic bag!

Diary entry by Johno

Firstly, a massive thank you to everybody for the lovely messages when I was not so well with my dose of colic. To be honest, I wouldn't wish colic on my worst enemy. It was very painful and quite distressing for all concerned.

I also think it was possibly a little harder for the Blind Chick as she couldn't see what was happening, she could only hear that I was in such terrible pain. Even though I was so distressed, I think being totally blind can be pretty scary.

On a more positive note, I'm feeling really good today, no tummy ache. We've had a lovely morning in the dressage arena doing some more desensitisation. Oh, my heavens the Blind Chick had this bag on a stick! It's on my ears, it's up my nose, it's between my legs! But I don't mind. I suppose this is why it's called desensitisation. Mind you, at the same time she had something on her mobile phone that played through the stereo. It was lots of different noises: firecrackers, racing cars and planes taking off! Guess what? I took no notice of any of it. I'm a star.

I've also thrown a shoe, oops. Thank heavens my wonderful farrier Troy. He's coming tomorrow.

This desensitisation thing the Blind Chick is doing is to hopefully decrease my anxiety. As Dr Sarah pointed out to the Blind Chick, my anxiety is not caused by man, it is clinical. So, this desensitisation thing might take a bit of doing, and it may not work. Either way, my Blind Chick is certainly giving it a fair go.

The first day she came out of the tack shed with the bag on the end of the stick, I nearly had a couple of kittens. It scared the heck out of me. Then she started waving it around. I was like "holy cow Batman, just hold the bag still!" It's only taken two days but now I'm taking absolutely no notice of it. And that mix of noises has become just a noise. After it finished, she played cool music, it was so nice I think the Blind Chick and I could dance to it, it was really lovely.

I must say, I enjoy it when the Blind Chick rides me to music. Hopefully when we get my anxiety attacks under control, the Blind Chick will be back riding to music. That would be nice.

We had a great training session with the desensitisation. You will see what I mean about the bag, it's everywhere! But I don't care.

Now I have my fly veil on, a lovely light mesh rug and I am vegging in my paddock. I had a couple of run arounds this morning, just a little anxiety attack. I think they might be getting less, well maybe not, but we believe in miracles here, and magic.

I hope everyone is having a wonderful day. I'm sending everybody lots of love and hugs. Have a spectacular day, Johno.

PS: I forgot to mention that a motorbike went past a couple of times and a couple of trucks and trailers came in, but I took no notice! I just kept eating and listening to the music. So maybe this desensitisation stuff might be working. Bring it on!

Playing Ball

Feeling Wonderful
26 November 2020

Diary entry by Johno

What a spectacular day on the Macquarie River. I think it's going to be 34°C, so I'm going to get a bit hot. But it's such a beautiful morning.

I had a lovely early breakfast, a carrot, a hug, and my medication. Then I was just chilling in my paddock wondering what the Blind Chick had in store for me today.

Well, an hour or two later I was not disappointed. It was something different. Here comes the Blind Chick with her white cane and a massive, big green ball! What is she going to do with that ball?

The first thing she does is come sit with me and have a chat . We had a bit of a cuddle, a bit more of a chat, then she started kicking the ball around! Wow, she pushed it to me. What the hell did she want me to do with this ball? She was standing there nodding her head, inferring "Push your ball Johno, push it Johno." Ooops! I had no idea what she was talking about. Then I shoved the ball with my nose and oh, the Blind Chick was ecstatic – "Good boy Johno, good boy." Apparently, I'd done what she'd wanted me to do, yay.

Unbeknown to the Blind Chick we were being watched! Matthew was on the veranda watching us play ball, he yelled out something about playing football and the Blind Chick called to him, inviting him to come play ball with us. He did, we had a lovely time. Yes, the Blind Chick missed the ball, a lot. She also got hit by the ball …. a lot! I missed it a lot to, but there was lots of cheering and carrying on. I got lots of pats and cuddles, it was so much fun. Matthew even bounced the ball off me and guess what? I took no notice! This was one of the desensitisation things, but it was a fun one.

We even tried to get our friend Kelly to come down and play with us, she was standing at the door laughing. I think she thought we were all daft, but it was good fun.

I'm having a pretty cruisy afternoon because my wonderful farrier Troy is coming at 3pm to shoe me. The Blind Chick is ready with her idea of walking me in between Troy picking up my feet and putting it down. Why this technique? It's so I keep moving, so I don't seize up because of my Shivers. Hopefully this might make the process of being shod kinder on me, and easier on Troy.

I hope everyone is having an awesome day. I've had the best morning playing with Matt and the Blind Chick. Who would've thought we would've been kicking a ball around!

Keep safe and well. Loads of love and hugs, Johno and the Blind Chick.

Even The Cockatoos Aren't Squawking

Feeling frustrated
27 November 2020

Diary entry by Johno

Holy cow, it's hot here!

I think it is 38°C and then it's going to get over 40°C on the weekend, aagh! So this morning the Blind Chickie babe has been putting out sprinklers for the birds. I think she's going to put one in my paddock, I saw her setting it up. Maybe tomorrow I'll have a sprinkler to stand under. Sadly, we don't have even a whisper of a breeze.

I'm so excited, I have my new shoes on! Amazing Farrier Troy was out yesterday with his lovely apprentice Henry. The job was done and dusted quite quickly. We had a few little tricks up our sleeve which made the shoeing much easier.

Today is my day off. I always have the day off after I've got new shoes. It gives me time to work them in.

Wow, unless you were working very, very early, it really is too hot for man or beast to be out playing in a dressage arena. You know what? It's so hot the cockatoos aren't even squawking. In fact, all the birds are incredibly quiet. They must be finding somewhere lovely and cool to sit.

All going well, I'll have some exciting things to share with you next week re-the Blind Chick and my training. But it all depends on what the weather is doing. If we continue getting these massive 40°C days and above, it'll be put off till a later date. It's something to really look forward to though, I can't wait to share it with you.

Re my medication I'm not sure if anything is really happening. I'm into my third week taking it but sadly it's not making a great difference. I don't think we'll keep up the trial. The Blind Chick is talking to Dr Sarah today, I'll update you on any changes.

I hope you are safe and well. Have a lovely day. Lots of love and hugs, Johno and the Blind Chickie.

Dreams Do Come True

Feeling Grateful
28 November 2020

Diary entry by Johno and the Blind Chick

Dare to Dream
"It doesn't matter what you did or where you were.
It matters where you are and what you're doing.
Get out there!
Sing the song in your heart and
NEVER let anyone shut you up!!"
Anon

Dreams do come true.

Thank you to my amazing two beautiful brown eyes that comes in the guise of an amazing horse called Johno. He is 18.3hh, 800 kg of absolutely spectacular, amazing horse.

Thank you also to the incredible angel Linda for your phone call, for reaching out to help us. From the bottom of our heart, we thank you for giving us hope, for keeping our dreams alive. We are so very, very, grateful.

There have been lots of magical moments in the last few days, and we believe they are going to continue.

So, everybody out there please keep believing, keep dreaming, keep making those dreams come true, and thank you to all of the beautiful people who believe in the Blind Chick and I. You keep us moving forward. We are so grateful to have you in our lives.

Have a spectacular weekend. Loads of love and hugs, Johno and the Blind Chick.

13
December

Summer Time

Feeling Grateful
1 December 2020

Diary entry by Johno

Good morning all and welcome summer! Today is the first day of summer and it's going to be a cracker. It's 45°C here in Dubbo today, not so pleasant for man or beast.

The Blind Chickie babe was up very early this morning to feed me, she then put the sprinkler on in my paddock and placed my hay under the sprinkler. What an awesome idea; I can stand, eat and keep cool all at once! Plus, the Blind Chick likes to soak my hay since my recent colic episode. I'm not sure it's necessary, but she just doesn't want to risk me having another colic attack. They are too scary and way to painful.

For the past few days, the Blind Chick has not been putting my mesh rug on. This is to alleviate me getting too hot under the rug. So, get ready, I may be a bit grubby in any photos you see of me lately. But grubby is better than overheating. And with overheating can come …. yes, you guessed it, another bout of colic. And we sure don't need that, again!

The Blind Chick has also turned sprinklers on in the garden for the little birds. I'm sure they will appreciate that, especially around midday.

It is quite amazing when it gets really hot and still here, even the birds aren't flying or chirping. Not even the noisy cockatoos squawk about anything. They just sit quietly somewhere in a shady spot on the river. I noticed the Blind Chick out calling for Thunder Paws this morning, to try and get the cat back inside, so he doesn't have an uncomfortable day in this heat.

Please look after yourself. I hope you have a safe day. Loads of love and hugs, Johno and the Blind Chick.

Soaking

😊 Feeling OK
2 December 2020

Diary entry by Johno

Well good morning summer! We're heading for a top of 45°C today, it's going to be a stinker. So, no work for me. The Blind Chick is being careful with what level of stress she puts me under at the moment, trying to manage my Shivers a little better. She's working really hard to try and keep stress out of my environment.

She was up early to feed me this morning, up with the sparrows. She put the sprinkler on in my paddock and guess what else? She put my hay under the sprinkler. So here I am enjoying my hay, and the sprinkler. What a cool idea.

This also saved her job. She is soaking my hay, not for long, just long enough to give me a bit more moisture and reduce the likelihood of any more colic attacks. I'm not saying that the hay caused it, but anything we can do to keep me from having another attack, the better.

Oh, my heavens, the past few days have included horrific winds. I look forward to a reprieve tomorrow. It's a Total Fire Ban here today. Everyone please be extra careful. Please keep cool, keep safe and don't forget to check on your neighbours and older family members.

Loads of love and hugs, Johno.

Trialling New Meds

Feeling Wonderful
3 December 2020

Diary entry by Johno

Wow, what a spectacular morning. We have a light breeze and it's not going to be 40°C or above. It's going to be low 30s. How cool is that?

The Blind Chickie babe came down to feed me early, as we've made our work time earlier, 8am, to try and get away from the heat of the day. I had an awesome work session with the Blind Chick. We went into the round yard. I know she did this as a precautionary move, in case I had a fruit loop moment. But I didn't. I was really relaxed and enjoyed my work.

We are trialling a couple of new things and at the moment, they seem to be working amazingly well together. I know the Blind Chick would love to take me off my medication, but we will give it a little longer and see how things go.

I'm totally loving having a sprinkler in my paddock. I've been standing under it this morning, it and the lovely breeze, the water gently sprinkling on me, it's really refreshing.

It's going to be a lovely day just relaxing in my paddock. I'm really looking forward to it. Now the plumber is here. He's putting new guttering on my stable. I'm not sure what I think of this guy walking around on my stable roof!

I hope you have a spectacular day and are all safe and well. Loads of love and hugs, Johno.

Guess Who Is Driving?

Feeling Excited
4 December 2020

Diary entry by Johno

Welcome to another beautiful morning on the Macquarie River. There are a few clouds sneaking about, but I think that rain will wait until tomorrow.

I had a great day in the arena yesterday. Today is no riding involved, just lunging and a bit of ground work desensitisation. Our session went for 40 minutes and my walk was lovely with a big over tracking swinging through my back. I felt good.

I have to share with you a fun observation yesterday while Matthew and the Blind Chick were in the header, finishing off harvesting the wheat. It really did look like it was going to storm, so they wanted to get the stripping finished and the back of the truck safely closed up after that was done. Matthew and the Blind Chick got back in the header but I saw the Blind Chick get into the …. driver's seat!

Yes. The next thing the Blind Chick is cruising across the paddock driving the header, under Matthews close supervision. She was turning left, she was turning right, she went up the hill, she went round to near the shed, and then she asked Matthew did she have her license to be a header driver? Ha ha ha. The answer was a definite, NO!

So, all the stripping is finished which is great Matthew will come home this afternoon and move irrigators to put on the lucerne. He is always so very busy

Ooops! I did a ripping job on one of my rugs, so Matthew dropped it off this morning at Horse-Wear Repairs, a friend of the Blind Chicks who does rug repairs. Neeni is going to try and get it done by this afternoon, so we can take it with us on our road trip next week

Watch this spot! We have some exciting things happening next week which we'll share with you. The Blind Chickie babe is getting ready all the things we need and packing up the horse feed to pack into the horse float on Sunday.

Whoohoo and I have the wonderful Tanya Hind coming to do a Craniosacral Treatment on me on Saturday at 8am. I totally love my treatments with Tanya, I can't wait.

I admit that I'm feeling pretty terrific at the moment. Changing my diet has been very effective. The Blind Chick is still soaking my hay and I must say I don't mind it like that. It's like freshly pressed hay, it smells lovely.

I hope everyone has a wonderful weekend. I think we're in for a shower tomorrow, maybe even some storms tonight. Keep safe and well. I can't wait to share our journey next week.

Loads of love and hugs, Johno and my Blind Chick.

Focus On Ability

🙂 Feeling Blessed
4 December 2020

Diary entry from the Blind Chick

Did you know that yesterday was International Day for People with a Disability?

With this in mind, I thought some reflection was needed. I'd like to share with you.

What are the things I Celebrate?
I Celebrate my Ability.
I Celebrate how very blessed I am to live in this amazing country, where you can have dreams and make those dreams come true.
I Celebrate being surrounded by beautiful people that believe in me.
I Celebrate friends and friendship.
I Celebrate the feeling of sitting on my beautiful horse Johno and riding across the arena.
I Celebrate these two beautiful brown eyes that guide me around when I ride him.
I Celebrate the amazing things I have experienced in my life: representing Australia at the Paralympics twice, and riding at the World Championships in Denmark.
I Celebrate the ability to make a difference to sit on a horse and ride 16,000 km for different charities and raise over $3.2 million.
I Celebrate everything I have in my life. I take time to reflect and thank God for this amazing life we have.

I Celebrate my disability. Because it has made me the person I am today.
I Celebrate the fact that Vision is much more than Seeing.
The Blind Chick

Have a wonderful day, take care. Lots of love, the Blind Chick.

Amazing Adam

 Feeling Excited
8 December 2020

Diary entry by Johno

Well, hello everyone. Have I got some news for you!

Yes, you need to grab a cuppa as this might be a long diary entry. Hang onto your seat because it's full of ups and downs, and lots of Holy Cow moments!

Well, it started on Saturday morning with my treatment with our wonderful Tanya Hind, Craniosacral Therapist. Wow, man oh man did I have the most amazing treatment and transformation. Things have been so different since my last treatment. Like bring it on massive changes.

Then bring on late Saturday afternoon/evening. Holy cow Batman, a mini cyclone! Yes, it came through tearing our trees; ripping off branches, picking up field bins that the day before had wheat filled to the brim in them, sending them rolling across the paddock heading for Matthew's mum and dad's place before being stopped by a tree! That tree finished up broken off at the stump, its branches flung and stacked high on top of Lee and John's house!

It's lucky the Blind Chick and Matthew's house wasn't blown away. It was horrific. Winds of up to 130 km an hour. Holy cow, I'm lucky to have my tail!

Then on Sunday oh my heavens, the place looked like a war zone. Thankfully Matthews wonderful friends Brian and Pete arrived to help clean up the place. Matthew's mum was busy getting the electric fence working again because there are trees down all over the electric fence. The Blind Chick was pulling big limbs to the burning heap with her white cane leading the way; tap, tap, tapping. Oh, my heavens, so many people putting in so much work to clean up such a massive mess.

Oh, my heavens – the dressage arena! The majority of the arena white edging was in the next -door neighbour's paddock. It had just been totally uplifted and moved to next door. A massive thank you to Andrew and Emma and the Blind Chicks wonderful husband Matthew for putting it all back into place again, so gratefully appreciated.

Now keep in mind, the Blind Chick and I are off on our road trip on Monday! So, as well as all this mess to clean up she still had to pack the horse float. The Blind Chicks wonderful husband got the float organised and parked it near the tack shed so the Blind Chick could pack it.

Okay, bring on our road trip on Monday. Our wonderful Tanya my Craniosacral Therapist is driving us down to Lochinvar. We're heading for the New South Wales Equestrian Centre where I'm going to meet the amazing Adams Sutton and have some training.

Now keep in mind, I have Equine Shivers! This degenerative neurological condition affects my limbs, and my neurological condition. Bring on hypersensitivity to sounds and to what I see. Hence why like the Blind Chick affectionately calls them my 'Fruit Loop Moments'. But we need to work out what's triggering these and how to work with them. So, the wonderful Adam is going to work with us and see what we can do. This is critical because unless we can get this under control and the Blind Chick can control what is happening, then things are looking a bit grim.

So, roll on Tuesday morning and my first session with the amazing Adam. Mind you I need to reflect a little on Monday evening first. Oh, my heavens, numerous fruit loop moments!

I do apologise to Tanya for being so rude with my objectionable behaviour and rearing and not being very nice at all. My excuse is I was anxious and okay, I did have friends either side of me, but I obsessed about a couple of other horses that I thought were my mates and I was very naughty. Apparently, this not nice behaviour is about to change!

So, Tanya and the Blind Chick arrive at Adams, give me a good brush, put my boots on and wait a while. Then the lovely Adam arrived and takes me off to the indoor arena. Wow, what a lovely place this is. Okay on the way to the arena I admit, I had a couple of little fruit loop moments, but Adam let me have them then we walked on.

Once we got into the indoor yes, maybe I had another couple of moments, but my mind was asking where are my mates? What's happening? Why am I here? All the while Adam kept me busy, he got my concentration and focus. There was no forcing, just asking. Plus, I must say, no bad behaviour was accepted.

Adam was very quick to pick that I was probably a little bit of a bully and pushy. So, he got me to respect his space and what he was asking. He didn't allow me to walk all over him. This worked a treat. Quite quickly I worked out my boundaries, where I was, where I was allowed to be and what I was allowed to do, all done without any cruelty and done very subtly. Like a lead mare in the paddock, Adam would just stop, and if I didn't stop, he would kick back with his foot as if to say – 'No! This is not a go zone, stop.'

Holy cow! This only took two or three times and I all of a sudden had respect for him and his space. I totally got what he was doing and if he stopped, I stopped. If he walked, I walked. If I got a little distracted and wanted to be a bit pushy, he'd just lift his leg and kick back at me, and just touch me on the chest. Oopsie, okay overstepping the boundaries! Listen Johno, listen. This process worked a treat. It was so subtle, but so effective.

Then Adam introduced …. a stick with a flag on it! Well, Blind Chickie babe and I have been there and done that, or so I thought. Adam used it a little bit differently. Holy cow! I was a little bit confronted, a little bit worried, but very quickly I worked out the flag wasn't going to hurt me. Then he brought out a bigger flag, the beautiful Australian flag, and he did desensitisation with it. It made a lot of noise when it was flapping beside me. I admit, that didn't worry me when it was going over my body, but when it was flapping beside me, that got my attention! But slowly and surely, I learnt to trust Adam. He wasn't going to hurt me.

After all the ground work in the indoor arena, Adam also introduced whips. He cracked them, and their whooshing noise was a bit disturbing, but quickly I learnt that it was just a whooshing noise. Ignore it.

Then Adam took me outside. Whoohoo, holy cow! There are other horses here. Instantly I started to whinny and get excited. Adam stopped and gave me a kick in the chest, just with a lift of his foot, not cruel, just getting my attention and making me back up. Then BAM! It was like a lightbulb moment, I got it. Maybe I don't need to be so pushy and over the top.

Okay everyone, don't overreact to the kick in the chest thing. It's like a lead mare behaviour. If you come up behind her, she'll lift her hind leg, and just kick back at you. This is what Adam was doing to get my attention. It wasn't done cruelly, it was just like 'Stop, don't do that. That's rude.' It didn't take long for me to realise what he was trying to say to me.

Then Adam took me for a walk down the road, a trot down the road, then back. Keep in mind this amazing young man has two broken ribs! Yet he's still doing lots of really good quality work with me.

Once my great session was over, Adam took me back to the paddock, took my boots off, my halter off and let me go with a lovely big pat of appreciation. "Job well done mate."

I can't wait to see what tomorrow brings. I was a bit of a fruit loop tonight when the girls came to feed me, but I'm sure I'll get better as each evening goes on. It's just a matter of settling in, getting the feel of the place, and being okay with the other horses coming and going.

I must do a little bit of reflection at this stage, because after my treatment with the amazing Tanya on Saturday I'm not having as many moments of my mind not connecting with my legs. Especially my front legs. When Adam worked with me, I was backing pretty good, except for my near side hind, it was having weird movements. But I wasn't anxious and freaking out! So, thank you Tanya for looking after me. Her amazing Craniosacral Treatments really are amazing. I can't wait for my next one.

Also, I have to share with you something really special. The beautiful Tanya offered me Sponsorship today! This means she'll continue to look after me. Oh, my heavens! The Blind Chick and I are so very grateful. Out of all of the treatments we've tried over the last 19 months, it's Tanya Hind's Craniosacral Treatments that are the only ones that have made a difference with my degenerative neurological condition, Equine Shivers. Thank you, Tanya, from the bottom of our hearts. We are so very very grateful and privileged to have you Sponsoring us.

I hope you have enjoyed your cuppa, maybe a couple of biscuits as well? We forward to letting you know what happens tomorrow. According to Adam there are new and exciting things in store for us, we can't wait.

Stay safe, keep smiling, love and hugs Johno.

Adam's Story

From Cowboy to Horseman!

Adam Sutton, owner, and chief instructor at Allroundhorsemanship, is not your run of the mill cowboy. He's always got something quirky or funny to say.

Adam has had over 24 years' experience working with horses from riding unruly horses in rodeos, setting traps for catching brumbies in the snowy mountains, campdrafting, to now travelling around Australia teaching his methods of making connections through transitions, for horses and riders from the basics to the more advance stages in all disciplines.

Everything comes together to form his own unique way of working with horses.

"Based on the experience I've had with some of the finest horseman here and overseas, I've developed a systematic approach to horse training that works well for me. It's a system that allows each horse to develop suppleness and obedience in their own time. My approach involves eight separate steps and exercises that build upon each other. There's no point expecting exercise three to work at 100 per cent if the horse is still only comfortably being 70 or 80 per cent effective with exercise two."

Adam starts all his exercises on the ground first. This allows both the horse and rider to understand which zone controls what movements.

Adams's calm, caring, knowledgeable, fun personality allow him to communicate openly and freely with clients. This allows the building of confidence and restoring trust essential to progress through the levels.

"I can be flexible on how I utilise my horsemanship to my clients. This allows me to develop better relationships with clients. It's a privilege to watch them succeed together and through a harmonious balance and developing their confidence at their own pace."

He has a great ability to understand people, horses and the processes involved with achieving their desired outcomes. He uses a more holistic approach to his training methods and can break down the barriers in a simple, and humorous way.

Adam has developed a reputation of success in turning around problem behavioural issues within both horse and rider in his popular clinics.

"I love teaching and being able to pass on knowledge and understanding for people to achieve ongoing success with their horse, and themselves!"

"I love taking something that isn't/wasn't working, taking it apart, and putting it back together."

Allroundhorsemanship has evolved into a successful Educational Business in Australia, moving away from its origins of mainly breaking in horses from the one home base in NSW.

Now Adam is a mobile horsemanship business, more able to tailor the training and learning to the individual needs.

"We enjoy helping people develop their connections and strengthen partnerships through confidence and trust."

Desensitising Day 3

🙂 Feeling Excited
10 December 2020

Diary entry by Johno

Absolutely this is a grab a cuppa diary entry.

Wow what a spectacular morning here in the Hunter Valley. I can even see …. balls in the sky!

I heard Tanya and the Blind Chick talking about them. Apparently, they're called balloons and they have a basket on the bottom that carry people. It was such a surreal beautiful morning here with a lovely cool sea breeze. It must have been spectacular with the most beautiful view from the basket.

The Blind Chick and the beautiful Tanya were here very early this morning to feed me. I had finished my brekkie before my session with the amazing Adam Sutton. Oh, my heavens we are learning so much, the Blind Chick and I, me in particular. I've been learning about personal space and manners! I thought I had good manners, oops no! I think I lost them.

Adam worked one on one with the Blind Chick and I. Instead of me leading her, she was leading me with Adam's stick in front of her. She used her body to stop me and then making her body bigger and flapping her arms, I'd back up and halt. Then we'd walk on. Wow what a new way of doing things. All this was a matter of me watching for what the Blind Chick was wanting; whether she walked out with bigger strides, whether she slowed her stride, whether she stopped. I had to work in with what she was doing. It was so cool and guess what? I had to concentrate and be responsible!

It's amazing the little things that creep into your life that become habit, possibly not good habits! Like feeding treats and always patting around the muzzle. Guess what's behind that muzzle? Very sharp teeth!

Adam has a policy 'Don't pat or caress below the eyes.' I don't know whether I like that idea, but the Blind Chick thought it was a great idea, it may stop my mouthing and always looking for food, especially if I'm not being stimulated by someone patting my muzzle all the time and I can smell carrots, I can smell liquorice, I can smell something yummy on their hands! Hence. I get mouthy.

After the Blind Chicks session with Adam and I, Adam took over control again and did more desensitisation work. Wow, this stuff is becoming a breeze, and I am learning not to be so reactive.

Adam then put his saddle on me, and we went for a long walk, not with Adam in the saddle, just me being lead, being very attentive and mindful of what Adam was doing. I got 10 out of 10! I didn't put a foot wrong. I didn't whinny at other horses, I didn't get excited, I just plodded along behind Adam. He had my undivided attention, as he should.

Then Tanya and the Blind Chick gave me a bath. Oh, my heavens did I so need a bath, I was filthy. Filthy, partly because I've not had a rug on since I've been down here. Why? Because I'm beside two youngsters that would probably pull my rug off. I admit it's been nice not having a rug on. But, man oh man I was filthy. Lots of dirt, lots of sweat as it's quite muggy here in the Hunter than it is in Dubbo.

Then to my surprise after they all sat in a lovely, shaded area for lunch, supplied by Adam, the girls came back down with the halter and got me. What's happening? I generally have the afternoons off! So back up we go to Adam, who does a little bit more work with me in the indoor, then we go out to a strange paddock. Strange because it has all these weird things in it.

The first thing I meet is a giant teddy bear! Adam walked me around it and all these colourful things: boxes on the ground, bridges, seesaws, and even a big rack that had coloured pool noodles on it. I'm not sure what they were going to do, plus poles on the ground set up like a maze.

So, the first thing Adam does, is takes me and faces me up to this box with water in it, like what the heck did you want me to do with that? Have a drink? He just stood to the side while I decided what I was going to do. I certainly wasn't walking through it, that was my decision. But Adam had other ideas! What I liked was he let me come to this conclusion myself. I went to the left of it, I went to the right, I went to the left. Then I thought oh my heavens, this isn't working, so I put one foot in, then I put my second foot in and walked straight through it.

We did it a couple more times, each time on a different rein. No problem. Then we mosey over to a …. bridge!

Well okay, the bridge was a bit of a mental stumbling block for me. No way was I going to walk on that thing. Again, Adam thought differently to me. Once again, I went to the left, I went to the right, I went to the left, all the while Adam just kept tapping me, encouraging me to come forward. Adam was consistent. I went on the bridge! First, I got my front two feet up there and just stood awhile, then Adam allowed me to back off.

Adam is extremely patient but consistent with everything he does. So eventually I did a couple more steps onto it with my front legs and then you know what? It was a bit like my Shivers, I never know what my hind legs are doing because we're not communicating very well. So, it took me a bit of time to sort out with those hindlegs, and get them up on the bridge, but eventually we did. I stood there so very proudly, with Adam by my side giving me a pat on the shoulder.

Then we walked through things like cafe curtains. I must admit I wasn't impressed with that either, but I could do it now with my eyes closed. It all came down to Adam allowing me to assess the situation, and me working out what I had to do and guess what? It's not that hard! You just have to think about things and be mindful.

While Adam was working with me on the bridge, I could see to the side another scary looking thing. They call it a seesaw! Other horses were going on it and everyone was giggling and encouraging, but I thought yeah, no, that one is not for me. Next thing I know, I'm facing up to the seesaw!

Once again with Adams's consistency, patience and allowing me to assess the situation, I eventually put my two front feet on the seesaw. But I wasn't going any further. No way! This thing moves.

Well guess what? Adam had his way eventually. I had all four feet on the seesaw and One Step at a Time, I walked up it, then down the other side. Yes, it was really cool. Later on, a cute little pony called Rosie was on the seesaw and they were making it go up-and-down. She was amazing how perfectly balanced she stayed. How awesome was that?

All up, I did about eight different obstacles. It was such an amazing learning experience. Being given the time to assess, to make up my mind and to work out exactly what Adam was wanting me to do was brilliant. These were all foreign things to me; I'd never done obstacles before. The biggest obstacle I've ever had in my life is …. getting on a horse float!

So, all in all it was an awesome learning experience. Lots of desensitisation is happening. Plus, it's making me more mindful about my environment, what I'm doing, where I'm putting my feet, and what is expected of me.

After the session, the girls took me down to my paddock and let me go. My heavens didn't I have lots of food for thought, didn't I learn so much. This being mindful and being attentive is so important for things to work out. It all starts on the ground.

In my paddock I've got feed up to my knees. I'm having the rest of the afternoon off. I think I might go down and hang with my two young friends down the bottom of the paddock.

I hope everyone has had a wonderful day. I've had a massive day of learning.

Loads of love and hugs, Johno.

Day 4 – The Earth Moved!

 Feeling Surprised
10 December 2020

Diary entry by Johno

It's another spectacular morning here in the Hunter Valley. There is a beautiful sea breeze which is making it a bit crisp. I think it might turn into a bit of a warm day.

Tanya and the Blind Chick came down to get me this morning. We had a nice walk up through the yards in to greet the wonderful Adam. What does he have in store for me today?

We started with a little revision on desensitisation. Then Adam did some work on getting me to line myself up with the mounting block. This was really interesting. I had to work out where I had to stand, which took a little bit of doing. But once I got the gist of it whoohoo! I was on fire, I nailed it.

Then Adam walked me to the side of the arena, put a saddle on me and off we went walking. Okay we went for a walk yesterday with the saddle, so I thought this might be on the cards, then the Blind Chick got her bridle. But Adam was not putting it on me! It was just a bit fancy with nose bands etc, Adam wanted to keep it simple. So simple it was. Adam put his bridle on me and we did some more work on the mounting block.

Adam was explaining how important it is just to keep everything very low-key, no fuss. When you get on, don't always just move off on a mission to do something. Maybe sit there and do nothing, maybe get off again. Mix it up. So, we did that for a while then Adam dismounted. We did some mounting block work again, but this time Adam got on me. We rode around the arena; we went outside and off down the road. Oh, my heavens, I don't do rides down the road! I have never done a ride down the road. I've always been in a dressage arena or round yard. But this was a pretty neat experience. It was a lovely road with trees down each side, horses here and dare I say, I really was a little excited.

But I was very, very good. After we'd gone about 200 metres Adam quietly eased me into a trot. As we trotted down the road the horse beside me was going absolutely crazy. Wow, I was such a good boy. I did a little bit of jogging but that was it. I really truly didn't get too distracted.

Adam then trotted me the other way down the road awhile the Blind Chick and Tanya stood and listen to me go on my second ride down the road. It was lovely big and relaxing trot. I was still listening and looking, but I was quite relaxed.

Then I thought we were all done. According to Adam, we were not! Off we headed for that area where we were in yesterday. The one with all weird things. But he was on my back. What do you think he's going to do with me in there with him riding me?

Whoohoo! What a ride. Straight over the bridge I went, onto the seesaw then across the water, through the curtain of pool noodles and up onto that stationery block. Oh, my heavens I was on fire! It was totally awesome. I was so confident doing it all. Even big Ted sitting there watching me had a smile on his face.

Adam took me for a trot around the obstacle course then we cantered. It was really lovely. I was relaxed. Yes, I was still a little wary, but I was listening and attentive. It was awesome.

So, watch this spot. Who knows what will happen tomorrow or where I'll be, or what I'll be doing. I must say I'm loving the training and loving Adams laid-back attitude. He's letting me enjoy myself. It's such an amazing learning curve, but so much fun.

I heard the girls talking, they've had a very busy afternoon having retail therapy! I think it was Christmas shopping.

After our Adam session tomorrow we'll be driving the five hours back to Dubbo.

We hope everyone has a lovely afternoon and is safe and well. Loads of love and hugs, Johno.

Language

🙂 Feeling Blessed
12 December 2020

Diary entry by Johno and the Blind Chick

So much to tell you today. Grab a cuppa.

Well Friday brings another spectacular day in the beautiful Hunter Valley. I'm up to my knees in horse feed, there's a couple of hot air balloons in the air on this pristine beautiful morning, and I'm so relaxed.

I wonder what the amazing Adam has in store for us today.

Things happened a little differently this morning. The Blind Chick is in charge of taking me up to the indoor arena. I'm a little looky and inattentive, but the Blind Chick puts into practice the skills that Adam has been teaching her. What to do when I'm looky, what to do when I'm being a little rude and pushy. She did a great job. By the time I got to the indoor I was totally focused on the Blind Chick, we walked quietly in.

Oh, my heavens. Today was very busy though. There was another coach in the indoor, lots of people around and lots of other new horses. Adam started with us doing a little bit of revision, more de-sensitisation. Wow, those flags didn't bother me at all. These days flapping bags, you name it, bring it on! I've got it all nailed.

Adam then saddles me up and we do more revision on the mounting block, me positioning myself. Straight away Mother Magoo I was there! Everyone was a bit proud I think. I lined myself up perfectly, my wither aligned with Adam's belly button while he stood on the mounting block.

Adam then quietly mounts me, sits there for a bit and has a bit of a chat. No hurry, just very cruisy and relaxed. We go for a walk around the indoor arena and have a bit of a walk, trot and canter. Then Adam takes me out for a walk down the road. With all the traffic coming and going there was lots to look at today. Even though I was pretty good, I could have been a little bit more attentive. I was looking around a lot, but all in all we had a lovely ride up and down the road a few times. Then Adam took me to the amazing obstacles.

Even though I do say so myself, I think I've taken to these obstacle things really quickly. I'm enjoying them. Once I knew what I had to do it was a breeze. So, in we go, straight up over the bridge, round to the seesaw then down through the pool noodles, through the cafe curtains, over five or six ground poles, they're getting me to use my hind legs really well. All the while, sitting in the middle of all this was big Ted, watching me with a big smile! I even walked up to an obstacle and put my two front feet on it. Mind you this obstacle is quite high! So, it took me a little bit of time to work out what I had to do. But now I know, it's awesome and so easy.

After all this, Adam gave me lots of praise. I thought my day was finished, get the float, let's go home. Well, this didn't play out exactly how I thought.

So, Adam and I headed back into the indoor arena, Tanya and the Blind Chick following behind. Next thing the Blind Chick is putting on her helmet! Whoohoo the Blind Chick is going to have a ride. I'm so excited. I think she was very nervous.

Keeping in mind the Blind Chick is struggling a little bit with the loss of her confidence. This is totally explainable since her untimely dismount when I was a bit naughty about six months ago. She broke her knee. So, it's been a while, since she's been back in the saddle. Hence, we're back with Adam to build up our confidence and get things happening again for the Blind Chick and I.

There wasn't any hesitation with the Blind Chick getting back on. It was amazing when Tanya said to her, "It's lovely to see the smile back on your face." I don't think the smile moved.

So, under the careful guidance of Adam, the Blind Chick and I went for a ride around the indoor arena. She rides me a little bit differently than Adam, with more contact. This is understandable also keeping in mind that apart from the slip in confidence, she is totally blind.

We poke round the arena for a little while, changing reins and with Adam talking to the Blind Chick all the time, giving her feedback, getting her to relax. It was really nice. He truly is such an amazing trainer with horses and people who have lost their confidence. This is really great for the Blind Chick and I.

Next thing Adam is talking to the Blind Chick about going for a walk …. down the road! Well that certainly caused some hesitation, I felt that. I'm not sure she's keen on that idea. But she said "okay".

Off we go, keeping in mind it was really busy with quite a few floats and extra horses around. But off down the road we go until we've gone about 50 meters and guess what starts going passed us? A car and horse float! Oh, my heavens I could feel the tension in the Blind Chick. I think she stopped breathing! She may even have gone blue. But Adam kept quietly talking to her. I was fine, I had it all in hand, so we started walking again. Then another car went passed, but this time, we didn't stop walking and the Blind Chick was much more relaxed.

So, we had a lovely time going for a ride with Adam by our side. This gave the Blind Chick lots of confidence. I think this is the start of a very important building block, taking the time it takes.

The Blind Chick and I thought we'd call it a day, but Adam had other ideas! Off we go to the obstacle course. I'm pretty sure the Blind Chick was scared stiff. It's one thing riding around in a dressage arena where it's really flat but riding a horse with it all up and down and obstacles everyone, obstacles that move like the seesaw!

Oh, my heavens. Let me tell you what happened.

We walk into the obstacle course area with Adam giving the Blind Chick feedback about what is around her, what we're doing next, at all times. Next thing I'm lined up in front of the bridge and we just walk quietly up over it. Well, I must say, the Blind Chick was so excited, she swore a couple of times! She said things I can't repeat, but she was so excited. Then we turned to the left and went back, up and over the bridge again! We did it on both reins, up and over, no probs.

Then comes the dreaded seesaw. I know the Blind Chick was dreading this one because …. it moves! No dramas, I have this one totally nailed. Plus, we have the amazing Adam by our side, so nothing is going to go wrong. Voila - we walk straight up to the seesaw, up we go and down the other side. The Blind Chick was totally elated. She swore again! We should have had a swear jar.

Then we went through the pool noodles a couple of times and over the ground poles. It was really cool doing the ground polls as the Blind Chick could really feel me using my hind legs. This is a great exercise for my Shivers.

I have to tell you about big Ted. He is one of Adams obstacles. He stands about 4 foot tall and is a fluffy stuffed brown teddy bear. All he does is sit around all day watching us. He has a twinkle in his eye and a smile on his face. I'm sure I saw him wink when I walked past.

And I'm sure if his arms weren't so floppy and stitched on, he would've given me the thumbs up for a job well done.

Well, I must say after all this the Blind Chick was so excited. When she jumped off me in the indoor arena, the first thing she did was wrap her arms around Adam and give him the biggest hug. There were tears running down her cheeks, she was so so grateful and so very excited to be back riding me. The next thing she did was attacked me with lots of cuddles, pats and telling me how good I was. It was so nice to have my Blind Chick back on board.

There was a lot more chatter, lots more excitement, then Adam unsaddled me, and the lovely Tanya put me on the float. Off home we headed.

It's been a pretty cool trip. I'm learning so much. I'm learning about being responsible for my actions, learning about other people's personal space, and learning about becoming a team once again with the Blind Chick.

A massive thank you to the amazing Adam Sutton for his patience, his resilience in being able to cope with the Blind Chick and possibly me as well! I think we should be doing the desensitisation with the Blind Chick though, hee hee. She is really quite nervous, so maybe a few flags and things going pop might be good for her desensitisation! But yippee, we're on track because of the amazing Adam Sutton. We're so very grateful.

To his beautiful Manager Mel, thank you for everything you do behind-the-scenes. You make this all possible, you two run such an awesome business. We're so very grateful you even took the Blind Chick and I on. We really are a pretty scary combination!

Wow, wow, wow! We have lots of homework to work until we're back training with Adam again in January. Who knows what we'll be doing next time? I know one of the things the Blind Chick has on her bucket list is to ride me on the beach. Maybe not next time, maybe the time after that it will happen. So, watch this space! There are lots of exciting things on the horizon. The main one being the Blind Chick getting fully, confidently, back in the saddle.

We hope you are having a spectacular day. Keep safe and well. Lots of love and hugs, Johno and his Blind Chick.

Reflections

Feeling Thoughtful
14 December 2020

Diary entry by Johno

Well good morning. It's a beautiful morning here on the Macquarie River. Mind you it's a tad windy.

I had a wonderful weekend of doing absolutely …. nothing! Just vegging and relaxing in my paddock after our busy week training with the amazing Adam Sutton.

So much has come out of these five days training with Adam. The desensitisation stuff was awesome, so many things I thought might scare me, but don't anymore. Flags, balls, noisy plastic things. It's quite amazing what can be achieved if people take the time it takes to get used to things. Adam is certainly a master at this.

The Blind Chick also learnt lots of new skills. The best one being what to do when she's leading me. I know they spent a lot of time teaching me to guide the Blind Chick, but it's possibly not how things should be. The Blind Chick should be the one in front, she should be the lead mare. This has been a great learning experience for the Blind Chick and for me. I've learnt about being in my own space, about not taking over.

Plus, I've had my manners just a little bit realigned! I possibly had forgotten them on the odd occasion, not very often, but I'm more mindful of my manners now.

I'm also more mindful about being present in the moment, about listening to what Adam and the Blind Chick is asking of me. It's not good when I leave the room and I am not mentally present. So, the

Blind Chick has learnt different strategies for keeping my attention, keeping me at all times focused on her.

Then enter these amazing obstacles!!! Ha ha, I know what the Blind Chick thought of those. Especially when Adam said he would have her going over the bridge and the seesaw! That threw her a little bit, especially since she is still building up her confidence. Those obstacles were a really big ask. Again though, Adam took it One Step at A Time. At no stage did he over face me or the Blind Chick. This is so so very important when rebuilding confidence.

Yes. Adam had done all of the obstacles with me in hand first. He taught me about going over the bridge, lining up to go over the seesaw, through the water and through the pool noodles. Everything was done on the ground before it was transferred to the saddle.

I think this is a very important lesson in itself. You need to have the respect and knowledge on the ground before you go facing up to things you have never seen before from the saddle. The success of this process was clear when Adam rode me towards the obstacles. I didn't hesitate, straight over the bridge and seesaw, and around the rest of the obstacles I went. They were all a piece of cake. The time had already been spent getting me used to going over them and learning that they weren't scary. I'd already learnt I could do it. I'd already had my confidence built up.

I think it when I was being ridden over the obstacles it was a great confidence builder for the Blind Chick. She was able to hear me going over the bridge with such confidence, no hesitation, no jumping around, no jibbing. It was lots of fun and nice to be doing something so different. I really did enjoy my ride out with Adam each day. Out of the dressage arena.

I think the Blind Chick is going to look for someone to take me for a ride out at least once a week, maybe twice a week. That would be good for my headspace and doing something different. Getting out of the dressage arena.

As for the Blind Chick and her confidence building, Adam was conscious to keep everything just One Step at a Time, and manageable for the Blind Chick and for myself.

We started off in the indoor arena with Adam leading the Blind Chick around, then eventually as the Blind Chicks confidence built-up, he just walked at my shoulder and let the Blind Chick be responsible for turning and stopping. At all times he guided her on where she was and which way to turn. Having Adam by our sides helped both of us.

Then when we walked down the road, I think the Blind Chick was very nervous. We'd never done this before and there were lots of other people and horses. But again, Adam led me and talked quietly to the Blind Chick; making sure she was still breathing.

We coped with each thing One Step at a Time. Whether it was a float going past or horses being saddled up, we just kept focused and keep walking One Step at a Time. Ever so quietly we walked down the road. Yes, we were a little tense and yes, the walk back was more relaxed and swinging through the back. I started striding out.

This time to reflect is very important, I think. Because you can think of all the other things that were happening around you, that you cope with, and okay it doesn't sound like much that the Blind Chick was being lead down the road, but don't forget. This was totally unfamiliar surroundings. It was not something she's familiar with, that she could orientate with, like a dressage arena. Plus, she's on the journey of building her confidence back up. These are all big things. None of which happen overnight. There is no miracle cure for this. It will take the time it takes.

As for the obstacles! I think they may have been the highlight of the Blind Chicks ride. As well as her being back in the saddle of course. Watching her go over the bridge then onto the seesaw, Tanya mentioned how big the smile on her face was. I think she was smiling from ear to ear. That huge smile was happening from the time she first sat back in my saddle. Having her riding me is how it's meant to be, the Blind Chick and I.

So, we are building on everything Adam has taught us since we've been home. The respect, being mindful, being present when you are being worked, and being consistent. But by no step of the imagination has the Blind Chick got her confidence back. That will take time. It will also take time to help me with my anxiety. But wow we've just taken the most amazing step towards all of this happening.

This rebuilding process reminds us of our saying - One Step at a Time. Let's see where this takes us. Who knows where we might end up just doing it One Step at a Time.

We so hope everyone is having a lovely day. Keep safe and well. Loads of love and hugs, Johno and the Blind Chick.

Colic – Not Again!

Feeling Grateful
17 December 2020

Diary entry by Johno

Morning all from a steamy Macquarie River. Yes, it's quite muggy here today. We had a storm yesterday followed by some lovely rain.

Sorry I haven't written in my diary for a few days. Things have been a little bit hectic.

Monday started off brilliantly. The Blind Chickie babe and I did some wonderful work in the dressage arena practising homework that Adam Sutton had given us. I was attentive even when the trotters next door visited. I didn't take any notice of them until I went to leave, then I was a little inattentive. But I came back to the Blind Chick quite well, she was very pleased with me.

So then bring on Tuesday. Well Tuesday was not such a crash hot day. I had another one of my Shivers anxiety attacks followed by guess what? Yes, I got colic again!

The Blind Chick had been talking to me, trying to calm me down. I did calm down quite a bit, so she thought things were okay and she decided to go for a walk to the front gate. This generally takes her about 20 minutes. On her way back she was met by William, her nephew.

The wonderful Lee, the Blind Chicks mother-in-law, saw me distressed, pawing, and then spotted me going into my stable to do some more pawing and …. trying to lie down! Well Lee hot footed it down and got me out of the stable. Thank heavens or that could've been a disaster if I'd gone down in the stables and not being able to get up. Getting cast was a crisis averted. William came around the corner with the Blind Chick, halter in hand and they catch me. Then the Blind Chick walks me.

While she is catching me, she's putting a phone call in to our amazing vet Dr Don Crosby. She speaks to the beautiful Wendy. Oh my, thank heavens for the wonderful Wendy. Don was out to treat me within 15 minutes. We are so very very grateful.

Dr Don quickly assessed the situation, by then I'd stopped pawing, my breathing was a little more normal, but my heart rate was up a bit. Dr Don gave me something for the pain but as my gut was making some noises, he didn't need to give me paraffin or sedate me to do any procedures, which is rather wonderful. All the walking helped but thank heavens Lee spotted me. Colic is one of these insidious things that gets bad very quickly if not attended to.

As you can imagine I was feeling a bit sad and sorry for myself that afternoon. Then Wednesday rolls around and it was raining. So, no work for me. Then we had another of those horrible storms come through, more trees down. A particularly massive tree in my paddock snapped off so Matthew was out chain sawing it at about 8 pm last night, plus clearing limbs off electric fences etc. These horrible storm cells are quite destructive. Aaagh, we've had two in less than a week!

So today, I am having the day off again. There's no power at home because of a power pole getting replaced so the Blind Chickie babe is going to visit her lovely friend Jenelle.

All in all, it's been a very full week, and we're only halfway through it! The Blind Chick had a big talk to Dr Don my vet about trying some ulcer guard for eight days. We'll see if that makes a difference.

At this stage we are trying everything we can! We're also using Stress Paste, from Poseidon Equine. This product deserves amazing praise for the difference it's making to me. I haven't had a massive anxiety attack for quite a few weeks now, just the odd little one. I think with the new products I'm on it is definitely making a difference. We just need to be able to pick the triggers for when I have massive anxiety attacks, so we can avert getting colic as well.

Oh, my heavens. I apologise another one of these very long diary entries.

I hope you are having a wonderful day. Keep safe and well. Lots of love and hugs, Johno and the Blind Chick.

Chainsaws & Chaos

Feeling Frustrated
20 December 2020

Diary entry by Johno

It's an overcast morning here on the Macquarie, but what a beautiful, pleasant day. I think there might be rain coming through tomorrow.

Firstly, a massive apology to all of my wonderful Facebook friends who have sent me notes or responded to my diary entry. I've not been able to respond as there's still a lot of clean-up work after the really bad windstorm going on. Plus, Christmas has brought extra jobs to do.

I noticed the Blind Chick out with her white cane hunting for dressage arena bits and pieces yesterday. That's the third time this week she's had to put the arena back up! This week the winds have been terrible. She is still missing parts that are over the fence in the next-door neighbour's property. Matthew will have to go fetch them.

I think the Blind Chick is planning on giving me some time off over Christmas. Maybe two, maybe three weeks. Let's see how things play out.

Matthew will be in my paddock later today, doing some chainsaw work. Another tree came down, a beautiful big gumtree. It just totally snapped off about 8 foot above the ground. So, he'll be clearing that off the fence next door as well. Never a dull moment here that's for sure.

I hope everyone is having a wonderful weekend.

Keep safe, keep smiling. Lots of love and hugs, Johno.

The Lady With The Magic Hands

Feeling Grateful
22 December 2020

Diary entry from the Blind Chick

What an honour to be able to do a reference for an amazingly talented therapist.

I am referring to the amazing Tanya Hind who our Craniosacral Therapist. She has been looking after Johno and I for the past nearly 2 years.

Tanya and her magic hands have been the only therapist to make a difference to my wonderful Johno's Equine Shivers, keeping in mind Equine Shivers is a neurological degenerative condition. It is Tanya who is keeping this condition quietly under control.

It's worth looking into the diversity of what Tanya can treat in humans and in horses. You may ask – "Does it work?" Absolutely! The first time Tanya did a treatment on Johno there was a marked difference. His last two treatments have been absolutely amazing. Johno's Shivers had moved into his front legs and with Tanya's expert Craniosacral Therapy he is no longer showing symptoms in his front legs! How totally awesome is that! She has also alleviated a lot of his stress, which is so gratefully appreciated.

I have also had treatments with Tanya. I found them able to relieve bad pain and help with anxiety and a couple of other things I suffer from. She's been able to help in a big way.

So, I strongly suggest if you or your horse has back pain, headshaking, shoulder pain or just feel as if you both could do with a tune up, get in contact with Tanya. This amazing lady has magic hands! Her Craniosacral Therapy has the ability to work wonders.

My wonderful horse Johno and I are so grateful for Tanya's treatments and support. Give it ago, you will not be disappointed.
With love the Blind Chick.

The Amazing Angel

Feeling Grateful
23 December 2020

Diary entry by Johno

This is a really special message about an amazing angel who, out of the blue, contacted the Blind Chick to help me after my second bout of colic.

Grab a cuppa and I'll tell you all about it.

We have a lovely friend on Facebook called Jean. She is a great mate of the Blind Chick and I. She was most disturbed by me having colic, again, so she contacted her beautiful daughter Jade enquiring if Jade knew of anything to help me. Jade is a professional eventer who straight away contacted the amazing Linda.

Jade informed Linda about this Blind Chick and her horse that's frequently getting colic. Jade wondered whether Linda could do anything to help.

This is what happen next.

Out of the blue the day after my bad colic attack, the Blind Chick received a phone call, which she missed. There was a message for her to get in contact with a lady called Linda.

So that afternoon the Blind Chick rang Linda. Oh, my heavens! You know how the Blind Chick is always talking about Angels and Magic, well this beautiful lady came in the guise of the most amazing angel offering help! Linda wanted to make a difference. She and the Blind Chick talked for ages and ages.

The Blind Chick was absolutely hanging onto every word this amazing lady had to say. You'll never guess what the topic was mainly about… gut health! Until meeting Linda, the Blind Chick didn't know managing stress was so connected with gut health. Linda's approach was all about being holistic and how you treat your horse.

Linda spoke about this amazing paste you could give your horse called Stress Paste. Next thing in the mail the very next day came a box of Stress Paste! I was started on this amazing paste straight away. Plus, we received an absolutely massive tub of a great product called Digestive EQ.

Linda asked the Blind Chick to send her a list of what I had in my diet, so they could make sure I had a balanced diet with no grain in it, but lots of fibre. The Blind Chick was totally chuffed when Linda gave her the results of my diet analysis. The only change needed was to add a little salt, and everything was perfect.

But getting back to the Stress Paste! Oh, my heavens it made such a difference. It reduced my anxiety attacks nearly straight away. With the Blind Chick adding the Digestive EQ to my diet that has been the icing on the cake. Just think about it for a moment. If your tummy is not right, nothing else in your life is quite right. It's so important to get that gut health correct.

Then a few days later another product arrived, Digestive VM. This super charger is a Vitamin and Mineral mix in pellet form. I quite like them. So, wow things have changed a lot. I'm really starting to feel a little different … better. Okay I still have Shivers, but I honestly think in time this holistic approach with my gut health and these vitamins and miners will make a difference for me.

The other day the Blind Chick was pretty stressed because I'd had that massive anxiety attack, followed by colic, again! If she'd known about Stress Paste before then and been able to give me some as soon as I'd started showing colic symptoms, I'm sure it would have made the world of difference. As you can imagine the Blind Chick was pretty stressed out with walking me, calling the vet, and trying to stop me from rolling. But next time she'll be more on the ball and remember to give me the Stress Paste.

The Stress Paste has also been amazingly helpful for when we travel and on really scorcher day, like when we've been 40°C. It helps my body cope with these extreme conditions.

Watch this space! Things are on the improve. Okay we're not going to be able to stop the Shivers, but through having good gut health we might be able to make a difference to managing the Shivers. That would be totally awesome.

So, don't stop believing in Miracles, Magic, and Angels! They are out there. There are beautiful Angels out there watching over you all the time. Our Angel came in the guise of a beautiful lady called Linda, to whom we are so very very grateful.

The beautiful Linda owns the company Poseidon Equine and the Blind Chick, and I are both so very grateful for her phone call, for her caring and for believing that we can all make a difference in the world. You just need to reach out.

So dearest Linda, from the bottom of our hearts, we are so grateful.

We hope everybody is safe and well. I'm feeling magnificent. Loads of love and hugs, Johno and his Blind Chick.

The Angel Called Linda

Diary entry by Linda, Owner and Creator of Poseidon Equine products, our Angel.

You should never underestimate the power of a phone call and kindness.

Three phone calls is all it took to change the journey of one special horse and his rider.

The phone rang, it was a friend of mine, Jade Findlay. Jade and I met a few years ago, when she'd reached out for help with her beautiful horse, Heidi. Heidi was a high-level eventer whose performance had been affected by gastric ulcers. Jade was seeking help from our company, Poseidon Equine, to address Heidi's gut health issues. Two years on, Heidi's performance had long since improved and there were no more signs of gastric ulcers, but Jade was now asking for help with another horse …... Johnno.

Jade's mother, Jean, a long-term admirer of Johnno's, had asked Jade to contact me. She had seen first-hand the improvement in Heidi and was hoping Johnno could enjoy the same outcome.

It was an easy call to make. Once I knew of the generosity of spirit that Sue Ellen had shown through the years with all her fundraising and her obvious love for Johnno, I knew I had to help. I had experienced first-hand the power of improving my own gut when I suffered a life-threatening illness the year I turned 40.

In 2007, just after celebrating my 40th birthday I fell very ill, and my life changed forever. I didn't know it at the time, but a virus had impacted on my brain, which led to me being hospitalised and ultimately never returning to my job. I was bed ridden – unable to work or exercise – for a long period of time. I went from being incredibly independent to vulnerable and completely dependent on my family and friends for basic functions.

The loss of both my health and job were huge blows for me and I spent the first few years in denial of the severity of my illness. I suffered severe cognitive dysfunction and chronic fatigue for years. Despite this, I remained optimistic and was determined to restore my health. When life throws you challenges, you can either accept the prognosis or look for an alternative approach; I chose the latter.

I began learning about the role of gut bacteria and the importance of gut health on human health overall. Back then, I had no idea of just how important the microscopic community that resides in our gut, truly is.

Our gut does much more than just digest food – it houses microorganisms (ie. gut bacteria) who have a role to play in everything from supporting our immunity, to influencing our emotional health. When the gut is unhealthy, it can show up in many ways including: skin conditions, abnormal or sub-optimal behaviour and appetite, constipation or diarrhoea, the list goes on. There is also emerging research that links gut health to fertility and neurological conditions. We are learning more and more about the importance of supporting and managing helpful gut bacteria every day.

As I started looking after my own gut with supplements and changes in my diet, I was amazed at the huge improvements I experienced in my health and happiness overall. They were literally life changing. From then on, I spent every waking moment learning as much as I could about improving gut health; amazingly, despite my professional education in the area of health, I had never even heard of the gut microbiome. I wondered how this incredible opportunity for improving human health had been so ignored.

It didn't take long for me to realise that the gains I had achieved through improving my own gut health could also be applied to horses.

Horses have always been a big part of my life, and I have always tried to feed my horses as natural a diet as possible. But I had one particular horse that I was having ongoing problems with. He was losing weight; he had trouble getting the right canter lead; he would grind his teeth and tilt his head; and one day he even randomly bolted out from underneath my daughter, putting her in the hospital. Something was clearly amiss.

It occurred to me that the root of his problems could be an unhealthy gut. It seemed an obvious step to apply what I learned about human gut health to him and to other horses too.

So, I tried most of the horse gut health supplements commercially available, both prescribed and non-prescribed, but with little or limited results. In desperation I reached out to leading animal and equine nutritionists and spoke with them about what I'd learned from my own gut health experience; and my frustration in trying to improve the gut health of my horse. Together we pieced together what a good gut health supplement for horses should be comprised of, and after comprehensive testing, Poseidon Equine and our first product, Digestive EQ, was born. Truly a case of necessity being the mother of invention.

The day I rang Sue-Ellen, it was clear that she adored her horse but was losing hope of ever being able to enjoy him again. Ongoing anxiety-related behavioural problems plus a vet diagnosed medical condition meant that 17hh Johnno was now becoming impossible for

Sue-Ellen to enjoy. Our conversation that day was emotional for us both, as I tried to understand the complexities of meeting Johnno's needs, and also the emotional fragility of Sue Ellen as she poured her heart out to me and shared her despair at the current situation.

Two years along the path of learning about the power of restoring gut health, meant that whilst I could never promise we would improve Johnno's condition, I could at least use my knowledge of gut health and nutrition, call on the expertise and dietary advice of my team of incredible equine experts and supplement Johnno with some Poseidon Equine products, to see what would happen if we improved his gut health.

A thriving population of 'good' gut bacteria create helpful by-products for the horse including energy, and B vitamins such as thiamine, which assist in creating calmer behaviour and a gut free from pain and inflammation. A stressed gut has more unhelpful or 'bad' bacteria that cause pain and inflammation in the horse and can result in anxious behaviour. The level of anxiety in Johnno pointed to an unhealthy gut, which meant that restoring his gut health could result in a huge improvement in his behaviour. Well at least that's what we were hoping for...

Looking back on those early conversations, what stands out to me is that above all, Sue Ellen needed hope.

I asked her what her dream outcome would be, and she said, "to ride Johnno again".

When I shared with her the transformative power of gut health, it offered her a new approach to managing Johnno. The joy in her voice was unmistakeable.

I spent time understanding the journey that Johnno had been on and tried to establish what may have resulted in his poor gut health. The next step was reviewing his diet and making sure we were feeding to optimise his gut health. That meant using FeedXL – an incredible online software program – to balance his diet based on gut health principles. This meant switching him to a health-promoting fibre-based diet, with minimal starch and making sure that his vitamin and mineral intakes were sufficient and balanced. The addition of Digestive VM (Poseidon's Vitamin and Mineral supplement) to his new high-fibre diet ensured we ticked that first box.

We also spent time discussing what gut health is all about and the emerging research with poor gut health in humans and links to neurological disorders. I wanted to have Sue Ellen understand the *why* before we spent time discussing the *how*.

The slow addition of Digestive EQ (Poseidon's complete gut health supplement) into Johnno's diet was also an early step. EQ is designed to restore and then support gut health in horses. We added this to his feed very gradually, because when the gut bacterial populations are out of balance, any sudden changes can actually create further behavioural problems. We also used Poseidon's Stress Paste every day for the first two weeks, because this offered acute support to the gut, whilst the EQ was slowly being introduced. Management practices such as feeding lucerne hay whilst Johnno was being tacked up before a ride, and the need to manage the stress associated with travelling were also discussed.

Slowly, together with Sue Ellen's amazing veterinarian, trainer, farrier and body worker, Johnno began to improve. His anxiety reduced, which provided a good foundation for all the other work that Sue Ellen was undertaking. At times there would be small setbacks, but it was important to remember how far Johnno had come and the fact that changing gut bacteria to create a healthy, resilient gut, can take 12 months. We had really only just started the journey.

Sue Ellen's name would flash up on my phone and I'd hear squeals of delight as she told me that Johnno stood for the farrier for the first time …. Early steps … Early wins. The next call was to tell me that he didn't pace up and down the paddock anymore. Another small but important win. Then there were more phone calls, and more updates, until finally I heard the words I'd been waiting to hear.

"I rode Johnno today!"

Her gratitude was overflowing and so too was the joy in her voice. Hope had returned in abundance. My heart was full.

www.poseidon-equine.com

Chrissy Pressy

Feeling Excited
24 December 2020

Diary entry by Johno

Well, I am loving these Christmas holidays and this cooler weather. It's been superb at night, perfect for sleeping, and the days aren't too hot.

Oh, my heavens you will not believe what happened yesterday! Matthew and the Blind Chick went shopping for my Christmas present. They brought it home in the back of the ute. Guess what I got?

You'd never have guessed. My present is …. things called ground poles. Yes, poles that I stride over for exercise. I'm not sure yet if this is a cool present, or not. It sounds like serious work to me. They're just pine logs and need to be painted, so here goes.

I think the ground poles have had a very good covering of paint. Why? Because, when the Blind Chick came to feed me yesterday afternoon, she looked a little like a zebra or maybe a leopard! There were stripes and spots all over her boots. Her legs even had spots and there was even the odd spot on her face! So, I'm hoping she got some of the paint on the logs. She looked like a leopard cross zebra. Hilarious.

I know I shouldn't be ungrateful; she was doing her very best.

So, I guess when my holiday is over, I'll be out doing ground polls. The wonderful Adam Sutton introduced them to me when we were down training with him. I think the Blind Chick is also going to ask Matthew if he could possibly build me a bridge. That'd be just a pallet with a sheet of rubber on top. I guess it'd have to be extra thick rubber though. I weigh 800 kg!

Oh, the other thing I want to share with you is with these big winds we've been having, the dressage arena has been put up three times in the past week! The last time the Blind Chick put it up herself, so she ran the string lines and everything but one of the arena pieces is sticking out past the end by about 4 feet! I think something went wrong with her string line. That's okay though, we can work in a weird rectangle! Ha ha.

It's so exciting it's Christmas Eve here in Australia. I wonder what Santa's going to bring me. I might leave some pellets out for the reindeers and a bit of molasses, what do you think?

I know Matthew and the Blind Chick are off to Matthew's mum and dads for dinner tonight. Then they're off to Mudgee to have Christmas breakfast with his sister and family, then it's off to her brothers' place for lunch. It sounds like they're going to be doing lots of celebrating. How lovely to be spending it with family.

I'll let you know how I go on the Santa front tomorrow. Hopefully he doesn't forget me. I have been trying to be very good you know.

I hope everyone has a wonderful day. Don't forget to let somebody know you love them and that you care. Keep safe and well. Loads of love and hugs, Johno.

No Show

Feeling Thankful
25 December 2020

Diary entry by Johno and the Blind Chick

We hope everyone is having a wonderful day. We wish you all a very Merry Christmas and may 2021 bring all of our wonderful Facebook friends health and happiness.

Well, I waited for the Santa Claus guy to arrive with his reindeers. But they were a no-show! But a really nice fellow on a blue tractor turned up with a big load of hay to go in my stable. I think we'll call him Santa Matt.

The Blind Chick and Matt had a lovely day with the Blind Chick's family in Mudgee.

I also got lots of extra carrots in my breakfast for Christmas Day. I'm looking forward to tomorrow as I might be going with the Blind Chick to try out my new ground poles that she painted. Her boots are still sporting paint on them. Luckily, she had a shower and washed the paint spots and stripes of herself.

We hope everyone has a wonderful Christmas day. Loads of love and hugs and thank you for your friendship and support, Johno and the Blind Chick.

Reflections

Feeling Grateful
29 December 2020

Diary entry by Johno and the Blind Chick

Well, another amazing year has nearly passed us by! It has been full of highs and lows. From training with the amazing José Mendez down in the Southern Highlands to oopsy the Blind Chickie babe taking an untimely tumble off me, busting her knee and dinting her confidence.

To the visit down to Scone and meeting the amazing Dr Sarah Gough, her helping us manage my Equine Shivers. The Blind Chick has been trying to manage it all the way along, since Matthew bought me. But now we have a plan of attack with the wonderful Sarah and our amazing vet Don Crosby here in Dubbo.

Plus, our training with the amazing Adam Sutton, helping desensitise me and helping the Blind Chick regain her confidence. This has been a great Work-in-Progress. It's definitely making a difference and the Blind Chick and I are both enjoying doing the exercises Adam has given us on the ground. While the Blind Chickie babe is not fully back in the saddle yet, we have lots to practise at home and she has ridden with Adam on a trail ride and done obstacles in the arena. Which she was absolutely chuffed about.

I have also had three pretty bad bouts of Colic! They were scary things for man and beast, understandably the Blind Chick was quite distressed. I was in so much pain, there was lots of walking me, and thank heavens for our wonderful Dubbo vet Dr Don Crosby, who between he and his fantastic staff, were here when we really needed them. We're so very grateful.

Then enter into our lives came an amazing angel, beautiful Linda. Linda helped readjust my diet and put us on a new program to look after my gut health. Wow! What an impact this is having on my life. I am feeling so much better, so much so that for the past three weeks, fingers, toes and hooves crossed, I've had NO stress attacks! Yes, how totally amazing is that. Okay, I still have Shivers and we're managing that, but the stress was making the Shivers so much worse.

Linda owns Poseidon Equine. Her help is about nothing else other than me having a good quality of life, doing the best for me and optimising everything we can. We are so very grateful to Linda and her amazing products: Digestive EQ and Digestive VM. Plus, her seriously amazing product - Stress Paste. This has been a break-through product for us. It has gotten me through some pretty tough times, like travelling and days with 45°C heat. It is totally amazing.

So, as you can see it has been a pretty full-on amazing year. We even had a mini cyclone go through and devastate the house yard and the horse yards. We are so very lucky no horse or human got hurt.

We would also like to thank our amazing Facebook friends who have been there through thick and thin, giving us love and support and always encouragement. We are so grateful.

I have also had a few people contact me for signed copies of our first Johno and the Blind Chick book, which has been a real buzz, happy to do it.

So, all going well next year there will be another book out - Johno and the Blind Chick Mark II. Very original don't you think?

A special thank you to the beautiful lady Tanya Hind with her magic hands and treatments. Her Craniosacral work on me, oh my heavens, it gives me such relief and makes such a difference. I went from having the Shivers in four of my limbs, to now it is just affecting my hind legs. It's so nice not having it so bad in my front legs as well.

To the amazing girls who drive us to lessons and who come out and help the Blind Chick and I five days a week, we are so grateful for their support. None of this would happen without their help and support.

As you can see, to keep this well-oiled machine going there are so many people that make it possible.

I'm sure there will be another diary entry before New Year, but this is just a rundown to New Year's Day.

Have a wonderful day. Stay safe and well. Lots of hugs and love, Johno and the Blind Chick.

Be Brave, Take Risks

Feeling Optimistic
30 December 2020

Diary entry by Johno and the Blind Chick

Hey there wonderful friends. We came across this quote today. What do you think of this as a New Year's resolution?

Quote of the Day
"Be Brave and Take Risks: You need to have faith in yourself.
Be brave and take risks.
You don't have to have it all figured out to move forward."
Roy T. Bennett

We hope everyone has had a spectacular day. We are sending you loads of love and hugs, Johno and the Blind Chick.

14
January

No Limits

😐 Feeling Excited
1 January 2021

Diary entry by Johno and the Blind Chick

We're wishing all of our wonderful Facebook friends a very happy New Year. May 2021 bring you health and happiness.

Onwards with a New Year, a new chapter.

Quote of the Day
"Do not let the memories of your past,
limit the potential of your future.
There are no limits to what you can achieve
on your journey through life, except in your mind."
Roy T. Bennett

We are so looking forward to what this new year holds in store for us. We're looking forward to an amazing journey with our beautiful Facebook friends. Thank you for all of your love and support over the past year.

Keep safe, celebrate, loads of love and hugs, Johno and the Blind Chick.

Psycho Trotters

🤍 Feeling Loved
5 January 2021

Diary entry by Johno

Happy New Year everyone. It's a sunny Sunday here in Dubbo. A nice change to the showers of rain and thunderstorms we had as the introduction to the New Year.

Aaagh, the dressage arena has been full of water, hence no work. But all good things come to an end and it's sunny now. With the dressage arena having dried out the Blind Chick worked me today.

Firstly, she gave me a carrot, then put my lunging cavesson on, then gave me a pat and a scratch for a while. Then her lovely husband Matthew turned up.

We quietly wandered out to the dressage arena and Matthew took me into the round yard. Then guess what happened? Matt worked me! Keep in mind I'm quite unfit and carrying a little extra Christmas cheer around my belly. So, we just did 10 minutes each side …. walk, trot and a little canter. That was it.

I had one moment when my friends the trotters came and visited, they stood and watched for a while, admiring my work, then took off with great haste, which upset me just a little. So, I had this wee moment of being a bit of a turkey, but it was more exuberance, feeling very healthy and happy to be back in work. It wasn't a fruit loop moment. Plus, it was over quite quickly. It was only because the trotters left, so Matt cut me some slack. He had me to do a few extra canter circles to get my attention back.

So, it looks like my Christmas holidays are over! It has been nice not working, but I must say, I did enjoy being in the arena today.

I've got a secret to share with you. It happened last week. As you know the Blind Chick isn't supposed to work me by herself. But she did! Don't tell anybody. She came down, caught me, took me to the dressage arena with her trusty white cane and work me for about 25 minutes. I was good, I tried very hard to be on my best behaviour. I just one little moment of whinnying to the trotters next door, but that was it. But don't tell anyone or the Blind Chick will get into trouble.

Let's see where this next year takes us, and what we can achieve. I'm looking forward to seeing what happens tomorrow. Will it be Matthew that works me? Or the Blind Chick? Who knows? It was a real family event today though.

So happy New Year everyone. Loads of love and hugs, Johno.

Thank You Stress Paste

🙂 Feeling Excited
6 January 2021

Diary entry by Johno and the Blind Chick

Oh, my heavens what a day! Our amazing Farrier Troy Lomax came today to shoe me, remembering I have this horrible degenerative neurological condition called Shivers which generally makes it very hard for Troy to shoe me.

The first time Troy shod me, it took about two hours and it was not pleasant for man or beast. I found it so hard to keep my legs up. I didn't know what my legs were doing. it was rather distressing.

The next time Troy shod me, things were a lot better. The wonderful Linda from Poseidon Equine had sent the Blind Chick some Stress Paste, which she gave me, so my shoeing was much easier for Troy.

But you will never believe what happened today I have been on the amazing Digestive EQ and the Digestive VM now for about six weeks there have been massive changes and shoeing today was a breeze the Blind Chick came and gave me a Stress Paste about an hour before Troy arrived and voila, I was a saint and shoeing was so good and Troy was very impressed.

Okay the Stress Paste does not take away the Shivers but it stops the symptoms of my anxiety and stress which is just so cool. It makes me so much easier to shoe and to pick up my hind legs in particular, it was just so very, very cool.

So very grateful for Troy's amazing patience shoeing me and his wonderful apprentice Henry, who also has this amazing patience thing happening.

But the most amazing thank you to the beautiful Linda who owns Poseidon Equine the Digestive EQ and the Digestive VM and the Stress Paste just makes things work for me thank you from the bottom of my heart we just have no idea how very important having good gut health is.

Things are going really well. I am not having my anxiety attacks, so the next thing is getting things right for the Blind Chick to get her back in the saddle. Watch this spot …. so very excited.

Thank you to Matthew for holding me for Troy while I was being shod, it's been quite a busy day.

Just a thought maybe we should get the Blind Chick some Stress Paste now it is just a thought might help with her confidence, hee hee.

Hope everybody is having a wonderful day loads of love and hugs Johno and the Blind Chick.

Ouch

Feeling Grateful
13 January 2021

Diary entry by Johno

We hope everyone's New Year is off to a great start

Mine started off totally awesome but as they say all good things come to an end. I am now back in work, but that's okay. I'm not working too hard, but I definitely need to get some of this Christmas pudding from around my tummy off.

As I mentioned in my last diary entry, the amazing Troy Lomax came and put new shoes on me the other day. Each time Troy has come to shoe me, it's got easier because of my dietary change. Thank you so much Poseidon Equine and the amazing Stress Paste. They all contribute to my calm mind these days.

So, I'm back to work and our first day was a real family affair. Matthew worked me and the Blind Chick timed everything we did. All went really well. Again, on Monday Matthew worked me. Okay I had one wee moment of distraction, but it wasn't related to my Shivers. It was because the trotters came to visit and then decided to leave in a great hurry. I thought I should've been going with them, so I had a bit of a run around, but then I settled back into work very quickly.

On Tuesday we did something we don't normally share with everyone. The Blind Chickie babe came and got me and took me out to work me. I was so good and everything was going so well until .... yes, you guessed it. The trotters! They came to the fence then ran off in a screaming mess, absolutely flat out, plus some cars came and went next door. I thought Oopsy, I should be going with them. So, I had a wee run around being a bit of a ninkompoop until the Blind Chick got me back under control.

Oopsy, when I had my little run around, I was a little strong, I gave the Blind Chick rope burn on her hand. Oops, not so good. Thankfully her wonderful mother-in-law Lee dressed her hand so it's all good now. But I must say these trotters do cause a lot of trouble. Yes, I have to learn to ignore them. I'm working on that one.

Now I have to tell you about my anxiety moments, the ones I was having in the paddock due to my trotter friends leaving me. Well touch wood, fingers crossed, hooves crossed, I've not had any anxiety attack in the last six weeks. How cool is that! I know the Blind Chick is so excited and so very proud.

This is because of our wonderful friend Linda from Poseidon Equine. She got the Blind Chick to change my diet to a very basic one, with absolutely no extruded food and absolutely no grain. Then we add to this the amazing Poseidon Equine's Digestive EQ and the Digestive VM. On stressful days, like floating me for lessons or on those very hot summer days, the Blind Chick always gives me some Stress Paste as well.

I think it is totally amazing how quickly things have changed since we've been looking after my gut health. I no longer play with my feed each day; I usually have it all eaten within the hour. Then I go and eat my lovely home grown lucerne hay.

I am also very grateful to our amazing Craniosacral Therapist Tanya Hind. I can't tell you the relief Tanya gives me from my Equine Shivers, and the improvement that's happening between the change in diet. Tanya's amazing magical hands this has all been quite life changing for me in the last three months.

So, I think we need to get the Blind Chick to look at her gut health! This might help with her stress and anxiety. It has made the world a difference to me.

It's exciting today as the amazing Tanya is coming to do a treatment on me. I love my treatments, can't wait.

Another exciting thing about next week is we're going down for more training with Adam Sutton. Doing more desensitisation work, obstacles and getting the Blind Chick back in the saddle. Bring it on.

Oh, my heavens! I wish you had been here to witness what I saw happened yesterday evening.

Matthew and the Blind Chick were wandering across the front yard, then they went across to the wheat paddock. They were heading for the two tractors that had been used earlier in the day to collect wood from the bad storms. Matt had chainsawed it up and put it on the back of the trailer with the front-end loader. What are those two up to?

Next thing I see, the Blind Chick is in the driver's seat in one of the tractors! She has her phone up to her ear. What's going on?

Matthew is on the other tractor, giving her directions to drive one of the tractors back home. How cool is this, and what amazing trust Matthew must have in his Blind Chick. Next thing the Blind Chick is driving the tractor into the shed with Matthew sitting beside her giving her directions. This must be such an amazing experience for the Blind Chick and having a husband that has so much faith in her, and gives her opportunities to experience all different things. How super cool.

Well on that note I would like to wish you all a wonderful day.

Keep safe and well. Loads of love and hugs, Johno.

Not A Massage

😎 Feeling Relaxed
14 January 2021

Tanya doing her magic

Diary entry from a very relaxed Johno

Sorry this diary entry is a bit later than usual, but I've been just so relaxed after my Craniosacral session this morning.

I must also clear something up. Craniosacral Therapy is not a massage, it's not what some of you may be thinking. There is no rubbing of muscles like a body worker would do, oh heavens no. You can't compare a Craniosacral treatment under the gifted hands of Tanya to a massage.

You see, when I have a treatment, our energies combine. When I let Tanya into my energy field, she can follow the rhythms in my body tissues to find the ones that are restricted or not moving/gliding correctly and help me to release the tissue in the most natural way that the body can work with right there and then.

It also penetrates much, much deeper into the layers of the body tissues, sometimes I can feel her in the fluid that is around my brain! When this happens, let me tell you, magical things happen within my body, and my body rebalances itself.

As you know I've been receiving treatments from Tanya for over twelve months now, she can read me like a book. I only have to think where I would like her to place her hands, and she's on it in a flash. I think you could say we have quite a spiritual connection at times, especially when she is releasing the anxiety that has built up in my body tissues.

The Blind Chickie says she is very special, and her gift of healing is very unique compared to others. I whole heartedly agree. Since my last treatment my Shivers has improved out of sight. So much so that the Blind Chickie can hear that it is only minimally affecting one of my hind legs.

My stress levels have also decreased. I don't get as anxious about my legs not moving when I want them too.

Today my session was quite unique. Once I entered into the meditative state there was a very calm and peaceful atmosphere around us all, even the Blind Chickie could feel it. This calm peaceful relaxation stayed after the session today as well. This session was amazing. I had so many stretches after particular muscles and joints where released. I almost stretched my neck and head up to the top of the breeze way roof. I feel a million dollars.

Oh yeah something exciting is coming soon. The girls are going to video snippets of my treatments so you can see what happens when under Tanya's spell.

So, stay tuned.

Beautiful Tanya I'm so very grateful for the healing and magic you bring to my life and making living with Shivers a little easier. In-fact it's probably a lot easier. I'm so incredibly grateful.

I hope everyone is having a spectacular day. I'm truly just so very relaxed and grateful.

Keep safe and well. Loads of love and hugs, Johno.

A Lot To Smile About

Feeling Happy
19 January 2021

Diary entry by Johno

Oopsy! Many apologies for being slack on doing a diary entry. It's been pretty special here. We have been on a family trip to the Hunter Valley - wine and horse country, Matthew the Blind Chick and me. We've come down for me and the Blind Chick to train with the amazing Adam Sutton.

So, before I get on the float, I was given my life changing Stress Paste from Poseidon Equine. This Stress Paste helps me cope with the anxiety and the stress of travel. We arrived down to Lochinvar after about five-hours, which went quite quickly.

I was lucky enough to be put back in my usual paddock where there is lots of green feed. Head down, bum up eating. Bring it on.

Matthew and the Blind Chick came back about five-ish to feed me. By then I was surrounded by three horses, but thanks to my Stress Paste and that I'd had my Digestive EQ that morning, I wasn't really stressing out. But things went a little pear-shaped after that. I didn't eat my dinner that night or my breakfast the next morning, Oopsy! This has caused a few dramas. My anxiety is back up, I can't concentrate and my obsessing about things and anxiety is totally making me feel terrible.

But I hear on the grapevine that the Blind Chick has been speaking with the amazing Linda. I'm to have my Digestive EQ over my tongue tomorrow, plus another Stress Paste. The Stress Paste always makes the world of difference, things will be on the improve very quickly.

Today was totally amazing, training with Adam Sutton. We did more desensitisation; it was no drama at all because I'd done it before. It was all a piece of cake, so chilled, easy pesi. Bring it on.

Then my wonderful friend Adam saddled me up and did a little desensitisation work in the arena. Do you believe it the beautiful Mel was chasing me with bags! I then followed her with the bags, she lay them on the ground, and I walked over them. Wow this gig is pretty cool. I love playing games.

Adam also congratulated the Blind Chick on the homework she'd been doing with me. I think she was pretty pleased that Adam had noticed.

Then Adam took me out and, keeping in mind it was pretty blowy and overcast and most horses are bit spooky in this fresh weather, but we went for a walk down the road. I was so good Adam felt confident we could step up to trotting. I trotted back to the Blind Chick then Adam took me for another trot down the road. It was definitely a big improvement on our last visit early December. I don't mind this riding outside an arena gig, it's pretty okay.

Adam just gives me so much confidence. Taking me out of my comfort zone has been a brilliant thing. The plan for tomorrow is the Blind Chick is going to ride me, doing more desensitisation stuff. So, watch this spot.

The Blind Chick and I love training with Adam. His confidence building methods are engaging and challenging. They really work. Plus, he makes the Blind Chick smile a lot. I know she is extremely excited to be getting back in the saddle.

I think an important thing to realise amongst all of this confidence building is …… nothing happens without a Team. We are so grateful to the amazing Linda who reached out to us nearly eight weeks ago and who, because of her unreal products at Poseidon Equine, has made the world a difference to my life. My anxiety is now virtually non-existent when I'm in the paddock. We just have to work on my manners when working with the Blind Chick in the dressage arena, but this will come in time, it's early times.

Adam's work on my anxiety and my hypersensitivity is making the world a difference to me coping with different situations. This will follow on and help the Blind Chick. Mind you I think Adam probably should flap a few flags around the Blind Chick and throw a few balls at her and desensitise her! She's pretty jumpy sometimes. But then again, she is totally blind and not used to different noises. Don't we make a grand pair.

I'm so incredibly grateful to the Blind Chick's lovely husband who has taken the time to have this family trip away. The only one missing is our pussycat, Thunder Paws is at home. It would've been fun bringing him along, well …. no maybe not!

I'll give you another update tomorrow.

I hope everyone is safe and well. Loads of love and hugs, Johno.

Highs And Lows

Feeling Grateful
20 January 2021

Diary entry by Johno

Oh, my heavens, what a day. It's been full of highs and lows.

Okay the anxiety and stress has returned, but keep in mind I have a degenerative neurological condition called Shivers. I don't adapt to change very well, but we're on Day 3 of my stay and things are starting to change. Also keep in mind I haven't eaten all my amazing products from Poseidon Equine in the past three days! Because I'm not eating all my meals. But I have been having my Stress Paste which has helped amazingly.

So, let's get to the exciting stuff. The amazingly talented Adam took me to the front gate and back in a walk, in a trot and …. a canter, all on a long rein. Okay I was little bit like a giraffe looking left, looking right. The horses either side were cantering around, calling out. So, what do I? I stayed with Adam, I listened, and I just cantered ahead. It was so cool. I cantered on past Matthew and the Blind Chick and then came back, and we did it again. The next time I was even better. I took no notice of the other horses, I just focused on Adam and what he was asking me to do.

Adam had previously done desensitising work with me in the indoor arena. There had been three people running at me with flags on poles, bells and whistles, all sorts of stuff. And guess what? I didn't care, I kept focused on what Adam wanted to me to do. So, it's onwards and upwards. This training is rocking out, I'm loving the experience and I not missing a beat.

But I must reflect on the last few days; I haven't eaten any of my hard feed with my amazing Poseidon products in it, but I have been supported by the Stress Paste, which made such a difference. I'm so very grateful to Linda and her amazing team. Thank you, this was my saving grace.

Then my amazing Dr Sarah came from Scone Equine to be part of the filming. It was so cool to catch up with her. We're so grateful for Dr Sarah's support and knowledge, we are moving forward because of this.

Then, guess what? The Blind Chick was on board! We started off in the walk and okay, I was a bit lazy. The Blind Chick was riding me in our usual dummy spurs, but she had to work hard to keep me moving forward with a lovely soft contact. Then we went into the trot. It felt so nice to have the Blind Chick back on board.

I know the Blind Chick was extra proud when she was in the saddle with Dr Sarah watching us. Okay a walk probably wasn't the best we could do, and I was a bit lazy, but we were doing it, and the Blind Chick was on board. Her smile didn't move off her face. I am so immensely proud of my Blind Chick. Go girl, you rock.

A massive thank you to Adam Sutton for believing in the Blind Chick and I; for the gorgeous Dr Sarah driving all the way from Scone to be part of what we were doing, and for enlightening us about my degenerative condition - Equine Shivers. I'm so very grateful for the amazing team we have behind us.

So, watch this space! Adam has so many more things for us to experience. He'll continue to build up the Blind Chick's confidence. Thank you to everyone for believing in us and helping us make our dreams come true.

I hope everyone is having an amazing day. Today was the most spectacular day I've had in a very long time. The Blind Chick is back on board - that totally rocks!

So loads of love and hugs to everyone, take care, Johno.

Woohoo Blind Chickie babe is back on board, bring it on!

Equine Shivers & Desensitisation

Feeling Excited
23 January 2021

Diary entry by Johno and the Blind Chick

In so many ways this journey has many facets. Like learning to live with a degenerative neurological condition called Equine Shivers! We are managing it to the best of our ability, the Blind Chick is not leaving a stone unturned in her quest to give me the best quality of life possible.

The desensitisation that Adam has been doing with me has been invaluable. I'm now not so hypersensitive to sound or things I see that might be a bit different, unusual. This has taken heaps and heaps of work. It's taken consistency, time, dedication, and me taking the time to feel safe with my person I'm with. Whether they be Adam or the Blind Chick.

Adam spent quite a lot of time getting the Blind Chick to stand behind him and put her left hand on his left hand, and her right hand on his right hand. It may have looked a little awkward and a bit of a back to front dance move, but it allowed the Blind Chick to feel what Adam was doing with the reins, and with getting my hindquarters to disengage, and how much pressure he was using. It was really cool and quite out of the box. What an amazing trainer, so confident and competent. His confidence definitely rubbed off on the Blind Chick.

Adam eventually had the Blind Chick doing all the exercises by herself. The confidence she was building was so cool, we were both feeling pretty terrific. Then we went out to the outside arena. It was a lovely sunny day and guess what? The Blind Chickie babe was back in the saddle again. Bring it on! This is what it's all about.

The Blind Chick didn't ride in Adams lovely stock saddle though, I had my dressage saddle on with my beautiful saddle cloth and my own bridle. Again, the Blind Chickie babe was in her element, very confident in the arena. Adam's goal was to work in the arena then go down the road. He even got the beautiful Mel to bring a pushbike in, so he could ride down the road beside the Blind Chick and me. I don't know whether the Blind Chick was keen about that idea, but you'll never guess what happened.

It was pretty cool; the Blind Chick was following Adam's voice around the arena. Then he stood in the middle and she worked around him on a circle. We did changes of rein in the walk and in the trot. I think the scariest bit for the Blind Chick might be going into the canter, as this is where she had her not so elegant dismount when I was quite naughty, for want of a better word. But her friend said I did two massive, big leaps in the air. The Blind Chick said it felt more like a buck. Either way she hit the ground and busted her knee! Definitely not a good look.

So, the Blind Chick did lots of leg yields, walk pirouettes, half pass, shoulder-ins and travers. It was all so much fun, and all done with 'Ask - Don't Tell'. All very quietly done in the walk first, then a couple of leg yields in the trot. It was quite amazing how easy it was. This time it was a much easier ride for the Blind Chick and her dummy spurs. I was definitely a little more responsive.

It was also very cool following Adam around on the pushbike in the arena, getting ready for our ride down the road the next day. We did this very confidently in the walk and trot.

The Blind Chickie babe had a couple of small canters which I didn't put much energy into. It was a very lazy canter, but again it comes to One Step at a Time! The canter will come, we'll pull it all together.

I think now is a good time to mention about gut health. Oh, my heavens! Me not eating and being stressed each day hasn't been good. But keep in mind I was surrounded by horses. This stress is just a side-effect of the Equine Shivers. So, using the Blind Chicks language, I was off my chops and nothing settled me! Until the Stress Paste, it made the world of difference, especially before I was being worked. Thank you so much Linda and your amazing Poseidon products. Once I started eating it was a total game changer because I was getting the main ingredient into me …. the Digestive EQ.

This trip has been totally so cool, especially because it's been a family trip. The Blind Chicks wonderful husband has been part of every aspect. He takes her down to feed me, he helps Adam with the desensitisation and is learning so much. Family holidays totally rock.

Watch this spot! I know Adam has a massive challenge for the Blind Chick tomorrow. Definitely it will take her out of her comfort zone.

I hope everyone is safe and well and you are having a lovely day. We're sending you loads of love and hugs, Johno and the Blind Chick.

Challenges

 Feeling Grateful
25 January 2021

Going down!

Diary entry by Johno

Again, apologies for the late diary entry but things have been hectic. Grab a cuppa and I'll tell you about it.

Well Thursday brings an absolutely spectacular morning. We're all up early so Sean can film the balloons, that is the hot air balloons, above my paddock here in the Hunter Valley. I will still a little stressed, but when Sean put his drone up, I took absolutely no notice at all. Isn't it interesting what upsets me and what the triggers are!

I was given my Stress Paste, thank heavens for it, it's held me together for the past three days, but I'm slowly settling down. I think the Blind Chick is really appreciating this as she gets stressed when I get upset.

Today is a little bit more desensitisation work with the awesome Adam Sutton, then I'm pretty sure the Blind Chick is having another ride.

I get taken up to the indoor arena where I'm totally worked over by the beautiful Mel, Brooke and the Blind Chick. They hit me like a race car pit crew; brushing, cleaning, shining. I think I'll look extra handsome after my work over. I have to look my best for Sean and his camera, and for the Blind Chick of course.

I come out of the indoor arena sparkling like a new pin, all saddled up to go to the outdoor arena. It truly is a beautiful day for the Blind Chick to be riding, it's very sunny so she'll be able to use the sun to orientate herself in the arena.

So, Adam had the first ride, then the Blind Chickie babe was on again. We did a bit more work with Adam riding the pushbike around the arena and me following Adam, such fun. I took to this like a duck to water. Matthew was talking about him going for a ride down the road on the pushbike at home with the Blind Chick. I'm not sure the Blind Chick is convinced that is a great idea. Who knows, time will tell.

The Blind Chickie babe had a wonderful ride, I was much more forward as the Blind Chick had her dummy spurs on. I really am a little bit lazy without a little bit of encouragement. We did lots of lateral work, lots of transitions and we just took the time it takes. There was no rushing, but there was lots of fun and lots of laughter. Always lots of laughter around Adam.

And I must say it is really interesting when everyone is laughing and having fun, the stress level is way down, and much more is achieved.

But I know there is something at foot! I heard the Blind Chick talking to Sean, the film Producer, about something she was going to challenge Adam to do. But Sean said "No, no, leave it till tomorrow." So, roll on Friday, let's see what the Blind Chick is going to challenge Adam to do.

Well, another beautiful morning here in the Hunter. It's a very busy day ahead, we're going to be doing obstacle work and then going for a ride down the road. I still think the Blind Chick is a little apprehensive about the ride down the road, but I'm sure, with Adam's guidance she'll be just fine. I'll look after her of course.

I was so cool; the obstacles were awesome. We did the seesaw, we did the bridge, we walked over balls, we walked over plastic on the ground and over wee jumps. I met big Ted, he winked at me, he told me he was embarrassed, and I asked him why. He said because he had no clothes on!

The Blind Chick and I absolutely blitzed the obstacle course, it was so cool. Then we were getting ready to go out for a walk down the road, still apprehension from the Blind Chick. Next thing the Blind Chick is calling out for Adam. She said "I have a challenge for you! You've been challenging Johno and I for the past five days, so my challenge to you is for you to do the obstacle course blindfolded."

Wow, it was interesting. You can imagine Adam's response, he wasn't going to back away from a challenge from the Blind Chick. But he was a little apprehensive. How the heck was he going to do this? He'd never been blindfolded before. The Blind Chicks idea was that Matthew her wonderful husband would be Adam's guide, guiding him around the obstacle course. I think it truly was an amazing eye-opening experience for Adam because he couldn't cheat and open his eyes, have a peek. He really was riding blind.

So, they shook hands, Adam was given the eyepatch, then he mounted me. Matthew did a couple of laps around the arena so Adam got the feel of riding with absolutely no eyesight. Then it was on for young and old.

Being able to direct me with my new precision when you can't see, is just so important. Left isn't always a big left turn. It could be just a little leg yield. When Adam is guiding the Blind Chick, the movements are really little, because she rides like that all the time. So, this was a little hard for Adam, getting the set up to each of the obstacles.

Yes, I can do all the obstacles, they're easy, but when your rider is feeling a little disorientated it's really important to approach all the obstacles straight on, not at an angle. You must keep the body straight and ride straight forward. Sometimes it's really difficult to do this when you can't see! But Adam had a go at all the obstacles, and he ticked all the boxes. Okay he had to have a go more than once at quite a few of them, but it was a great learning experience for him. This gig is not easy when you can't see.

I know the Blind Chick was so, so proud of Adam for having a go at being blindfolded. You need to be brave to step outside the box like that and have a lot of confidence in your horse. I know Adam believes in me, I also had his back, but he had to learn to direct me and guide me.

And then came the challenge Adam had put out to the Blind Chick, to go for a ride down the road. Not just a walk, but a trot as well. So, they rode down the road, then out onto the main road and down the road on the grass. I could definitely feel the Blind Chick being a little more tense once we went out the gateway and down the road. The fact that the garbage truck had just been through made her worried it was going to come back. Matthew stayed on the road to make sure that nothing got to close to us.

And then the big test!

I went back in the gate, riding back down the road, back to the indoor arena. Then, without any warning or time for the Blind Chick to prepare Adam said …. "On the count of three we will trot. 1, 2, 3." And guess what? We were trotting! Adam was jogging beside us, what a great coach, he's a legend. We did this often going back down the road. I don't think the smile moved off the Blind Chicks face. She would love to be able to do this with me each day. It is so good for my mind to be out of the dressage arena.

So, this has been the training session where so many goals have been achieved and boxes ticked. The Blind Chicks anxiety level is not as high and while I know she has such faith in Adam, she is also starting to believe in me once again. Okay it'll take us a little while to get the canter right, but we will keep moving forward - One Step at a Time. That's all it takes. We may have the odd hick-up but who doesn't?

I can't wait for our next training session with the amazing Adam. He might even be coming to Dubbo. How cool would that be? I'm so excited.

I hope everyone is safe and well. Remember, never give up on your dreams, keep poking away at them - One Step at a Time. You never know where you might end up. Have a spectacular day, loads of love and hugs, Johno and the Blind Chick.

Because Of The Horse

 Feeling Grateful
27 January 2021

Diary entry by the Blind Chick

Because of the horse.

What a profound and honest statement. It is all because of the horse.

Before I could walk, but not before I could talk, it has always been because of the horse.

I have been driven by this amazing thing inside me to spend as much time living, loving, and learning from these beautiful creatures. They have brought so much joy and happiness to my life, whether it be playing with the horses in the yards, just standing and talking to the station horses, or jumping on bareback. Sometimes with a bridle, sometimes with a halter. Off I'd go and ride down around the river, just because we could.

It was lovely this freedom, this independence, this amazing feeling of being one with an animal, sometimes even knowing what they're thinking and feeling, and the desire for it not to stop.

We would wade into the river and the horse would splash the water. It was so exhilarating the days we spent meandering down around the willow trees, just taking time to enjoy the moment and the bliss of being on this amazing animal.

I've been very blessed with having many amazing horses in my life. While there are one or two super standouts, they have all been stars. I've had the most amazing connection on the ground and in the saddle with all my horses. I have this ability, this gift, I'm not sure what you'd call it, of being able to tell when horses are in pain or things aren't right. It's a feeling in my gut or my heart that badgers and bugs me until I do something.

One beautiful horse I remember in particular, a lovely chestnut mare, I remember saying to the people who owned this beautiful mare that every time I rode past her, I could feel this horrible pain, she was so uncomfortable. I think the people thought I was loopy. But after three weeks it became quite noticeable how profoundly lame and sick she was. They took her down to the main stables, but they left their run too late! The mare had toxicity to clover affecting her muscles, then she got chronic founder in all four feet. In no time, she was in so much pain she couldn't move.

On my way through life with these magnificent animals, I've been on this journey of learning and transitioning I suppose you'd call it. At the moment I'm at one of those stages of a major transition. I've done dressage now for so many years, it's the most majestic, beautiful discipline.

Personally, I see flaws in it because often it's not a matter of working with the horse, it's often dominating and telling - not asking. At the moment we're exploring other ways of doing things. Our aim is working with the horse and not so much telling the horse. I'm not sure where this will take me, but I'm having a lovely time with the learning with my beautiful horse Johno.

My last two horses, Johno and Desiderata, have both been taught to guide me around like a Guide Dog. So, for all intents and purposes, they are my Guide Horse.

This has been an interesting learning experience, having a horse take the lead and be the responsible one for getting me from Point A to Point B, which is often from the paddock to the tack shed, then safely into the arena. I think it's amazing when you give the horse a responsibility to fulfil a goal, and a challenge and they do it so very well. They are so underestimated with what they can bring to the table.

Desiderata was a challenge in himself. We never had a ride where there wasn't an argument. Then he'd go okay and happily do it. I'm working with a totally different mindset in Johno. Johno is just so willing and wants to please you every minute of the day. Everything is so easy, so uncomplicated. If there's a problem, it's generally me the rider that's causing this issue.

So Johno and I are exploring a few different things and introducing them into our training. Johno is learning quite a bit of liberty with a very good friend Karen. She is working on getting him to move off the leg, setting him up for half pass and getting him to cross his legs over.

He is if anything, airing on a little lazy when it comes to the half pass. I try not to nag but when you aren't getting the impulsion and the movement you need, you end up nagging! Not a good thing.

So, we're working on getting him more responsive and crossing his legs over. Johno was going forward and a little sideways, but not crossing his legs over. So. today's exercise was on doing that, doing it One Step at a Time and breaking it down into the individual elements you're wanting. You want sideways, you want forward. So today we just worked on the sideways and getting him to cross over. It was very cool, and he didn't get over faced. Then it was like a lightbulb moment, he said it's all good, I've got it. In our next ride we'll do a little more along the same lines plus we'll introduce the trot and see if it's any easier.

All of this training stuff, ever since a young child, has come easily to me because of the relationship I've had with all of my horses. Their willingness to please and be as one. Okay I'd be telling fibs if I said there wasn't the odd disagreement or confusion, probably caused by me or me not listening to what the horse was telling me, or what the horse was objecting to, but again this journey has been amazing because from every horse I've learnt something different.

Stay safe, stay happy. Love and hugs the Blind Chick.

Grinning From Ear To Ear

Feeling Fantastic
29 January 2021

Diary entry by Johno

Wow what a relief, it's been so windy here over the past couple of days. The wind has been strong enough to blow a dog off its chain. Not pleasant at all for man or beast.

With this morning being so overcast I thought the Blind Chickie babe would definitely not ride today. She doesn't normally ride if there isn't the sun giving her orientation, but guess what? She did! And guess what? She was pretty excited, so I'll share with you what happened today.

I was fed nice and early this morning at 7am, then I got a cuddle, a carrot, my hard feed and hay. Then the Blind Chick went back to the house to do her domestic goddess duties.

I was surprised when she returned again around about 8.45 am with halter in hand. I wondered what was a foot, she took me up to the tack shed, took off my dirty rug, then proceeded to give me a haircut! Yes, she hogged my mane again. I admit it was getting a bit long, so I had a big brush and some fly spray put on me. Okay things are looking very ominous. I thought I was to be doing some work today, but no one was here with the Blind Chick.

Then about 9 am two vehicles pulled up. My Blind Chick's great mates Jenelle Waters and Jacqueline Benn arrived. Jenelle is a professional showjumper and coach, and her great mate Jacq. They are assisting with continuing on with the wonderful Adam Sutton's training, with getting the Blind Chick back in the dressage arena, and hopefully, fingers crossed, getting her to ride a dressage test.

So, I was saddled up and taken to the round yard where Jenelle gave me a bit of lunging. I was feeling very fresh since I'd not been worked or ridden for a week, so I had a little bit of a play. But Jenelle very quickly put a stop to that, and I knuckled down to working hard. My excuse was I'm not very fit.

And guess what? Whoohoo the Blind Chick was so relieved there were no trotters today. It was awesome without the trotters interfering with my work program.

Jenelle then took me into the dressage arena and gave me a lovely long walk on the lunge. Then she put me over some ground poles! They'd been my Christmas present. Yippee, this was the first time I got to use my pressie. I was very clumsy the first time so I walked over them. But once we got sorted, I had that sorted very quickly. I just needed to pay more attention.

All the time Jenelle was working me, her wonderful friend Jacq was explaining to the Blind Chick what Jenelle was doing with me. Next thing Jenelle is taking me up to the mounting and wow! The Blind Chickie babe is getting on board. Whoohoo how exciting, she was grinning from ear to ear.

And guess what, we had the loveliest ride. Jenelle just kept everything very simple; lots of transitions in the walk, some leg yielding, some halts and no tension. Then after about 15 minutes she got the Blind Chick to going into the trot. Again, lots of transitions, softness and getting the Blind Chick to concentrate on just going nice, slowly and relaxing. By the end of the lesson, in the walk we were on the end of the buckle. We were so relaxed, we'd had an awesome ride. Watch this space. The biggest smile didn't move off the Blind Chick's face. She was so excited.

When she finished, she jumped off and gave Jenelle and Jacq a massive, big hug and thanked them both for believing in her and taking the time to get her back in the saddle. So next week they'll be back on Monday. I know the Blind Chick is excited about her next lesson and moving forward.

Then I was taken back to the tack shed and given lots of carrots. In fact, the Blind Chick had to go back into the kitchen to get more. I was such a good boy, I had a lovely bath and then put back in my paddock where I was relaxing and watching the girls. They were on the veranda doing a debrief of our ride and the plan for next week. They were enjoying a quiet drink of champagne.

Do you know this confidence thing is a biggie? It's often two steps forward and one step back, but it's important to take the time it takes and find the right person to help you move forward. The Blind Chick is so fortunate to have her amazing friends Jenelle and Jacq.

Well, the girls did lots of plotting and planning for Monday, so watch this space and let's see what happens.

While we were working in the dressage arena the Blind Chick's wonderful mother-in-law Lee was sitting in her house, watching the proceedings. She sent the Blind Chick a lovely message saying how proud she was. The Blind Chick so appreciates Lee's support and love. We are so lucky you know, to be surrounded by so many beautiful people.

I hope everyone is safe and well. I wish you all a spectacular day, loads of love and hugs Johno and a very excited Blind Chick.

Confidence – One Step at a Time

🐑 Feeling Determined
31 January 2021

Diary entry from the Blind Chick

What a beautiful day here on the Macquarie River.

I started my morning the best way any girl can start, I went down to feed my beautiful Johno. Then it was the domestic goddess duties. While I was hanging out the clothes, I gave a lot of thought to this confidence issue I have.

I have come to the conclusion that it's a matter of doing the doing. My phone has read me many books on regaining your confidence and people guaranteeing you after you read the book you will have oodles of confidence. I even had a go at hypnotise. Well, that didn't work either. One thing that did work was surrounding myself with very positive people and getting some one I trust to help me move forward.

Hence the steps Johno and I are taking to move forward. Getting the amazing Adam Sutton to help with Johno's desensitising. His help with building up my confidence. Each time we work together he takes us a little out of our comfort zone. Each time he works with Johno, Johno gains more confidence and is less sensitive to noise and what is happening around him. This is making the world a difference for us. But I respect that the confidence journey is very different for everybody.

With confidence, I think there is always going to be two steps for-ward and maybe one step back. Until you both believe and you both have each other's back. This rebuilding is not going to happen overnight. It is a matter of building a very solid base with your confidence level on the ground first, then looking to get back in the saddle. It's critical you aren't being pushed or shoved; just give it the time it takes - One Step at a Time.

So, moving forward with Johno and I, as you would've read in our last diary entry, we have our amazing coach Jenelle Waters who is a showjumper, a World Cup showjumper and her beautiful friend Jacq Benn.

Personally, I've found surrounding yourself with positive encouraging people makes the world of difference. Also, knowledgeable people. Not someone that's going to bully you and make you feel inferior or rubbish you for not being able to do something. Surround yourself with people who understand and get the fact that you don't need to be taught how to ride, you just need help rebuilding your confidence and believing in yourself and your horse again.

This rebuilding process is rather massive and sometimes quite a struggle, but I am so very grateful for the help I have had from the amazing Adam Sutton and at home, Jenelle and Jacq who work with me two to three times a week. This is just awesome. We will be able to move forward - One Step at a Time. Not great leaps, not great bounds, just One Step at a Time.

It was interesting with my ride the other day on Johno, Jenelle said "Can you feel what is happening? Relax and enjoy the ride, you don't need to override, just relax and enjoy the ride." It was so nice for Johno and I to take away that pressure of how my head is wired, to ride forward more, more, get the horse on the bit, into the bridle, keep that outside rein, more, more. Instead, we just enjoyed the ride!

So hopefully I can rewire my brain to not overthink when I get on Johno. Just enjoy the ride! That's what I'd like to be doing, I want to enjoy riding my pony again, without having the Itty-Bitty Shitty Committee in my head undermining me.

I am resigned to taking the time it takes and I'm surrounding myself with amazing people that believe in our dream of getting me back in the saddle and riding. It will take the time it takes. It will be - One Step at a Time.

So, to everybody out there who is struggling with their confidence, give yourself a break! Take some pressure off. Have another look, surround yourself with people who believe in you and can help you make your dream come true. But please, give yourself the time it takes. This is something I've had to learn.

I can't wait until tomorrow. Jenelle and Jacq we will be out for my lesson tomorrow and it is okay if we only walk and trot. But …. we need to relax and enjoy the ride.

So come along with us and the ups and the downs. We share them all.

Thank you all for your love and support. Have an awesome day. Loads of love, the Blind Chick.

15
Febuary

Positive People

😊 Feeling Blessed
1 February 2021

© 2CPhotography

Diary entry by Johno

Well, I must say there was a very excited Blind Chick today who came down to feed me nice and early this morning. She gave me a carrot, a pat and was back to get me way before the girls were meant to arrive.

The girls generally arrive around about 9 am but the Blind Chick had me up at the tack shed way before that. She took my rug off, gave me a brush and put fly spray on me. I must've been as shiny as a new pin by the time Jenelle and Jacq arrived.

Mind you I do remember Jacq mentioning how lovely I looked. So all the brushing must make a difference.

So, the girls started saddling me up, they put my lovely saddle cloth on first. Then they put this funny skinny thing on that had rings on the side of it called a lunge roller. Then on went my work boots and my bridle. We were ready to go.

I was a bit slow moving off today. My Shivers was playing havoc with my hind legs when moving off, but this passed and off we went out to the round yard. Jacq and the Blind Chick followed behind Jenelle and I. They bring up the rear carrying the saddle, riding helmet etc.

When we got to the round yard Jenelle took the reins off my bridle and put these exceedingly long reins on. They went all the way from my bit, through the lunge roller and back to Jenelle. I was a little confused, I wondered what she was doing. Then she asked me to move forward while she was like driving me from behind. Then she flicked the rein up over my back and started lunging me but driving me at the same time. She had the connection with both reins which was really cool. But there was an ulterior motive to the long reining .... control!

As you can remember, sometimes I'm a bit of a silly Billy on the lunge. When we go into the canter I can play up and buck and want to take off. Well today I walked, I trotted and wow, the Blind Chick was so impressed with how I sounded. Just so beautiful in the trot. Jacq was explaining to the Blind Chick what was happening and how I was looking, but the Blind Chick said I sounded especially magnificent in the trot. It was a beautiful big forward trot.

Then Jenelle asked me to canter. Well, I cantered off quite nicely into one circle, then another circle. But then I thought I'd like to probably pig root and play and be a bit silly. Gee whiz! In about two strides I had halted. This never happens. I usually have control when

I'm being silly on the lunge. But that's not possible with Jenelle having a rein on both sides of me like she had while long reining me. She was the one in control! Amazing, it worked a treat.

So we moved off again and we did some more walk, some trot and canter. I thought I'd like to do it again being a bit silly, well straight away I was stopped and made to stand. Wow, I'm not winning this gig anymore.

Jenelle continued to lunge me with the long reins on both sides in walk, trot and canter. We eventually got some beautiful work in the canter, no me being a silly turnip. I'd worked out very quickly that I wasn't going to win this argument.

Jenelle then took me into the dressage arena and did some long reining in there. Again we did walk, trot and canter and I was so very, very good. Then we changed rein and did the same thing. I admit, I was excellent. I didn't put a foot wrong; the Blind Chick was so impressed.

The Blind Chick commented to Jenelle how cool the long reining was and how much control she had. It was the first time she'd seen me disciplined properly for being a bit of a silly boy wanting to buck and play on the lunge or being long reined. This is no longer an option. I'm not allowed to do it, it's rude. Jenelle had been very quick to point this out to me in the kindest way. She just made me stop and think about what I was doing. Oopsy, lesson learnt.

Guess what happened next? Yes, then the saddle went on and the Blind Chick got on board. She was absolutely beaming. She did lots of walk, trot, change of rein and a little bit of leg yield. I was so very relaxed in a long and low frame, both of us just enjoying the ride. The Blind Chick wasn't overriding. It was such a cool day. Both of us learnt so much.

I see what the Blind Chick means by surrounding yourself with positive people that encourage and can help you move forward. It truly was an exceptional day. I'm so grateful to our wonderful coach Jenelle and the beautiful Jacq.

Needless to say the Blind Chick can't wait for the girls to return on Wednesday. I think they are going to have music when we ride next time! Just to add a little bit of variety to what we're doing.

I also think Jenelle is planning to get the Blind Chick trotting over the ground poles. She has walked over the ground poles before, but not trotted. We'll see how this goes.

So, let's see what Wednesday brings. I must say I'm excited. I'm so enjoying the training with Jenelle. The Blind Chick is learning so much about doing less, which is a good thing.

One Step at a Time! We are slowly getting there, rebuilding confidence and I'm having a bit of discipline on the way, which is also very good.

I hope everyone is safe and well. I hope you've enjoyed this long diary entry. Keep safe and well, loads of love and hugs, Johno and are very excited Blind Chick.

Pig Rooting Is A No No!

Feeling Grateful
3 February 2021

Diary entry by Johno

What a spectacular day here on the Macquarie River. It's 29°C, such perfect weather. We had 25 mils of rain yesterday, you can hear the grass growing.

Well, I must say the Blind Chick has a newfound spring in her step. Her smile hasn't moved off her face. I wonder if it's got anything to do with the fact, she's back riding me?

Today was another one of those amazing learning days. The girls got me tacked up with the lunge roller on, then Jenelle took me out to the round yard to do some long reining.

It was very windy early on, so I thought the Blind Chick may not ride today. But guess how things played out?

Jenelle did some beautiful long reining work with me. I had a particularly powerful big trot happening. Powerful, coming through from behind and covering a lot of ground. My walk to trot transitions were smooth and beautiful but …. I wasn't as willing to go into the canter!

Jenelle had to work hard to get me to canter, but when I did it was a lovely, big and uphill canter. Oops, I thought I should try my tricks again. I did one lap, then on my second lap I wanted to play a little and have a pig root and maybe a little …. No! I wasn't doing any of the above. Jenelle stopped me in my tracks, pulled me up and let me stand for a while. Then we are off working nicely again.

Okay, I'm not a slow learner. Obviously, you do not play up on the lunge. The last time Jenelle lunged me I was a bit silly and wanted to play three times. Well today it was only once, and it was very mild. So I'm definitely learning about when it's right and not right to play on the lunge. When I'm being long reined I know, definitely …. don't play.

Jenelle then took me into the dressage arena. All the time the beautiful Jacq was sitting with the Blind Chick describing everything that was happening for her, so she did not miss out on anything.

We did some walk, some trot and went over the ground poles. Then it was the Blind Chicks turn. Off came the lunge roller, on went the saddle and my reins back on the bridle. Next thing the Blind Chick is on board and we're off walking around the arena on a lovely long rein walk.

Jenelle gets the Blind Chick to keep me thinking while we are riding. So we did lots of transitions, changes of rein and little leg yields. It was really good. One of the trotters wasn't that far away today, but

I took no notice. I was such a good boy. The Blind Chick was enormously proud of my behaviour. So was Jenelle.

Then Jenelle got us walking over the ground poles. Okay I was a bit clumsy over them at first while we just walked, but as soon as I went into the trot it was much easier. I think the Blind Chick was a little apprehensive about trotting over the ground poles. Why? Because she's never done this before, it's quite a new experience. Mind you, I took it in my stride. It was easy pesi.

We went over the ground poles in the trot three times on each rein then did some more transitions. Then we called it a day. Everyone was so happy with my improvement, plus the fact that I'd taken no notice of the trotters next door. Okay they weren't running around, but they were there, and I could've gone and had a look, but I didn't.

It was a four carrot day today because I was so good, my reward for being such a good boy.

Next was a lovey bath and back to the paddock for me and the girls sitting on the veranda with a nice cold drink, discussing what we're doing on Friday. This is going to be a big adventure as we're going to Janelle's place. At Jenelle's there will be lots of different horses, people and show jumps. Okay the Blind Chick and I won't be jumping; we're going out there as a new experience for me. I don't do new experiences very well. This will also be good for the Blind Chick's confidence.

So needless to say, the Blind Chick's smile didn't move off her face again. I think she's still grinning. We both so appreciate Jenelle and Jacq's help. We're progressing just One Step at a Time, but it's feeling so good, so right.

There is nothing quite like surrounding yourself with positive people to help you to move forward.

Watch this spot to see how things go on Friday!

I hope everybody has had a wonderful day and you are all safe and well. Loads of love and hugs, Johno and the Blind Chick.

Wow! Check Out My Trot

Feeling Grateful
7 February 2021

Diary entry by Johno

Wow what a crazy old day on the Macquarie River! It was a pea soup thick fog here this morning. It wasn't gorillas in the mist it was Johno in the mist. The fog stuck around for ages.

Well yesterday we were meant to go out to Janelle's for my lesson. I was really excited about this because I would've got to catch up with my little mate Kenny Kakadoo.

Kenny is a cool little pony that Jenelle has, he even goes into the house and visits her mum! He goes in harness and lets kids ride him. He is one ripper of a pony and he's my mate. I was hoping to get a photo with Kenny and I. Maybe next visit if it's not raining, we can do that.

Hence no work yesterday, but today Jenelle and Jacqueline turned up to work me. Jenelle long reined me in the dressage arena. The aim of the game today was to get me responding and listening when Jenelle said canter.

Oh my heavens did I impress the girls this morning with my trot work! It was massive, it was big, it was forward. Ha, ha everyone was saying "oh wow." But I wasn't as keen to go into the canter on the left rein. Yet with her gentle persistence, Jenelle got her way and in no time at all I was taking up the canter on the left lead quite easily. Then we went on the right rein, much easier for me because I'm not as affected by the Shivers on my right side. So we did some beautiful trot and canter transitions, everyone was pleased with me today. I think it was a five star day today. I definitely got some brownie points.

I must say the Blind Chick and I are so very grateful to Jenelle and Jacqueline for their time and Janelle's patience. There was no rushing, no yelling or hitting, it just took the time it takes for me to get the message when Jenelle said 'Canter.' It got so good she would say 'Canter' and I was straight into the canter. Beautiful big, bold, uphill canter strides.

Everyone was extra proud of me today with how I handled the trotter next door. It was not too far from me, watching me. It didn't take off or anything, but it was there, and I could've been distracted, but I wasn't. I was a star, such a good boy. I think the Blind Chick is really looking forward to riding me tomorrow, seeing how amazingly good I was today.

In fact, I was even a little proud of myself. I was really on the job today concentrating on Jenelle. I must say I'm looking forward to tomorrow and seeing what we get to do in the dressage arena.

I am pretty sure Jenelle is setting things up for when the Blind Chick canters me, just making sure all the buttons are in place and that I am being a good boy. There is nothing like putting in good groundwork.

Oh, we have had some lovely rain. I think around about 28 mils. The northern end of the dressage arena had a little water in it, but we weren't in flood so that's great.

I hope everyone has had a wonderful weekend. I hope you are all safe and well. I'm so looking forward to my training session tomorrow.

Loads of love and hugs, Johno and the Blind Chick.

Whoohoo

Feeling Fantastic
9 February 2021

Diary entry by Johno

Wow what a spectacular day, another 29°C. It's like Spring-Autumn here, a beautiful breeze, the sun is shining, and we've had some wonderful rain. The grass is growing, this weather is amazing. It's a perfect summers day.

I'm so looking forward to my work this morning. The girls are starting at about 9.30am. What's ahead is always something new and different, which is excellent.

I quietly got saddled up, work boots put on and out to do some long reining with Jenelle. I did some great work. My canter transitions are getting so crisp, so good. I'm sure she is planning for the Blind Chick to canter soon, but don't tell the Blind Chick this! It might make her break out in a sweat.

I must say I'm very proud of my work long reining today. I did beautiful transitions through the walk, trot and canter. When asked not to run through the movements, I listened. I think everyone was impressed. Then we finish the long reining, and the saddle was put on for the Blind Chick to have a ride.

We started off with just a lovely, relaxed walk on both reins. It's really helpful Jacq calls out the letters as the Blind Chick and I ride pass. Calling out helps the Blind Chick know where she is in the arena. Jenelle is very watchful of the fact the Blind Chick is sitting up nice and tall.

The aim of the game is no tension and no stress. We then go into the trot and do some lovely trot work doing the odd 10 metre half circle, doing more like a teardrop, plus changing direction exercises. When going back to the long side, it took the Blind Chick a little while to get the size of the circle right. I must admit we haven't done 10 metre or eight metre circles for a very long time. So she'll just need to get the feel again.

We then started working on the centreline. Jenelle looked after me doing the 10 metre half circles down to the bottom of the arena near B. Jacq would be calling and getting me centred on the centreline, calling out C, C, C, C all the time. This was so helpful for the Blind Chick to get orientated. Mind you she is still listing to the right a little. It's so important she keeps her right leg gently on me, so I say straight and keep me straight through the neck.

We did this exercise about three times in the walk. Then we had a couple of attempts in the trot. I think the Blind Chick needs to get her orientation a little better, but it was good fun. Having both girls giving feedback on my straightness on the centreline was really valuable for the Blind Chick.

Then we moved on and did some ground pole work in the walk. Firstly, I must say I'm still a little clumsy walking over the ground poles. But when we go into the trot, I'm big and bouncy, it makes the Blind Chick giggle. She really does like doing the ground poles. I think Jenelle is going to add one more ground pole next week, then we'll have four to go over. You may remember these poles were my Christmas present.

So many goals have been achieved today. All this good consistent practise helps the Blind Chick start to orientate herself in the dressage arena again.

So let's see what Wednesday brings. Hopefully it will be another 29°C day. That would be a great start. I'm so enjoying our training with our awesome coach Jenelle and Jacq.

Also I must say, I'm still feeling amazing. I haven't had a big anxiety attack for possibly two months now. I had a few moments four or five days ago for three days, I don't know what caused this though. It was like a relapse or something. Since we are dealing with a degenerative neurological condition there could be some degeneration. But the Blind Chick has her finger on the pulse and keeps an eye on how I'm travelling, and my diet. Which is all so important.

I'm so grateful to the wonderful Linda from Poseidon Equine for looking after me so well, and for her coming into our life. It has been a game changer for my gut health …. the Digestive EQ. We have not had to use the Stress Paste since travelling back from Lochinvar. Things have been going really well.

I'm so looking forward to my next lesson. I know the Blind Chick is having a ball slowly but surely rebuilding her confidence. I hope you are all having a spectacular day.

Loads of love and hugs, Johno and the Blind Chick.

Being My Best Self

🙂 Feeling Excited
10 February 2021

Diary entry by Johno and the Blind Chick

Well wow, how long can this amazing weather go on for? It's another 29°C and another spectacular morning here on the Macquarie River.

The girls had me ready in no time at all this morning, out for a little bit of long reining. Jenelle and I have a great relationship, I'm so tuned in to listening to her and being very obedient. Keep in mind, she is setting this all up for the Blind Chick. She's done an amazing job.

We did some long reining on both reins, some walk, trot, and canter. The transitions were crisp and my canter was beautiful, big and uphill and a big ground covering, swinging trot.

It doesn't get better than that, does it?

Then, Jenelle announced that it's the Blind Chicks turn! So we went down to near the round yard and they take my lunge roller off, my saddle on. The Blind Chickie babe dons her helmet and gloves.

We start off doing some lovely work just in the walk. We were working on 10 metre half circles and on getting a good centreline. Even though it was all at the walk the Blind Chick was much better today at the centreline than the other day. I'm starting to get the feel for straightness again, which isn't easy when she's totally blind.

Jenelle's sets the Blind Chick up off the 10 metre circle onto the centreline while Jacq starts calling out C, C, C, C. This helps the Blind Chick with her direction and riding a straight line. Jacq also let her know if she was drifting to the right, or to the left. We did some great work today.

Jenelle then set the Blind Chick and I up to do some ground poles, again keeping me nice, calm and steady. The Blind Chick isn't allowing me to run through the trot poles. It was such cool fun. We did a little bit on each rein. I know the Blind Chick loves the bouncy trot going over the ground poles. It was such a cool lesson.

We then came back to having a little bit of a walk, and relax and a talk about how I was travelling, and what the Blind Chick was doing. Jenelle suggested to the Blind Chick that she not rise so high out of the saddle. This will help her stay down and not be so long out of the saddle. As you can imagine my trot is very big, so this made the world a difference. It also helped her keep her shoulders back, making everything look quite elegant.

While we work around the circle in the walk, Jenelle said to the Blind Chick, "Now you're ready to canter," and the Blind Chick didn't miss a beat. We didn't even go into the trot. We did a beautiful walk canter transition. It was a ripper! We probably did three circles on the left rein and quietly back to the trot, then a walk.

Well they were yuppies, there were yahoos, everyone was so excited. The Blind Chick was absolutely stoked.

We did a few more canter transitions from the trot, then a few more walk canter transitions. Whoohoo Mother Magoo, it was totally rocking out. The smile was so big on the Blind Chicks face, she was so excited.

We then came back to a walk and a change of rein. Jenelle said "Would you like to canter again?" And once more we didn't go through the trot, we straight away went from a beautiful engaged walk into a lovely soft ground covering, up-hill canter. Oh my heavens, I think the Blind Chick had tears, but don't tell anyone. Tears of joy. Think of how long it's been since she has had the confidence to canter? Probably seven, maybe eight, months. What a great day and how very exciting.

It was made even more special, because today beautiful mother-in-law Lee was there to watch her lesson. It was so nice everyone was so very happy, so very proud of me. I was proud of the Blind Chick today, she was totally awesome.

We can't go past the fact that Jenelle has put a lot of work into getting me to this stage. We are both so grateful to Jenelle and Jacq. Without their dedication and belief, guidance, love and support, I don't think this would've happened. This is happening because the Blind Chick believes so much in the girls. And she's now starting to believe in me again. I'm so grateful to these two amazing ladies.

So whoohoo, the Blind Chick is back cantering. I can't wait for our lesson on Friday. They're predicting rain but hopefully they'll back of that prediction and we'll get a lesson in with the amazing Jenelle and Jacqueline.

I hope everybody is having a spectacular day. Our day totally rocks. Keep safe and well. Loads of love and hugs, Johno and the Blind Chick.

Living With Equine Shivers

Feeling Optimistic
11 February 2021

Diary entry from the Blind Chick

This is serious from the heart stuff.

Living with the neurological degenerative condition - Equine Shivers!

I've been giving it a lot of thought about writing this diary entry and I think it is an especially important one to share. This journey is not an easy journey for Johno or myself or my amazing support team.

Keep in mind it is Neurological and it is Degenerative. They are probably the two hardest things to be working with …. or …. trying to work with and manage.

The first time I rode Johno there was something magical that clicked inside us both. I had the most wonderful ride. Our journey was meant to be. But when I rode him, I asked him to back up a couple of times and he resisted quite badly, so I left it alone. I thought heavens girl, give him a chance, you've been on him 20 minutes and you ask him to back up! But keep in mind he is a medium advanced dressage horse.

Also keep in mind, Johno passed a vet check with this degenerative neurological condition.

After Matthew had bought Johno for me, Janelle my coach took me down to ride Johno before we brought him home. We also had a wonderful saddle fitting from the amazing Jason to make sure everything was right for when we came home to Dubbo.

On this occasion, again after walking, trotting and cantering and asking for some lateral work, which he obligingly did with no problem at all, I asked for another back up. Once again he resisted and put his head up and said "No, No, No, I can't do this". So once again, I put this down to giving the horse a chance for me to get to know him better.

Then we noticed when he was coming off the float, he stepped backwards in a really weird and awkward way. But again, I had a reason for that. He'd just spent six hours on the float travelling from near Penrith to Dubbo, so he could've been stiff. I'm always giving him the benefit of the doubt.

I had a lovely friend who is a Chiropractor come and have a look at Johno for me, to check him out. He simply asked Johno to square up. Based on Johno's back leg reaction, my friend said he wouldn't touch the horse as "Johno has a patella problem, commonly known as a locking patella."

I noticed how Johno often didn't want to step forward after I caught him in the paddock, or after being saddled, or when he'd stood still for five minutes. He wouldn't walk forward. I just thought he was being a bit stubborn, so I'd just wait for him to oblige. But once again, it's these little issues you don't know about, they meant something. They were all symptoms of Shivers!

I'd never heard of this horrid disease before.

So I continued working Johno, oblivious to everything other than the fact that he couldn't back and that he took ages to walk off after standing and when he did walk off, he had a funny spastic movement with his nearside hind leg.

I had no idea why. All I knew was it didn't affect him when he walked, trotted, or cantered after he walked out of this weird movement.

Then BAM! We went down to have lessons with the beautiful Melanie Schmerglatt and Melanie picks up within five minutes of us arriving, having seen Johno back off the float …. "Your horse has Equine Shivers!!!"

Everything went fast from there. We went and got diagnosis after diagnosis. We learnt that nothing can cure this hideous disease. It keeps degenerating! Johno's brain was not communicating with his hind legs; hence he was finding trouble backing and if he stands for a while, he has trouble moving forward.

The other thing that has happened with time, keeping in mind this is a degenerative disease, is it is affecting his front legs as well? Plus if Johno has a stressful time, like anything new in his life or a change, like going to Lochinvar for lessons, Johno's Shivers is greatly affected.

It affects his movement in his hind legs. His brain doesn't connect to his hind legs, so he has trouble moving forward and once he is moving, he is quite fine. But when I got him home the Shivers had really got worse, it was affecting his front legs as well. He was having trouble moving at all!

First thing in the morning he would stand there, wanting to come for his carrot and a pat, but he couldn't move because his brain wasn't communicating with his legs. I think it's important I haven't put any videos of this on Facebook, because I think most people would find it very distressing. As do I, having to listen to it every morning.

So all this time I'm hunting, hunting, hunting, for something to help this beautiful animal that does not deserve to have this hideous neurological degenerative disease. He has been on lots of different drugs to try and help him.

Under the supervision of the beautiful Dr Sarah Gough from Hunter Equine, we even tried a human drug. This didn't work well enough for me to ride Johno. Now he takes other medication. This medication doesn't fix the Shivers, it helps him manage the anxiety attacks he has. Hence my unceremonious buster!

He has these moments of explosion. Hence his big leaps in the air and me falling off. Also, out of the blue when lunging him, he can just explode and start bucking or running flat out. As his anxiety attacks in the paddock got worse and worse, he would run frantically for hours. I'd go to catch him and he'd rear at me. He was really quite dangerous.

We really needed to find something that was going to help this beautiful animal not be stressed out because of the Equine Shivers causing the anxiety.

Hence where the medication has come in. The only way that Johno is quiet in his paddock and for me to ride him, is by medicating him.

Otherwise, the only other option is euthanasia.

And that to me is not an option.

Along with his anxiety attacks, his mass running around, screaming and carrying on, being so out of control, would come colic! In one of his episodes, he had colic twice in less than 10 days. This is horrific for him to have to go through. All because of this hideous disease.

Sorry, this is not one of my more positive diary entries.

It is an honest sharing of what we go through on a daily basis to keep Johno sound. Okay we cannot stop the Shivers, but we can try and manage the episodes he has with his anxiety.

It's a one day at a time prospect.

Amazing Poseidon Equine products have helped us a lot to get Johno's gut healthy. But they aren't going to stop the Shivers. They help us manage it, but there's nothing that's going to cure this hideous disease.

I suppose the main reason for sharing this with you is so you get an idea of the huge amount of behind-the-scenes work that goes into managing this horrible degenerative condition Johno has. He had a relapse the other day that lasted for five days. It was so heartbreaking hearing him stressed again. Thankfully, with medication, we have this under control, for now.

So THANK YOU for reading this. I think it is important to share the good, the bad, and the ugly.

This is the sad side of things. All the other beautiful things that we do; the riding, the diary entries, rebuilding my confidence in getting back on Johno have all been rather massive.

It wouldn't have happened if he did not have Equine Shivers.

But, there's nothing we can do about that.

Hence everything here is one day at a time, trying the best we can to manage Johno's Shivers and giving him the best quality of life we can.

For now, while I can ride him and it is not too dangerous, what a bonus to be riding such a spectacular beautiful horse. When he has his moments, I know it's not Johno being naughty, it's his neurological condition. Which he has no control over.

I will continue to share our amazing journey. I think I'm very blessed to have Johno in my life even with as much stress as it causes me... we have written a book together!

We have another book to be published hopefully in July, all going well. We will keep sharing our journey.

So here's to one day hoping they find a cure for this horrible neurological degenerative disease - Equine Shivers: Here's to being able to give horses who have it a better life, including my beautiful Johno.

To be honest this would have to be one of the hardest diary entries I've ever written.

I'm so used to writing about all of the beautiful things we do, not about the hard things that make you cry.

A massive thank you to our amazing Team that keep Johno and I on track. Our amazing veterinary surgeons Sarah and Don, Johno's Craniosacral lady the beautiful Tanya, amazing Adam Sutton doing his desensitisation work on Johno and building up my confidence, the beautiful Linda from Poseidon Equine - the Angel that reached out to help us, and to my two beautiful, amazing friends Janelle and Jacqueline for getting me back in the saddle.

I'm now cantering again!

So many good things.

I hope you don't mind me sharing this.

Be safe and well. Loads of love and hugs the Blind Chick.

Automated Markers

Feeling Challenged
13 February 2021

Diary entry by Johno

What an overcast bleak old day it is here on the Macquarie River. A bit of a wind blowing and quite humid.

The Blind Chick and I are really looking forward to today, because Jenelle and Jacq are coming out for us to have a lesson. I'm not sure whether the Blind Chick will ride as it's very dark and overcast. When she doesn't have the sun to orientate her, it makes it quite difficult. So we'll see what happens.

Jacq messaged the Blind Chick that they were on their way, so she came down with a carrot and caught me. We walked quietly up to the tack shed. I was reasonably relaxed and by the time the girls got here the Blind Chick had me brushed, she'd hogged my mane again, so I was looking very handsome indeed.

When the girls got here I heard the Blind Chick say to Jenelle and Jacq that she would not be riding today, it was just totally black and there was no sun for her orientation. That was okay, the girls had other things to work on which were really interesting.

The girls quietly put my lunge roller on and Jenelle took me out to the dressage arena and started driving me while she followed on behind. Jacq and a lovely girl called Georgie were pulling a wheelbarrow type thing. In it was a big box and some other things.

To my surprise the girls were going around to a few of the letters around the arena, putting special devises at the letters. What they were setting up is called the Dressage Arena Marker Announcer (DAMA) system, it's really interesting.

Georgie was the one in control of the DAMA. When she pushed the letter C on the remote control the Announcer box at C would call out that letter. When she pushed the letter P, the Announcer box at P would continuously call out the letter. This was a new thing for me and with Jenelle driving me around the dressage arena and these letters being called out, it was all a little perturbing to say the least.

Needless to say, I didn't take to it like a duck to water. It took a little while to get the gist of what was happening. I didn't mind going towards the letters, but I hated the letters being called when I was going away, it was really disturbing. This took a little while to get used to, but Jenelle was very patient while Georgie was very persistently pushing the letters.

I was a little disturbed and definitely a little tense, but over the next few days of practising with it I got used to the Dressage Arena Marker Announcers. An amazing guy called Andrew invented these and they're so helpful for my training.

Eventually there will be a marker at each letter in the arena, and all it'll take is Jacq to push the letter on the remote control of the letter I'm heading towards, and it will keep calling it as I ride to it. This is what we're working towards, hence Jenelle and the girls desensitising me with it today. They're working on getting me use to it.

So get ready for tomorrow, I'll be a little more relaxed. But it was all fine today. Even with the four Marker Announcer things, they didn't disturb me in the least.

It looks like we have a storm coming in this afternoon, and more rain. Everything is so beautiful and green. I'm loving this mild weather.

Also, on reflection of the diary entry the Blind Chick did yesterday, we truly are both so very humbled with the love and support from everyone about me living with Equine Shivers. The Blind Chick is doing the best she can to manage this condition. But keep in mind this is not something they knew I had when Matthew brought me for the Blind Chick. I did pass my vet check with this condition! It's degenerated, which is so really sad, but it is being managed with medication, which I'm so happy and grateful for.

I'm hoping everyone is safe and well. Have a spectacular day. Loads of love and hugs, Johno and the Blind Chick.

Living Markers

🐷 Feeling happy
14 February 2021

Diary entry by Johno

Wow, what a spectacular morning! We had 5 mils of rain overnight, so everything is sparkling and clean. Although it's currently a beautiful fresh morning, I think we are in for some humidity.

I really look forward to our trips out to Waterville Park, Janelle's place, for lessons. It's a nice short road trip and I get to catch up with my other horsey friends, Janelle's professional show jumping team.

We also got there in time today to watch some of Janelle's young pupils have lessons. It was really cool as they were having flat lessons today, not jumping. I think they like the jumping more, but the flat lessons really paid off as the horses were going really lovely by the end of it.

Then it was my turn! I was a little edgy again today. I think the Shivers is probably rearing its ugly head a little bit. Remember it's a degenerative condition, so the benchmark changes daily, sometimes weekly, we just have to be aware of this. However, Jenelle was very quick to pull me into line and we had a great session long reining. Then it was the Blind Chicks turn.

What a team we had today! There were at least eight Living Markers, the A-Team from Waterville Park; Mary, Abbey, Elenore, Jacq, Claire, Matt, Tilla, Elyse and Ainsley.

It was super cool. Everybody was calling the letters and guiding the Blind Chick around, then Jacq started singing the ABC song! Well it was hilarious. Everybody was singing the ABC song as well as the Blind Chick. So much fun. This also helped the Blind Chick with her relaxation.

With me being a bit edgy this morning the Blind Chick wasn't sure she was confident enough to ride. But, as per usual, Jenelle had the Blind Chick onboard and we walked, we trotted, we cantered and we did lots of transitions. I was a very good boy. I'm getting used to going to these living markers as they call their letters, it is such fun.

Mind you, oh my heavens, it was very steamy and humid, so I was super sweaty and hot. But the girls gave me a big bath. I think it was at least an eight-star day today, so I got lots of rewards. While I dried off Jenelle gave another lesson, to Abby and her horse Rex. It went really, really well.

The crew are all off to Mudgee Show next weekend for the show jumping, so they're all getting in some practice with Jenelle they're super coach.

I am now back in my paddock, it's still very humid, feels like we could be in the tropics. But I don't think there is any more rain on the horizon.

I hope everyone is having a lovely day and you are safe and well.

Loads of love and hugs, Johno and the Blind Chick.

P.S.: I nearly forgot to thank a very important person, the Blind Chicks husband Matthew. He has taken us out to Jenelle's for lessons these past two days. On Saturday he came and left the Blind Chick and I, then he came and picked her up later. But on Sunday he stayed and helped by being a living marker. It was such fun. I'm so grateful to Matt for giving up his weekend to help the Blind Chick and I. We are incredibly lucky.

Who Am I?

Feeling Excited
15 February 2021

Diary entry by Johno

Okay, the Blind Chick is on a bit of a mission.

We would love it if our Facebook friends could help in any way, shape or form. I know this won't be able to be done by our friends overseas, but anyone in Australia that can put some light on my history would be wonderful.

Blind Chickie babe is trying to find out as much information as she can, to go back as far as she can, to see if she can work out when I might have started showing symptoms of my Equine Shivers.

Keep in mind when Matthew bought me for the Blind Chick, I was showing the symptoms then. I had trouble backing and had weird goose stepping with my nearside hind leg. I also showed a tendency to get quite anxious when put under light pressure. But these symptoms have reduced quite a bit now. So it's some investigating we need help with.

I am by the majestic stallion Gymnastik Star.

My registered name as a foal was Kinnordy Godolphin.

Attached is the only history we have. If you know anything at all about me, we'd love to hear from you.

If you know someone who might be able to shed some light on my history, could you please share this request with them. It really might make the world a difference to us. Thank you.

We think I may have come from Queensland, that's where the stud where I was bred was located.

I'm hoping we can shed some light on my history. Have a spectacular day.

Loads of love and hugs, Johno.

Confidence Building Never Stops

Feeling Positive
17 February 2021

Diary entry by Johno

Wow, I can't get over this spectacular weather! Anyone would think it was spring all over again. The Blind Chickie babe was out early this morning calling the kookaburras and the beautiful king parrots. She feeds them.

We had a later start than normal today, about 11-ish, because Jacq and Jenelle had five horses to work before they came and worked with the Blind Chick and me. They're busy getting their competition showjumpers ready for the Mudgee Show.

So, in no time at all I was all saddled up, boots on and ready to go. Jenelle took me out and we did some long reining first. I'm getting pretty good at this stuff. Jacq also put a Dressage Arena Marker Announcer letter outside the arena for some more desensitisation. Things were going grand: walking, trotting, cantering and then …. those trotters came for a visit!

Well, all was fine while they were visiting, until they thought they'd take off in great haste across the paddock. I grew from my 18.3 hands to probably 19.3 hands and thought it might be a good idea if I went to! Jenelle had other ideas. She asked me to stop. I was made stand and compose myself, then asked to walk on and get my attention back on working. This took no time at all and I was re-focused. But the Blind Chick heard all of these goings-on and it stressed her a little. She was concerned I might be naughty with her when she rode, so she mentioned to Jacq that she might not ride today.

I understand why she thought this way. For no other reason than that the confidence between us is still being rebuilt. Her hearing me be a bit naughty was a little disturbing for her. But I worked for probably another 10 minutes long-reining, focusing on transitions. Things were going great. Then Jenelle started to take my lunge roller off and the long reins! Whoohoo, the saddle was being put on. The next thing, before she knew it, the Blind Chick was on board.

I have to say she had a pretty terrific ride. It was a Five Star ride for me. I was a very, very good boy. We walked, we trotted, we canted - on both reins. We concentrated on keeping it nice and steady, relaxed. Our transitions from walk to canter I have to say, were lovely. The Blind Chick was just a little bit pleased with herself.

It was really funny after the Blind Chick had such a great ride, the girls were standing around discussing the fact that the Blind Chickie babe had mentioned to Jacq that she probably wouldn't ride today, then voila, she's on board! So there were lots of pats on the back and everyone saying to the Blind Chickie babe what a good job she did.

Truly it pays to surround yourself by positive, beautiful people. People that want the best for you. Jenelle and Jacqueline are such great support for the Blind Chick, and I.

We wander back to the tack shed where everything is pulled off me; I'm given a bath, my rugs and work boots are put into the washing machine and the girls go sit on the veranda for a cold drink and a chat. It's during this time that Jacq and Jenelle go through the photos and choose the best one for the Blind Chick to post that day. What a great Team!

There will possibly be another diary entry today. The Blind Chick has some really exciting news to share with you. In fact, there are a few things going on, but one thing at a time.

I'm now back in my paddock for a pretty cruisy afternoon.

I hope everyone is safe and well. Loads of love and hugs, Johno and the Blind Chick.

It's All In A Name

Feeling Excited
18 February 2021

Diary entry by Johno

I must say, yesterday was a pretty cool day, apart from us having an awesome ride. One of the Blind Chick's beautiful friends Jane has been doing some hunting. She discovered that my First Owner was a lovely lady called Peta.

It was so exciting. Jane spent about an hour talking to Peta about me as a foal, then she desperately tried to get in contact with the Blind Chick. But we were riding at the time!

Eventually Jane spoke to the Blind Chick and shared the absolutely super news. Then the Blind Chick dashed inside and rang the beautiful Peta.

Well, there were lots of tears from both ends of the phone, they were both so excited to be talking to each other. Peta told the Blind Chick all about me as a little foal and how I'd foaled down at Kinnordy Stud. Apparently, I was one of the best foals they'd ever breed! They were very proud of me.

My name is Kinnordy Godolphin.

Peta was sharing how I was such a beautiful foal and lovely to handle. I had a lovely nature and loved playing in the water trough. Well that hasn't changed! I still love playing in the water trough.

Peta sold me at six months old and spent the last 9.5 years looking for me! She even put advertisements up everywhere, trying to find me. But no one knew where I was.

So, there is a big part of my history still missing …. from when I was six months old to when the Blind Chick bought me from down near Camden. I'm pretty sure I spent a bit of time down there, maybe three years. But where was I before that? Probably somewhere in Queensland, because that's where the Kinnordy Stud was.

If you know of anyone who had a cute foal called Godolphin it might be me! If you could put your feelers out, we would love to know where these missing years of my life were spent.

I have the Hanoverian brand on my near side flank, and I think the Blind Chick is going to send a hair sample off to the Hanoverian Society to verify my DNA. How exciting!

I have some baby photos now, which is wonderful. It's fantastic knowing a little more about my history. I'm so grateful to Peta for the beautiful photos and sharing my baby stories.

I hope you have a super day. Loads of love and hugs, stay safe and well, Johno.

New Shoes

Feeling optimistic
18 February 2021

Diary entry by Johno

Wow, life is never boring! There is always something happening and it's always interesting.

First thing today, my amazing Farrier Troy Lomax came out to shoe me. The Blind Chickie babe was out about an hour before Troy arrived, to give me my Stress Paste.

Getting shod was a breeze, I was such a good boy. Having the paste made such a difference, I was so relaxed. Thank you so much Poseidon Equine for this incredible paste. Then the Blind Chickie babe put me in the paddock for an hour, so I could relax while she did some domestic goddess duties.

Then Jacqueline and Jenelle arrived, and my lunging gear was put on. The Blind Chick typically doesn't ride me after I've been shod, so we just did some light work in the arena with Jenelle long reining me.

Wow, did I do some pretty cool work? My trot was big and ground covering, my canter was beautiful big relaxed and uphill. Jenelle then asked me to walk, so I walked for a little while. Then she asked me to canter, so I started doing these amazing walk to canter transitions while on the long rein. How cool is this? I know the Blind Chick does this with me all the time, but this time I was being long reined. No one was there putting a leg aid on to get me to canter. Everyone was clapping and so proud of me, it was awesome.

We also did some more desensitisation with the Dressage Arena Marker Announcers. Well I must say, I take absolutely no notice of them now. I'm so good.

I can't wait for my lesson on Saturday at Waterville Park for more desensitisation work with Jenelle. All going well the Blind Chickie babe will then ride me. We need to practise me going to other venues and feeling relaxed. I can't wait for Saturday as I also get the chance to catch up with my good mate Kenny Kakadoo. He's a pony and ever so cute.

I have lots of exciting things coming up in the near future, so watch this space! I can't wait to let you know how things go at Janelle's on Saturday. I'll be on my best behaviour.

We are still having spectacular weather here. I can't believe it's still Summer, the weather is like a beautiful spring day. Sometimes maybe a little windy, but other than that pretty okay.

I hope everyone has had a lovely day. I'm sending you loads of love and hugs, Johno.

Lemon Trees Have Thorns

 Feeling Unsettled
21 February 2021

Diary entry by Johno

Wow, what a busy day Saturday morning. It started very early at 6am with the Blind Chickie babe coming down to feed me. Well that was a venture, probably an adventure, in itself! Why? It was totally dark, so she had no sun to work by. So she ended up in the middle of the lemon bush and the lemon bush has …. very long thorns! I don't think she was a very happy camper.

So, eventually I got my breakfast and was settling in for a relaxing day. Well that wasn't going to happen!

Then our beautiful friend Prue Crichton arrived. She's a photographer and is doing the cover photo for our next book, coming out very soon. So Prue arrived lovely and early at 7.30am so she could take advantage of the light.

This was going swimmingly until they thought they'd like my ears forward! Now remember all that amazing desensitisation work Adam Sutton has done with me? Well I'm not spooked or alarmed by anything these days. So there were bags being waved, towels being waved, people clapping, Matthew tooting the car horn and nothing worked. But the thing that did work was Matthew rolling across the lawn. Oh my heavens! I think Prue was flat out taking the photos it was so hilarious. Yes I did put my ears forward to check out what the heck was he doing.

After Prue had taken her photos, I thought cool, I'll go back to my paddock. Well, I was there for only about an hour when Matthew came and got me. Next thing I'm on the horse float heading out to Jenelle's place for a lesson.

You probably remember me mentioning that Jenelle is a professional showjumper and coach. Her lovely property Waterville Park is on the other side of Dubbo. When we arrived Jenelle was in the arena giving the beautiful Amanda and her new horse Arnie a lesson. It was a super-duper lesson, smiles all round.

I was put in a paddock where I met a few more horsey mates and given some hay, while the girls sat and had a chat under the tree for a while. Then it was my turn! Jenelle's arena is different to the one we have at home, hers has show jumps in it, everywhere. She started long reining me and how good was I? I didn't take any notice of the show jumps, I was quite at home. In fact, I was very relaxed.

This was another day where things snuck up on the Blind Chick. She had no intention of riding me but next thing Jenelle calls out "where is the saddle" and suddenly I'm being saddled up, reins put back on my bridle and then …. the Blind Chickie babe is on board! I think she was really worried about the new environment and no dressage arena sides to help orientate her, but guess what? It all worked brilliantly. Talk about a Team effort.

Jenelle got the help of Jacq's husband Andrew and the beautiful Amanda to be Living Markers around the area where the Blind Chick and I will be riding. So there was Jacq, Amanda and Andrew calling out to the Blind Chick to ride to them, they were call a letter or giving her a little bit more direction. More left, or more right, it worked a treat. All the while she was orientating with these amazing helpers, she was listening to what Jenelle was saying from the middle of the arena.

It was a super cool ride. Jenelle initially said to the Blind Chick "just have a walk." Well, we walked, we trotted, we cantered, and we even did a couple of sequence changes! I think we may have done three two times changes. They were pretty cool, and not planned. The changes did happen and they were perfect.

This was an amazing boost to the Blind Chick's confidence as she really was way out of her comfort zone with no arena sides and totally reliant on her beautiful friends to guide her around. I think it was one of the best rides we've had since the Blind Chick has started rebuilding her confidence.

So after our ride there was lots of clapping and yahoos, everyone was so happy. I was such a good boy, I had that Blind Chick's back, we just had the most perfect ride.

We are so very grateful to our wonderful coach Jenelle and Jacqueline had lovely husband Andrew and the beautiful Amanda for helping make yesterday so perfect. What a super-duper Team.

You know that smile I talk about, well it's still there. The Blind Chick was so elated I don't know how many carrots I got, I lost count. After the ride I was given a lovely bath and put back in the paddock with a biscuit of homegrown lucerne hay. I had time for a little rest before Matthew picked us up about 3pm.

After a lovely lunch with lots of laughter and talking we were back out to the arena and Jenelle had another lesson with the lovely little Abby. When Matt arrived he and Jacq loaded me on the float, and we were off home. Everyone was so happy. Matt took me down to my paddock, put my fly veil on and I had the rest of the afternoon to relax.

How cool is this doing it One Step at a Time? That's all it is, taking one step forward and look, we're slowly making progress. This has been such a big boost to the Blind Chicks confidence.

We hope everyone is having a wonderful day. Loads of love and hugs, Johno and the Blind Chick.

Joys Of A Squeaky Pig!

Feeling relaxed
25 February 2021

Diary entry by a very relaxed Johno

What a gorgeous morning. My Blind Chickie is with me here under the breeze way, brushing me. Oh I do so love it. You know it brings the oils up in my skin to help my coat shine and apparently mine is very shiny and soft. The Blind Chickie is telling me that the lady with the magic healing hands is coming today to check me over and iron out any little wrinkles that have appeared in the last month of work.

I can hear a voice, "good morning Sue-Ellen."

It's the lovely Tanya. The Blind Chickie was right, the lady with the magic healing hands is here, whoohoo!

Now I know these two ladies always have so much to catch up on when Tanya visits, and I'm usually very patient, I wait my turn, but I really need her to touch me! Typically she touches me straight away, but today she's still talking! I'll just push my energy at her and see if that gets her attention.

Mmmm, still talking about my last few weeks. I'll just put my nose to her shoulder. Oh, that worked, she has put her hand on my shoulder, I can feel her connecting with me. These girls are still discussing things about my movement when my shoulder is mentioned. Now I know there is nothing wrong with my shoulder so let's see what Tanya has to say. Straight away she tells the Blind Chickie that there's nothing wrong with my shoulder, everything is gliding nicely over each other.

I shouldn't have doubted her, she has always got it right since the first day she started treating me. I can't really explain what happens, she just seems to be able to connect into my thoughts and feelings, she knows exactly where to go and what to do. She is my little angel.

But today feels different for me. I don't normally give my head at the beginning of the session, but I know this is where I need her to help me today. In any case if I don't want her to touch my poll anymore, I can just put my head up because she can't reach it when I do that.

I lower my head to a height that Tanya can reach easily, and with just one light finger touch I can feel myself falling into a deep relaxation. All the tensions in the muscles and tissues, not only around my poll and neck areas but also my back, pelvis and hind legs, are releasing. Oh my, I am feeling so good. The stretching my body is doing whilst in this state of mind is amazing. If you'd been here to see me you would've thought I was a great big cat stretching after a nap.

I know I've reacted well because I can hear Tanya saying "good boy Johno, great work." I can't tell you how good this treatment makes me feel. As I've said in past diary entries if you have a horse please, do it a favour, get this lady to put her magic hands on them. You might think that there is nothing going wrong with your horse, but I bet this lady can make your horse feel even more super. Trust me when they feel as good as I do, they'll give you 100%, and love you even more.

There was another difference today, something that is very special indeed. I can feel this amazing lady in other parts of my body, parts she doesn't even have her hands on! Her intuition and abilities to feel and read my body Rhythms are getting so powerful. Yet at the same time they're very calming. Oh, I'm in horse heaven.

At this point in my session, I'm in a place so deep in relaxation I can feel this flow from my head to my tail. It's just so heavenly, the peace is so serene. I think I might stay here all day.

Tanya steps back from me to allow me to release even deeper. I can hear her calm voice and I'm happy to keep releasing. She makes me feel safe, so it's easy to stay in this heavenly place. Then, our time is up, as always good things must come to an end. But my muscles have relaxed and I've stretched out what I needed too. So, I have to come back to the real world.

Then I hear a gentle, "Hello Johno, welcome back." It's Tanya making sure that all is good, that I've come back safe and sound.

So folks, that wraps up another craniosacral session for me. Stay tuned for the next report, I guarantee it will be worth a read.

I hope everyone is having a lovely day. Don't forget the amazing Tanya does travel to do treatments and she does people as well as horses! I know the Blind Chick highly recommends her as well, so drop the Blind Chick a line if you'd like to get in contact with the amazing Tanya for you or your horse.

Have a spectacular day, loads of love and hugs, Johno.

Never Say Never

 Feeling Optimistic
26 February 2021

Diary entry by Johno

Quote of the Day
"Never say that you can't do something,
or that something seems impossible,
or that something can't be done, no matter how
discouraging or harrowing it may be.
Human beings are limited only by what we allow ourselves
to be limited by: our own minds.
We are each the masters of our own reality,
when we become self-aware to this:
absolutely anything in the world is possible."
Mike Norton

Have a spectacular day. Loads of love and hugs, Johno.

No 'I' In Team

🙂 Feeling Humble
27 February 2021

Diary entry by Johno and the Blind Chick

There is no 'I' in Team!

On a massive scale I think the Blind Chick and I have much to be grateful for.

But one of the main things is the amazing Team we are surrounded by and how important that above quote is.

There is no 'I' in Team!

In the Blind Chick's world, in my world, nothing happens without a Team effort.

Whether it be getting the Blind Chick ready to ride and have a lesson, this is accomplished by the wonderful Jenelle Waters and the amazing Jacq **Benn**. Jenelle is the coach and Jacq is the coordinator and organiser. Together we are a formidable Team.

Everything runs smoothly and everything is well organised, but most of all they have fun doing it, training with the Blind Chick. Always laughter. Always encouragement. We are so very grateful for their assistance.

Our awesome farrier Troy Lomax keeps me sound. He has spent quite a lot of time making sure everything is right when he shoes me, no rushing. His great apprentice Henry is full of empathy and understanding with my Shivers condition. So again, our Team of Troy and Henry.

To the amazing veterinarians in my life. The wonderful Dr Sarah Gough, Hunter Valley Equine Vets, who speaks with the Blind Chick regularly about: how I'm travelling with my condition, whether I'm degenerating, whether we change medication? So grateful to be able to ring Dr Sarah directly and get advice.

Then we have the amazing vets in Dubbo: Dr Don Crosby and his Team who are just a phone call away. The beautiful Wendy makes sure everything is just right for looking after me, especially when I have colic and Wendy has someone here within 10-15 minutes.

So very grateful. Once again there is no 'I' in Team.

Then we have my beautiful Tanya with her magic hands doing her Craniosacral work on me every couple of weeks. Without this I'm sure my condition would be degenerating much quicker and I wouldn't be coping as well. Lucky me Tanya is just a phone call away and she's only 5 km up the road! So she's here in a flash when we need her.

We are so very blessed to be surrounded by so many amazing, beautiful, talented people who make such a difference to the Blind Chick and me.

Then we have beautiful angels that enter our life because they want to help and make a difference to my quality of life.

Enter stage left the beautiful Linda Lord from Poseidon Equine and her amazing products.

Linda has educated the Blind Chick about the importance of gut health. I must say it really has made the world a difference.

I now have absolutely no grain and no extruded food in my diet. Okay it might be a bit bland, but I am healthy and my gut is very healthy. This will hopefully help slow down the Equine Shivers if we can keep my gut health improving every day.

We are surrounded by the wonderful Linda and her amazing Poseidon Equine Team. The lovely Nerida Richards does my diet and helps look after me.

So very grateful. Again, there is no 'I' in Team.

And where would we be without the amazing Adam Sutton? Adam has invested many hours in helping with my desensitisation, with building up the Blind Chick's confidence and with stretching our benchmark little bit, by little bit.

Definitely he is taking the Blind Chick out of her comfort zone. A couple of times I've certainly been taken out of my comfort zone. But Adam always does this with great confidence, and it's had the most profound effect on me.

A prime example of this was the other day when our lovely friend and Photographer Prue Crichton came to do photos of me. Ooops, no one could get me to put my ears forward. Why? Because nothing they did startled me!!!!

I was just taking everything in my stride, and it took the Blind Chicks husband Matthew rolling across the lawn to get my attention. I must say I looked at him with a peculiar look on my face, I wasn't startled or worried. I did happen to put my ears forward though, and Prue got some lovely photos.

The efforts people go to, to get you to put your ears forward, ha ha.

A special thank you for being a part of our Team has to go to the Blind Chick's wonderful mother-in-law Lee for all her love and support.

Then, there is the amazing team from EQUISSAGE. I so appreciate the back massager, it's totally awesome. Plus …. the hand held massager!!! The Blind Chick generally uses the hand held unit on me while I have the back pad massaging me. Oh my heavens! Isn't EQUISSAGE so good at getting into spots where you are a little bit tight and sore?

The amazing team from EQUISSAGE have Sponsored the Blind Chick for many years. I think I am the fourth horse that has had the privilege of the EQUISSAGE machine being used on them. Boy oh boy is it a great warm up before you start working, or if you have any sore muscles?

Plus the boss, Ian Bellion, is a good mate of the Blind Chick's. The EQUISSAGE Team have backed all the different projects the Blind Chick has done. Even when she did one of her long-distance rides to raise money for the local Oncology Unit here in Dubbo. They donated a beautiful EQUISSAGE machine to be auctioned off for the ride.

So very generous! Once again, it shows the importance of there is no 'I' in Team.

And then there are the behind-the-scenes people like the wonderful Jacqueline Thompson who is always just a phone call away to help the Blind Chick out. She helps her with correspondence and getting our next book ready. The book about the Blind Chick's amazing husband Matthew who brought me for the Blind Chick. I think we can both be very grateful to him for getting the Blind Chick and I on this journey together.

So once again we should be so incredibly grateful for these most amazing people in our life. They help us make our dreams come true. They help us have the best quality of life we can, whilst also living with Equine Shivers.

What an amazing Team!!!

To our beautiful Team THANK YOU, from the bottom of our hearts. We so appreciate all of the things you've done for us in the past and will do in the future.

We want you to know how incredibly grateful we are.

And to our amazing Team on Facebook!!!

What would we do without your interaction, love, support, and encouragement? You have got us through many a sticky situation, we are so grateful.

To all of our friends, we hope you're having a lovely day. Thank you for your support, your friendship, and your encouragement.

We hope you are all safe and well.

Loads of love and hugs, Johno and the Blind Chick.

Living Markers

Feeling Impressed
28 February 2021

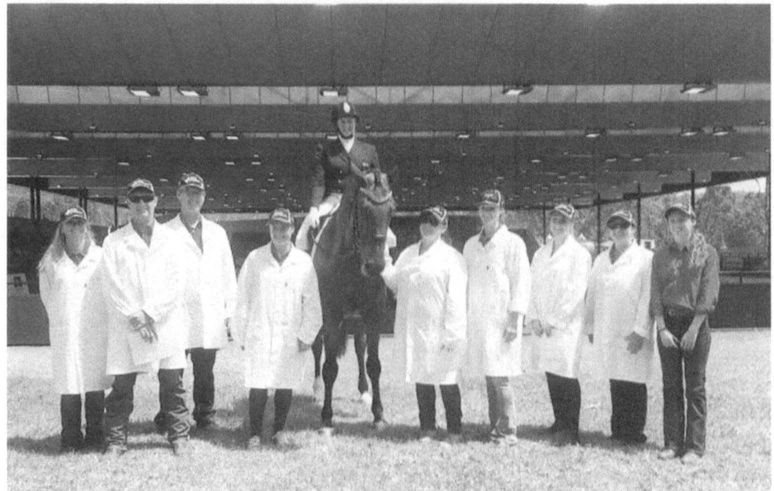

That other horse Desiderata, at Willinga Park with their amazing Living Markers

Diary entry by Johno

Good morning, what a spectacular day we're having, even though it was meant to be raining this morning. It was a little overcast at first, then it cleared, so the Blind Chick thought yes, she'd go out for lessons with Jenelle. Then it became overcast again so it was no she wouldn't. Then the sun was out again, and she made the decision to venture out to Janelle's for a lesson. Well, thank heavens she did.

We arrived out there in time to see a couple of Janelle's young pupils having show jumping lessons. Wow, they were so cool, so agile and so talented. Jenelle is such an encouraging coach, and the girls were all full of smiles after their wonderful lesson.

After the girl's lesson Jenelle, Jacq and the Blind Chick sat for a while under a shady tree and had a cool drink. Then they saddled me up ready for our usual long reining warmup with the wonderful Jenelle. I'm getting so good at this stuff. As per usual I took no notice of the show jumps or other horses. I knuckled down and did my best work.

Apparently, there was a storm looming, so they got the Blind Chick on board reasonably quickly. Today we had five living markers calling me around the arena, so the Blind Chick had somewhere to go. Jenelle was in the middle, it was totally awesome. Especially as I really thought today the Blind Chick may not have ridden.

Keeping in mind the Blind Chick is a fair-weather rider, she really relies on the sun for her orientation, so today she was totally flying blind, it was black sky. She was totally reliant on the five living markers on the outside of his circle and Jenelle in the middle. Jenelle talking to the Blind Chick all the time, keeping her thinking about being centred and having inside leg into outside rein, a little softness to the inside, but keeping me flowing forward. It was a super cool lesson. The Blind Chickie babe gets the diagonals wrong a bit, but so what! We walked, we trotted and we cantered. We didn't do any flying changes today, but it was a huge lesson in the fact that it was totally black for the Blind Chick. She had to rely on every one of those living markers calling out for her and on Janelle's guidance all the time giving the Blind Chick feedback.

How about you try something for fun. Be brave! Give it a try! Walk from your kitchen down to your bedroom; find a pair of shoes, put them on, walk outside to the clothesline, get the clothes off the line (or pretend to) then come back inside, get yourself a drink. All this with a blindfold on. This is how the Blind Chicks life is all the time, totally black, yet she soldiers on.

I'm so proud of my Blind Chick. She doesn't have the liberty of being able to take the blindfold off! It is what it is, she just deals with it and keeps moving forward.

This leads to the diary entry I put up yesterday. There is No 'I' in Team.

A massive thank you to the amazing team that made today possible. Our awesome coach Jenelle and Jacq, Tilla, Elenore, Mary and Andrew.

To these beautiful young people being a living marker was so wonderful. They had never ever seen the Blind Chick ride before or helped out. Yet they were totally awesome. To the beautiful Mary and Andrew, I'm so very grateful. To our super coach Jenelle and the beautiful Jacqueline who does the coordinating and organising, wow! What an amazing team and how very lucky are we.

To these very special beautiful people in our life, we are so grateful for you believing in us and for helping make our dreams come true. I'm sure people get bored with me saying thank you, but it's so very important.

We hope everyone is safe and well. Have a spectacular day, loads of love and hugs, Johno and the Blind Chick.

Final Reflections

16

Vulnerable and Frightened

Diary entry by Johno

I think this is something we never consider, being vulnerable and frightened.

We seem to blunder through our lives one step in front of the other and keep moving forward. I know for a fact the Blind Chick puts up this really brave front that everything is okay, she just gets on with it.

But over the past two years it has been really interesting watching how vulnerable and reliant on other people the Blind Chick has become. She keeps mentioning there is no 'I' in Team because her life does not work without a team. In fact our life does not work without a team.

I think that might be one of the reasons the Blind Chick gave up having a Guide Dog a couple of years ago. Being totally blind she felt quite vulnerable with a Guide Dog in town. There is always that element of what if? I know that's not a good thing because that steps right back into the confidence issue, but I think that was also an issue with a Guide Dog. Having the confidence to go out and brave the world by yourself, sometimes is pretty scary I would think.

I must say I admire the Blind Chicks attitude of Get On With It. But I also see the other side of things, where the wheels fall off the cart. She sits on the veranda crying because she doesn't feel good enough, she feels as if she's let people down, she's gone from riding a lovely horse at Grand Prix level to being frightened to ride at all! Some days my heart breaks for her with this, because she is so passionate. I know it doesn't help with my Equine Shivers that causes me to be a little bit unreliable under saddle.

You know some people think she should just probably retire me, maybe even euthanise me, because without the medication I am really quite dangerous. But she plugs away every day making sure I get my medication, making sure I have the best care possible. If she gets on a thread of information, off she goes hunting it down, seeing if it might be able to help me keep a good quality of life, and maybe help manage this Equine Shivers, which is quite a monster.

I watch the Blind Chick on these very overcast mornings, this is really what prompted me to write this diary entry. With rain forecast and it being very overcast, for the Blind Chick that makes it is as black as the inside of a cow. She relies on the sun for her orientation when she comes down to feed me, or just navigating around the house yard. Without that beautiful sun it really is quite difficult for her to orientate. I often again hear her sobbing as she's hit the electric fence, again! Tears of sheer frustration.

I'm not sure how things go inside, but I often hear some swear words coming from inside the house. Often I think it's because she has run into the kitchen table, again, or the wall in the hall has moved. I know Matthew keeps saying to her "slow down," but I think if she went any slower, she'd feel she was going backwards.

It's interesting how things work out. I've heard Matthew and the Blind Chick talking about her mum Mary, who is also totally blind, and how she gets disorientated and years and years ago the Blind Chick used to say to her mum, "just think where you are." Well you know what? It's not that simple for her now, just thinking where you are now.

She is walking in her mums' shoes being totally blind and getting lost, a lot. Imagine getting lost in your own bedroom! What the heck. How would that make you feel? I know the 'Lost In My Bedroom' occasions are guaranteed to bring on tears.

And you know what, on reflection if I were her, I think it would be really, really easy to give up and not do things. But because of her determination, stubbornness, and bloody mindedness to embrace life and live a full and happy life, she pushes herself every day, to keep a good quality of life. I know she loves cooking. Often there are cremated offerings, but them's the breaks. She keeps her life interesting and has lots of amazing, beautiful friends. I hear her talking with them on the phone each day. But it's the hours between the phone calls, the quiet time, what to do?

How would you fill your day being totally blind? I know the Blind Chick used to love doing craft. Well that's out now. I'm sure the frustration sometimes must be totally ginormous, quite overwhelming. But she keeps soldiering on. Sometimes I'm not sure why, or how.

All these things above I think are frustrations. But I know her biggest fear is, not knowing what to do next. She needs to have a plan, she needs to have a goal, she needs to have a direction. Why? Because it's so important, that - 'One Step at a Time'. By doing this you may arrive at the top of the mountain you quested for, having achieved your goals and perhaps even more! Doing so - One Step at a Time.

I know her wonderful husband Matthew has to step up a lot more, especially when the Blind Chick is having a big dinner party for 12 people, and doing it all herself! It was slow, but she did it all. She copes better with eight people; her wonderful husband Matthew cleans up afterwards. The Blind Chick can work in the kitchen and set the table by herself, but as soon as there are other people there it's difficult. Why? She runs into them a lot! I'd call her dangerous, especially when she has a knife in her hand cutting up vegetables or chicken.

In fact I often think she should count her fingers to make sure they're all still there.

So, even at home there's no 'I' in Team. Matthew and the Blind Chick are a great combination. Both are big stirrers, there's always quite a bit of laughter and cheekiness in the home, which is good fun to listen to.

But I would be stretching the truth if I said it was all a bed of roses. It's not.

I think it must be frustrating for Matthew living with the Blind Chick. Mind you I don't think she has burnt too many holes in his shirts ….. yet. After she's done the washing, he often picks up socks off the ground because they've escaped from the basket when she was getting the washing in. I think with the Blind Chick Matthew needs an extra set of eyes to make up for her sometimes.

Serving dinner out is often rather hilarious. Especially if there's a rice dish with a sauce. Matthew typically serves that out, which is much better on his plate than on the bench. That's where it's ended up quite a bit.

On a daily basis, I think a sense of humour is just so valuable. In fact, I think essential. Otherwise, I don't think the Blind Chick would get through the day. She loves our Facebook which is lots of fun and we have beautiful friends.

I suppose confidence comes in the same basket as the fear and frustration. Often it's the confidence level that is lacking that brings on the fear and the frustration.

Sometimes I don't think it's good for the Blind Chick to have too much time on her hands. If she does, she starts reflecting on what she was able to do quite a few years ago, and what she can't do now. The fact that Matthew lets her drive the tractor, with him by her side, is really cool fun for her. I know she loves going out and doing farm work with him, but often she feels she's more a hindrance than a help.

By the way this isn't a winge, this is fact. The fact that the Blind Chick is always smiling sometimes astounds me, because I don't think life is always that easy for her.

Interestingly I guarantee if you ask the Blind Chick if she had the opportunity to draw the cards again for her life, would she change it, I'm sure the answer would be 'No'. Why? Because going blind and being blind has shaped the amazing person she is today.

Mind you there might be a couple of little decisions she made on her journey that she'd change. But in general, the cards she's been dealt are okay, it's just 'One Step at a Time' and she will get there. Who knows what's around the corner? Time will tell.

I do know her greatest fear is not being able to do 'One Step at a Time'. I think with that attitude; One Step at a Time, One Day at a Time, Make your Goals Manageable and Achievable but Never Stop Driving and Moving Forward, we really can get through anything.

Go the Blind Chick, you rock!

17
Circle of Life

Diary entry by Johno

Wow, wow and wow!

Well another year has quickly passed us by, and oh my heavens, so many things have happened this year.

One of the major things is finding my identity. Knowing who I am wouldn't have even happened if the Blind Chick weren't so determined to find out about my past.

She was trying to find as much information as she could about my past, so she could ideally find out about where the origin of my Equine Shivers comes from.

Keeping in mind when Matthew brought me for the Blind Chick, I had the Equine Shivers then. I had a weird spastic movement with my hind legs, like a weird goose-stepping thing. Plus I had separation anxiety, which is part of the shivers disease.

And as you know, as time has gone on, my condition has got worse. This is because Equine Shivers is a neurological degenerative disease. Hence the communication between my brain and my hind legs has gotten worse, ditto with my front legs. I struggle quite a lot every morning, getting moving and my anxiety attacks.

We have slowly got that anxiety gig under control, which is just wonderful, especially in the paddock. I still have my moments when the Blind Chick rides me, which is probably a tad dangerous, but we're working on finding something that will keep me reliable and calm, and not have these trigger moments. At this stage we don't know what causes them, which is really frustrating. I think it is just part of the Equine Shivers and the way it manifests itself.

Some really exciting things have happened as you now know. I was bred by the beautiful people at Kinnordy Stud, Holger and Melanie Schmorl. I was out of a gorgeous mare called Vida.

But while I was in my mummy there was a special lady called Peta Bradley who came into our lives. She purchased my mum Vida with me inside. I was foaled down at Kinnordy Stud, then went to live with Peta on her farm when I was one month old, with my mum.

I was with the beautiful Peta for six months. In that time, she had me registered with the Hanoverian Society and I got ribbons! Even as a baby I got ribbons, what a clever lad I was. I was very pretty and very leggy, the latter shouldn't be a surprise to you given I'm now 18.3hh. I must have looked like a daddy long legs spider, lots and lots of long legs!

Then there was a really big missing piece of the jigsaw. Where did I go to after Peta's? At first Peta couldn't remember who she'd sold me to, it had been nearly 10 years ago after all! Then one day she remembered, and so we went on a hunt to find the lovely lady who brought me next.

The beautiful lady who brought me next is Libby Sander, I lived on her farm for the next two years. I was broken in quite early by a guy called Kevin who live next door. I seem to think he did a pretty good job because I have a lovely mouth and I'm a pleasure to do things with.

Then somehow, I ended up in New South Wales on a really big horse farm where they had over 150 horses. It was a very, very busy place. They do the pre-training of racehorses plus train showjumpers and eventers. My heavens there was always lots happening. Did I mention yet, it was a very, very, very busy place?

It was there, when I was four years old that I was introduced to dressage. From then on, I spent the next five maybe six years with them advancing up the levels of dressage. When Matthew bought me for the Blind Chick, I was a Medium training Advanced level dressage horse.

If you've read my first book, you'll know the Blind Chick fell in love with me the first time she rode me, I looked after her really well. We weren't to know what lay ahead of us with the Equine Shivers and everything like that, but I am so extremely glad I am in the home I'm in and I have the Blind Chick as my owner.

With our big hunt over the past two years to find my history, sadly even discovering all we have, it still hasn't put more light on my Equine Shivers. We still don't know where it came from, or what caused it. So it will probably stay one of those unsolved mysteries.

But whoohoo, we did find out what my full name is, and we've sent hair off for DNA testing to make sure I am the horse I'm supposed to be. The horse whose real name is really …. Kinnordy Godolphin.

I think it sounds like a very regal name. The Blind Chick is in the process of getting my name with Equestrian Australia changed back to Kinnordy Godolphin. I will keep my paddock name of Johno, which I like, a lot. When I was at the place where Matthew bought me from, they used to call me John Doe, which was a bit sad. But I like Johno, it's a pretty cool name.

They called me John Doe because they didn't know my history apparently. But the Blind Chick has fixed all that. There is nothing like knowing where you came from and your history. Like most people, the Blind Chick would not have bothered looking into my history if I had not had the degenerative condition Equine Shivers. She wanted to know more about where I had been and what I had done.

You now know how much the Blind Chick believes in making dreams come true. One day we hope we will be out competing, doing dressage with me wearing my beautiful name… Kinnordy Godolphin.

But things change!

Sometimes Life Sucks

😢 Feeling sad
6 April 2021

© 2CPhotography

JOHNO
Kinnordy Godolphin
8-11-2010 to 6-4-2021

Not all Angels have Wings

My beautiful Johno from the moment I stroked your beautiful soft muzzle and I stood and talked to you quietly, you gave me so much.

Right from that first moment, you made something glow so brightly in my heart. I can't even call it Love At First Sight - because I have never seen you! But your image burns so brightly in my heart and my mind. I found it hard to leave after I first rode you. There was something magical about being in your presence.

You brought so very much to our relationship. You brought love and joy and happiness to many.

My wonderful husband Matthew saw it, from the first moment we met..We had something special you and me. So, he brought you for me.

How very privileged I have been to have you in my life for the past two years and two days! The time has flown. They haven't always been easy times. We've been fighting that hideous condition - Equine Shivers. It has caused you so much grief and discomfort, but we both kept soldiering on. I kept looking for something to help you.

We both knew there wasn't a cure. Our aim has been to manage the condition and keep you comfortable. That's all that mattered. The times that I got to ride you, oh heavens! What a privilege and an honour. You are spectacular in every way.

What joy and fun we have had writing your books. The saddest thing is our journey is ending way too soon. We had many more stories to tell, adventures to go on and people to meet.

But this hideous Equine Shivers is degenerative and …. degenerate it has!

Okay we learnt to manage your anxiety attacks in the paddock, which made it safer for you, so you didn't hurt yourself. But the attacks are starting to override the medication. It's now become unsafe to ride you. We know this is not you. It is the Equine Shivers.

Do you know how hard it is to let go of somebody who is so beautiful, so perfect, who brings such magic to your life? Knowing you must do the right thing by them and let them go.

Oh my beautiful amazing Johno, how do you say goodbye and stop fighting for someone so beautiful and perfect in every way!

How do you convince yourself you are doing the right thing by giving the one you love peace, and letting them go?

My beautiful Johno, you have taken my love of horses to another level. Our relationship has been based on Magic and Stardust and Fairies. I am so grateful to all of the beautiful people who have helped keep you going, helped give you a better quality of life. ⊠⊠ So very grateful.

But my beautiful friend, my heart breaks. How do you move forward after losing something so perfect and beautiful?

But I know in my heart what you would expect of me, so I will endeavour to be strong. I can't promise there will be no tears.

But I will promise to lock all of our beautiful memories deep in my heart, I'll have them with me forever.

I thank God for every moment that I've had to spend with you.

I have lost my best friend and God has just received a beautiful angel. Run free my beautiful friend. Be at peace. I love you forever, I will miss you forever.

Our journey has been way too short, but thank you for the memories and the ride, totally awesome. Thank you from the bottom of my heart for just being…J ohno.

To our beautiful Facebook friends THANK YOU. You have been part of the journey with Johno and I. We are so privileged and so grateful to have you with us on such a sad day.

It is so hard to say goodbye my beautiful friend.

Rest in peace Johno.

P.S.: This decision has been made with the advice from two of Johno's vets. Please respect I'm devastated, but there was no other choice.

Thank you

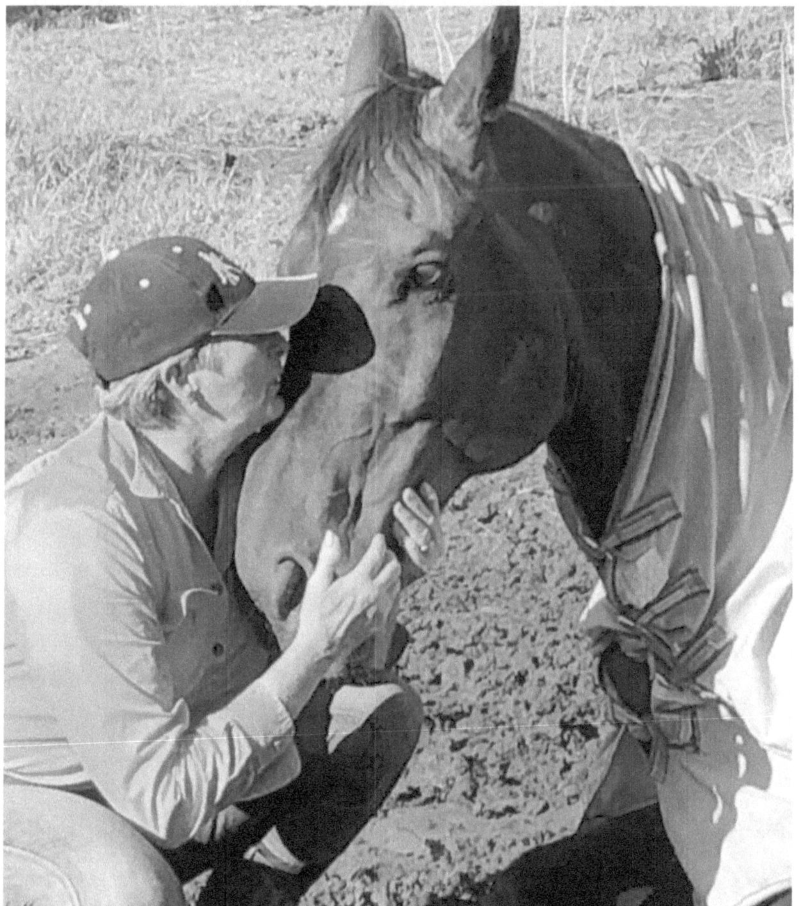

Wow what a year this has been! What a massive job pulling Johno's book together has been. I'm so very grateful to quite a few people that have made this all happen.

To my wonderful friend Jacqueline Thompson thank you so much for your patience, your amazing ability being the most incredible wordsmith, and for being able to unjumble my gobbledygook. As you know when I dictate with my iPhone, it often comes out gobbled.

We have spent many hours on the phone laughing at my phone's way of spelling particular words or saying particular things. It has been so much fun spending time working this gobbledygook out with you. You have made it such a pleasure and I am so grateful for all you've done with the book, but also for being a very dear friend.

My beautiful mother-in-law Lee was the first to read the book after Jacqueline pulled it into gear. Lee read the first book, *Johno & The Blind Chick: Vision Is More Than Seeing*, now she has proofread our second book Johno & The Blind Chick – Walk In My Shoes. I'm so incredibly grateful for Lee taking the time to read it. It's really quite amazing Lee has lived all of the journey but still enjoyed the book. I'm so happy about that! I'm so grateful for Lee's time and energy, her always supporting me and always being there as a confidant, a shoulder to cry on and a good friend.

Thank you to my beautiful friend Princess Prue! Prue Crichton has done all the photos for both my books and is always so much fun doing photo shoots or catching up. Prue and I been mates for a very long time. I so appreciate her love and support. This time we have pictures in the book for you to enjoy. Thank you Prue, I'm so grateful for all your help.

A massive thank you to my beautiful friend Jane Loxley. Jane is always there as a sounding board. I'm so very grateful for your contribution and your friendship.

A massive thank you to the amazing Belinda Crawford who does her magic in typesetting the book, setting it out, getting it to the printer and getting everything else done so it ends up on the bookshelf or being able to be purchased online. You are totally amazing! Everything with Belinda always seems to be done so easily, such an amazing professional. I'm so incredibly grateful for all your help, support and guiding me through everything that needs to be done. Thank you Belinda.

My thank you's wouldn't be finished without thanking all of my beautiful friends and support team that believe in me and help make my dreams come true. You are all mentioned in the book. I am so grateful for your support and love.

A massive thank you to my beautiful husband Matthew who supports me on all my endeavours. He takes the Mickey out of me and teases me, but always in jest and always supportive and helping me move forward. I'm so grateful for the wonderful things you bring to my life, those being love, support and caring. Thank you Matt.

A massive thank you goes out to all our wonderful friends on Facebook who have followed the beautiful Johno and I over the past two years – the good days, the bad days, the sad days. You have all been there holding my hand, supporting Johno, sending us love. I'm so grateful and humbled by the caring that comes from our wonderful friends on Facebook. From the bottom of my heart thank you, I'm forever grateful.

And last but not least to the beautiful horse with a beautiful brown eyes, Johno. Thank you for just being you. You have brought so much joy and love to so many people all around the world just being the beautiful horse you were. Rest in peace my gorgeous friend. We all have our beautiful memories of you locked deep in our hearts. Run free.

Testimonial

Oh Sue-Ellen...

I was so lucky the day I opened Facebook and found a suggested 'like' link to *Johno & The Blind Chick.*

These tales would certainly have room for book 3.

I have always grabbed a cuppa so I can read every word you share.

We all laugh, cry and smile with you.

Keep telling your story my friend, your inspiration continues

Robyn Alston

About the author

Sue-Ellen Lovett is a motivational speaker, two-time Paralympian and Grand Prix-level dressage rider. She's also blind, but she hasn't let that slow her down.

Born with a degenerative eye disease that left her legally blind from birth and without sight for the last decade, Sue-Ellen has a slew of awards, and has competed against able-bodied riders at the highest level of international competition. In 1996, Sue-Ellen competed in the Atlanta Paralympic Games, following it up by competing in the Sydney Paralympic Games four years later, and a four-year stint on the Sydney Paralympic Board of Directors.

In between Atlanta and Sydney Paralympic Games, she represented Australia at the World Equestrian Games in Denmark, where she was ranked 4th in the world and in the Bronze Medal team.

More than just dressage, Sue-Ellen is also a long-distance rider and has ridden over 16,000 kilometres, raising $3.2 million for numerous charities, including an epic trip 2400-kilometre trip from Cairns to the Gold Coast in 1988; a total of 55 days in the saddle!

Johno & The Blind Chick 2 is her second book. She's already hard at work on the follow-up as well as an autobiography from her own point of view.

Sue-Ellen lives in rural New South Wales with her husband Matthew, a cat called Thunder Paws and Lola.

Stay up-to-date with Sue-Ellen's adventures
via her website (www.sueellenlovett.com.au) and
Facebook page (www.facebook.com/JohnoAndTheBlindChick/).